EASTER RISING

EASTER RISING

AN IRISH AMERICAN
COMING UP FROM
UNDER

MICHAEL PATRICK
MacDONALD

HOUGHTON MIFFLIN COMPANY
BOSTON · NEW YORK
2006

Visit our Web site: www.houghtonmifflinbooks.com.

Library of Congress Cataloging-in-Publication Data
MacDonald, Michael Patrick.
Easter rising : an Irish American coming up from
under / Michael Patrick MacDonald.
p.   cm.
ISBN-13: 978-0-618-47025-9
ISBN-10: 0-618-47025-5
1. MacDonald, Michael Patrick—Childhood and youth.
2. Irish Americans—Massachusetts—Boston—Biography.
3. South Boston (Boston, Mass.)—Biography. 4. MacDonald
family. 5. Irish American families—Massachusetts—Boston.
6. Boston (Mass.)—Biography. 7. South Boston (Boston,
Mass.)—Social life and customs. 8. South Boston (Boston,
Mass.)—Social conditions. 9. Boston (Mass.)—Social life and
customs. 10. Boston (Mass.)—Social conditions. I. Title.
F73.68.S7M34 2006
305.891'62073074461—dc22   2006009767

PRINTED IN THE UNITED STATES OF AMERICA

Book design by Robert Overholtzer

CRW   10 9 8 7 6 5 4 3 2 1

Some names have been changed to disguise
or protect some identities.

"In Excelsis Deo," written by Patti Smith. Published by Linda Music (ASCAP). Used by
permission. All rights reserved. "Search and Destroy," words and music by Iggy Pop and
James Williamson. © 1973 EMI Music Publishing Ltd., James Osterberg Music, Straight
James Music, and Bug Music. All rights for EMI Music Publishing Ltd. controlled and administered by Screen Gems–EMI Music Inc. All rights reserved. International copyright secured. Used by permission. "Good Times," by Bernard Edwards and Nile Rodgers. ©
1979 Bernard's Other Music & Tommy Jymi, Inc. All rights administered by Warner-
Tamerlane Publishing Corp. All rights reserved. Used by permission. "Boogie Wonderland," words and music by Jon Lind and Allee Willis. © 1979 EMI Blackwood Music Inc.,
Irving Music, Inc. and Big Mystique Music. All rights reserved. International copyright
secured. Used by permission. "We Are Family," by Bernard Edwards and Nile Rodgers. ©
1979 Bernard's Other Music and Sony Songs, Inc. All rights for Bernard's Other Music administered by Warner-Tamerlane Publishing Corp. All rights reserved. Used by permission.

CHILDREN OF

Helen (MacDonald) King

DAVID LEE MACDONALD
b. May 10, 1956
d. August 9, 1979, age twenty-three

JOHN JOSEPH MACDONALD
b. April 25, 1957

MARY MACDONALD
and JOSEPH MACDONALD
b. April 4, 1958

FRANCIS XAVIER MACDONALD
b. November 24, 1959
d. July 17, 1984, age twenty-four

KATHLEEN MACDONALD
b. December 26, 1961
coma January–April 1981, age nineteen

KEVIN PATRICK MACDONALD
b. February 27, 1963
d. March 5, 1985, age twenty-two

PATRICK MICHAEL MACDONALD
b. March 21, 1964
d. April 15, 1964, age three weeks

MICHAEL PATRICK MACDONALD
b. March 9, 1966

SEAMUS COLEMAN KING
b. September 17, 1975

STEPHEN PATRICK KING
b. December 3, 1976

EASTER RISING

I LEARNED TO JUMP subway fares by tagging along with my brother Kevin and his friends on shoplifting ventures outside the project. Downtown Boston was only three stops but worlds away from Old Colony Project. I was ten, and Southie's busing riots of the past two years had now dissipated into the occasional scuffle with the police. Still, everyone in our neighborhood always said how dangerous it was to leave. It was still the world against Southie and Southie against the world. So for me there was a terrifying thrill in leaving the neighborhood at all. The more I snuck on those trains, the more it felt like traveling to another country, like I was a tourist about to see strange lands and stranger people for the very first time.

At first our technique was basic. We'd wait at the top of the stairs of Andrew Station until we heard a train arriving, then dart down the stairs, hop over the turnstiles, and bolt for the train's doors. By the time we were lined up at the four turnstiles, the train would be just making its final *wshhhh* sound, which Kevin said was the air releasing from the brake cylinder. We'd each lift off, hands on either side of the turnstile, and drive our legs over the bars feet first, landing as far out as we could. By the time we landed, the fare taker would be screaming and knocking on his scratched and blurry Plexiglas windows, mouthing what I imagined was "You little fucks!" Right about then I knew we would hear the train doors open with a collective rumble. If we did it according to Kevin's exact timing — if we started running downstairs at just the right moment, when the train was first coming to a halt with a long screech of the brakes — we'd usually make it inside just before we felt the suction of the doors closing behind us. No one ever chased after us in the early days, so we probably didn't have to turn it into the heart-racing caper it always felt like. But it was great each time to feel the breeze of those clackety doors nearly catching my shirt. I'd take a deep breath in relief, and then in expectation.

If the train we hopped came from the suburbs, it would be one of the brand-new modern ones, carrying all whites. But if it had come from Dorchester it would be one of the old, run-down ones and filled with blacks. I would go off by myself to grab a seat and silently take in all the newness, black or white. But my brother Kevin seemed interested only in "getting the fuck in, and getting the fuck out" — back to Southie. To him we were on a mission, and he was all business. He'd make me stand up so that we were all sticking together. He'd keep us huddled around him while he told us what to do and what *not* to do around all these dangerous blacks and goofy-looking white people from the world that was not Southie. And he'd whack me in the head every time I snuck a glance at the people he was talking about. But after a few minutes our huddle would fall apart. As we tried to keep our feet firmly planted on the bumpy ride, I always seemed to have the worst balance, flailing backward and sideways with the train's chaotic twists and turns. I didn't mind, though, as long as I never hit the floor.

Riding the trains was my favorite thing to do even before the trips with Kevin. Ma always told us we should *want* to go places, like Dorchester or Jamaica Plain. "For Chrissake, don't you wanna see the world?" she said. On my eighth birthday she took me all the way to Park Street Station and put me on the Green Line to Jamaica Plain, where Nana would be waiting at the other end to take me out for a birthday dinner. The old trolley looked like it was the first one ever built, with bars over square windows that opened. Best of all, it had a driver's booth at both ends — I guessed that was so it didn't have to turn around at the end of the line. That seemed like the greatest day in the world, being trusted to get on a Green Line trolley all by myself. I kept thinking that to drown out how nervous I was getting. I sat in the backward-facing driver's seat and waved to Ma on the platform while I pretended to myself that I was the conductor. Ma disappeared from view, and I distracted myself by trying to think up an excuse for why I was driving backward. But before I could, all the excitement and the backward driving made me puke out the window into the blackness of the tunnel. I went to sit in a normal remaining seat, to pretend like nothing had happened. On the forty-five-minute-long journey, I let my fears get the best of me, though, and imagined that I would end up on this one-way trip forever and never see my family again. Worst of all, I was soon the only passenger remaining. When the train came to a final screeching halt, the driver shut off the engine and the lights and barked, "Last stop! Arborway!" while packing up his things like he was going home. My heart was in my mouth until I saw Nana waving and running across the ghost town of a train yard. The sight of Nana was unmistakable, always in a loose navy blue polka-dot dress, shoes you saw at drugstores, and a flowered kerchief tied snugly under her chin. "For Chrissake, you look like Mother Hubbard," Ma would snap at her when Nana complained about Ma's miniskirts and spike heels. For me though, Nana's old-fashionedness was calming. And this day the sight of her was more comforting than ever. I hopped off the trolley stairs in one leap. Nana greeted me as she always did, not saying hello but spitting on a napkin that seemed like it had been in her purse forever and rubbing it into my cheeks until they hurt. Nana talked about rosy cheeks like they were the most important thing in the world for people to see. "We'll go for a wee supper now," she said in that Donegal way that made everything sound like both an exclamation and a question. Well over my fears, I greeted her by saying that riding the subways was just about the greatest thing in the world and that I couldn't wait to do it again.

Going home from fare-jumping trips with Kevin and his crew was easier than the trip out. We'd walk from Filene's to South Station and press the red STOP button hidden near the ground at the top of a wooden escalator so ancient-looking that Kevin convinced me it was from "colonial days." After we pressed the button, the escalator would stutter in its climbing motion and then come to a rolling stop. That's when we'd run down the steep and treacherous steps into the station exit. Each wooden step was about one foot square, and I always wondered if people were skinnier in colonial times. At the bottom of the escalator was an unmanned gate that was often left wide open. But even if it was chained and padlocked, you could push out one fence post to make a gap, just enough to slip through. It usually took a bit of teamwork, but it was a cinch. Kevin was the scrawniest and could slip through without anyone's help, so he'd go first and pull on the gate from the other side.

One day I discovered an even better way to get back home to Southie. Kevin was inside Papa Gino's, pulling a scam he'd recently perfected. When the cashier called out a number, Kevin would wave a receipt from the trash, all excited-like, as if he'd won the lottery. His performance was so convincing — or maybe just distracting — that he'd walk away with a tray full of pizza and Cokes. Okie and Stubs would distract the waiting customers even further by asking if anyone knew where the bathroom was. I was outside on Tremont Street, playing lookout — for what I didn't know — and daydreaming that Kevin would get a whole pizza pie. But Kevin cared more about scamming stuff for everyone else than for himself, and I knew he would give away his only slice if that's all he got. While I was supposedly keeping watch, I spied groups of black people gathering nearby and then disappearing through an automatic door to a steel shaft sticking up from the sidewalk. As soon as one cluster of mothers, teenagers, and babies in strollers disappeared through the mystery door, more groups would gather around, press a button, and then loiter at a slight distance. They tried hard to look inconspicuous by rubbing their hands together or jumping up and down in one place as if they were cold, but I knew by their watchful eyes that they were just looking out, like I was supposed to be doing. The door opened, and again the busy sidewalk turned empty. I walked closer and saw through little steamy windows that everyone was squeezed like sardines onto an elevator and then whisked away to some place below Tremont Street. I pressed the button and waited for the elevator to come back up again so I could investigate.

"What are you, a fuckin' losah?" Kevin screamed down Tremont Street just as the doors opened and more people looked around before hopping on. He was running toward me with a single slice of pizza, yelling at me for always wandering off. "You were supposed to keep watch!" he barked, grabbing me by the collar. Okie and Stubs were running behind him, pizza-less. They seemed like they thought they were being chased, and I told them to follow me. We squeezed into the elevator and pushed our way to the middle, surrounded by whole families of black people. Kevin punched me for staring up at them, even though there was nowhere else to look but up. In the end I would get high marks for finding a whole new and simpler method for getting a free ride home. The service elevator led from the street right into the subway system, beyond the conductor booths, and we all filed out nonchalantly. That day I earned the only slice of pizza Kevin was able to score.

In the days that followed I was so proud of my find I put the word out all over Old Colony Project about the new way to get home from downtown. That pissed Kevin off — he said the more people knew, the sooner the MBTA would cop on and shut us out. For a time the elevator was the one place in Boston

5

you'd see my neighbors from Southie squeezed into a small space with black people. A key was required for the elevator to work, but the keyhole was always turned sideways, in the on position, either because it was broken or because some transit worker was doing us all a favor.

Kevin and his friends didn't care about leaving Southie except on scamming missions — they never went just to wander. And I could never get my own friends to leave the project, so it wasn't long before I was venturing alone to see the strange lands and strange people beyond Southie's borders.

I'D SPENT ANOTHER roasting-hot afternoon on the kitchen floor with my little brothers. In the project we were lucky to have cool concrete floors, and to me lying low was just about the smartest thing to do during an August heat wave. We played with their toy fire engines and conjured up emergency scenarios that included their WWF action figures. It didn't bother Seamus and Stevie that Hulk Hogan was too big to exist in the smaller world of the fire engines, or that George "The Animal" Steele had no arms or legs. I even pulled out my ramshackle Planet of the Apes Treehouse from when I was eight. I was thirteen now, but Seamus and Stevie gave me a good excuse to play with my favorite old toys. I pretended the Treehouse was on fire so we could move the whole scenario to the coolest place in the house, the bathtub. We showered it with water, and soon the tub became Seamus and Stevie's wading pool, clothes and all. The little kids were almost three and four, and they were able to adapt to almost anything. And since they never seemed to notice that the day was hot as hell, being around them sometimes made me forget about the heat.

After Stevie dozed off for a midafternoon nap, my brother Frankie dropped over, rousing cheers from Seamus. On seeing Frankie, Seamus put Stevie in a WWF headlock, waking him up red-faced and screaming. Before long the "two little kids"

— as we called our ninth and tenth brothers — were jumping up and down on the couch with their fists raised, ready to spar with their boxing-champion brother. Frankie always said you could never start them boxing too young. But that day he called a time-out and told them to settle down, saying it was too hot for so much action. He went to the freezer and stuck his head inside. "It's hot as fuck out there!" he hollered. His aggravated voice sounded muffled and cooled, and I wondered why I'd never thought of the freezer for relief.

I was always paying attention to everyone's different ways of coping with days like this. It seemed like a game to me, each person on a mission to discover the best ways to deal with the heat. Kevin had stopped in and said he was going to sneak onto one of the new air-conditioned trains to Quincy, and then into an air-conditioned movie theater. Joe — the mechanic of the family — was spending the day lying on the cool concrete beneath a neighbor's car that needed fixing. Kathy and her friends had broken the padlock off the door to the cool basement below our building, which they'd furnished with a couch from the dumpster. I could hear Chic's "Good Times" blasting on their radio, coming up through the stairwell.

Billy Cuddahy from the first floor had dragged his son's plastic kiddie pool to the curb and was sitting in it, leaving no room for the neighborhood kids who stood around watching the water overflow. Sure enough, relief came with the sound of the first gushes from the fire hydrant down the street. Cheers echoed from the swarms of little kids who poured out of the brick buildings to get drenched. Some raced to the action two and sometimes three to a bike — one on the handlebars and one hugging the driver's back for dear life.

Left to hog the kiddie pool alone, Billy Cuddahy let out a relaxed moan. "Christ, I'm sweatin' like a whore on a good night!" he said, then slid down on his back and immersed all but the solid dome of his belly. The easygoing laughter of the ladies on the stoop — who themselves were coping with the heat by wearing loose house smocks — made me think how much I loved sweltering days like this. "Well, it's not the heat so much as the humidity!" I heard one of the ladies on the stoop affirm, like it was the surest thing she'd ever said. It was the fifth time I'd heard it that afternoon, and I felt like I could hear it fifty more. I lay on the couch waiting for afternoon cartoons to come on. To me, hot days like this were the greatest, when all anyone could think about was just how hot it was and when nothing else really mattered.

A woman screamed, *"He jumped!"* And more hellish cries followed. My eyes caught Frankie's, and in that moment I knew everything had changed. The panicked rumble of feet up our hallway stairs came close, and the banging of fists on our door left no doubt in my mind. I knew exactly who had jumped. Davey had been in a bad way the past couple weeks, marching up and down Patterson Way talking about Jesus. And ever since he'd stood on the roof's ledge one evening talking to God, I had tried to tell myself that I was just being a worrywart. Davey had been schizophrenic for years, and by now most of us had gotten used to our oldest brother's strange fixations and rants. But recently, since his psychiatrist had gone on August vacation, he'd been getting worse.

Frankie raced downstairs, five or six steps at a time. I felt the entire world slip away from me before I could even make myself look out the window. I didn't know how I was still standing because I couldn't feel my legs anymore. I couldn't feel any part of my body by the time I laid eyes on Davey, lifting himself up from the ground and collapsing again and again. He was covered in blood, and his face was filled with rage. Somehow he gained the strength to throw flailing punches at anyone trying to help him, including Frankie. But his legs failed him again and he stumbled backward, as Frank leapt forward to catch him. I had no feeling left, not even in my fingers, when I tried to dial 911, but I got strength for just one moment when I suddenly had to grab Seamus and Stevie, who were running to the window to see what all the commotion was outside.

Davey died in the operating room overnight. When Johnny, the second oldest, arrived home at daybreak — on emergency leave from the navy — Ma opened the door and said calmly, "He's gone." I'd stayed awake on the couch through the night and was pretending to be asleep, too nervous to find out whether Davey was in stable or critical condition. When I heard what Ma said, I stuck my face into a pillow to silence myself. And I stayed like that until I went numb again. I let go of everything. Johnny stood completely still listening to Ma as she told him the doctors had said Davey died of a burst spleen. I didn't even have it in me to wonder what a spleen was, or to care. I felt connected to nothing and to nobody. I had no choice in the matter. It just happened.

That lazy afternoon before Davey jumped, when all anyone could think about was how hot it was, was the last time I felt like a kid with nothing much to worry about. The feeling I carried with me from seeing Davey strapped to a gurney and fighting for his death was a feeling I knew my whole family now had in common. But it was a feeling I could only bear to be alone with. I think none of us wanted to make it worse for Ma by crying or anything. She had the worst of it, having lost her own son. I would shrug whenever Ma asked in the following weeks, "Mike, how are you taking it?" Sometimes I would ask back, "Taking what?" I felt ambushed to have the subject brought up at all. In a way it felt good that Ma knew I might not be feeling so well. But one thing my family all knew was that you had to be tough, so I changed the subject fast.

On the day of Davey's funeral, Ma finally disappeared into her room. She'd spent a couple of days and nights playing jigs and reels on her accordion for friends and neighbors. "We gave him a great sendoff, didn't we?" Ma said. I didn't know what a great sendoff could possibly be. But I knew Ma's accordion was the main reason Grandpa didn't come back to our apartment after the burial. Grandpa said what he always said about

Ma's accordion playing, that it was "an awful fookin' shame." Ma retired to her room with her head held high, though, proud of the only kind of sendoff she knew. I wished Grandpa could see her, walking slowly to a room I knew was darkened by shades pulled low.

After most of the neighbors had gone, I realized that life was carrying on like normal for the rest of the world. Kids were playing in the fire hydrants outside, the ladies had returned to the stoop, and the rooftops were filled with teenagers sunbathing. Chic's "Good Times" blared once again from every radio on the block. Johnny was packing his duffle bag to head back to some top-secret location with the Navy SEALs. My older sister Mary took Seamus and Stevie to her apartment for a few days to play with her own two kids. Kevin had disappeared with his friends. Joe went to score some pot from someone who needed an engine looked at. Kathy had joined her friends tanning on the roof.

After Johnny yelled goodbye to Ma through her bedroom door, I sat in the window and watched Patterson Way stir to summer afternoon life. It was like nothing had ever happened. I tried to pay attention to the same old stories unfolding outside, from kids playing blindman's buff to teenagers dealing on the corners. It all reminded me too much that Davey was missing from the street below. He was always pacing up and down Patterson Way. On a normal day I could count on him to appear out of nowhere, round a corner, and walk in a straight line with a bounce in every step, his trademark walk, which some of the smaller kids in the neighborhood had started to imitate. Only a few days before, a gang of them had trailed behind him, single file, playfully mimicking his straight-as-a board posture, arms to the sides like a trained Irish step dancer. The kids imitated the spring in his step to the point of lifting entirely off the ground. Davey would often stop dead in his tracks to think more intensely, like he was lingering on a thought or was on the verge of breaking through to a conclusion about something. On this day, with the neighborhood kids trailing behind him, he stopped short and was startled by one of them bumping into him. The long line of kids fell behind him like dominoes. "What is this, the Pied Piper or something?" Davey said. He didn't mind their laughter. He brushed it off, warning them to stay away from the Pied Piper if he should ever come to Southie.

"Who the fuck is the Pied Piper?" one of the kids shouted up at him. Davey was shocked. "You never heard of the Pied Piper?" he asked, looking serious and worried now for the kids. In no time, as usual, all the little kids were sitting around on the stoop across the street listening to Davey's storytelling, their jaws slack and a faraway look in their eyes. I watched from the window, hoping my own friends wouldn't show up and see Davey acting out everything in the story, from the Piper playing the flute to rid the town of rats to the town's kids who would pay the "ultimate price," lulled by the Piper's tune.

Davey was always foretelling the last days of Southie, but the little kids in the neighborhood never looked scared by his warnings. Whether he was imitating superheroes like the Incredible Hulk or telling an apocalyptic tale, it was all the same to them, and they laughed with Davey like he was on their level. After entertaining the kids on the stoop that day, he turned away with a lingering smile that they couldn't see. He looked proud to have done his duty, but then he turned serious again and got back to his job of pacing up and down Patterson Way, trying to figure it all out. Even though I was drawn to watching Davey, whenever a friend said, "Hey, there's your brother Davey! Let's get him to imitate the Incredible Hulk!" I quickly changed the subject and the direction of our trail around the neighborhood.

At first, remembering all of this made me forget Davey was dead. I looked out the window toward a brick wall, thinking Davey could come around the corner any minute. And then it hit me, even harder than the last time, at the funeral Mass that morning, that he'd never be seen on Patterson Way again.

As hot as it was outside, I closed the window. I went to sit on the couch and wished the remaining funeral guests would leave, while half wanting them to stay. There were a couple of cans of beer left. Maureen O'Brien and Billy Cuddahy were sitting on the couch across from me saying, "I shouldn't," but I knew they would. Finally, to get away from the lingerers, I went to the clothes room, an otherwise empty room piled high with the castoff clothes worn by the ten of us kids in years past. Before it was the clothes room it was the room where Davey lived after he got out of Mass Mental, before he got accepted for a project apartment across the street with Frankie. I threw open the door to the clothes room, wanting to escape from everyone. But Frankie was already in there, sitting on a trunk and staring blankly across the room toward a flowered hippie suitcase that Davey had carried home from the mental hospital years before.

Frank wasn't crying or anything. It seemed even worse than that. He was just sitting there, completely still, his hands folded like he could have been praying. Whatever he was doing, it was private. When I barged in, he said nothing, and his frozen expression stayed frozen. But he reached out and pushed the door closed on me; slowly, not like he was pissed off at my barging in, but locking me out just the same. I was actually relieved. I didn't want to go into that room anymore, not after seeing him alone like that, looking the way he did. I had never seen him so still and silent. Frankie was usually the center of activity, being the champion boxer of the family, and one of Southie's rising stars. There was always a lot of life around him, whether the little kids in the project were jogging after him or he was huddled on a street corner telling stories from the ring to "the boys," as we called our gangsters.

I knew Frankie would take Davey's death badly, since he had been living with him. In the apartment across the street he'd hung a heavy bag in the center of the parlor and was teaching Davey to box in case anyone messed with him in the streets. He was even working on teaching Davey to talk to girls again instead of scaring them away with talk of the Bible and how we were living in "the end of time." Frankie and I were the only ones in the family who had seen Davey on the ground that afternoon before the EMTs took him away. And I knew too well that Frankie was the last one of us to be with Davey. Seeing him sitting in the clothes room only brought back the picture I wanted to erase, of Frankie pinning Davey to the ground, both of them soaked in blood, before the ambulance finally arrived.

After seeing Frankie sitting alone that day, I never wanted to see him — or anyone else — looking so emptied and expressionless again. It was hard to look at my family in those days, for it only brought me right back to Davey.

At his graveside I had promised myself, and Davey, that I would think of him every day for the rest of my life. I wanted never to forget him, and I was afraid that I could. In the weeks after his death, though, it seemed impossible not to think of him constantly. I wondered if I could ever make it stop, if I could ever live a day without him on my mind, without the sadness and the guilt I felt about his final decision. That's when I felt most like a monster. I wanted Davey to go away — to have never even existed. Everywhere I turned in my family, though, there he was. I didn't want to see Davey's suicide anymore in the numb expressions of my brothers and sisters, or in Ma's defeated slow walk, or even in the partying on the rooftops. I had to get away from all the memories and connections to the small world of Patterson Way that had witnessed Davey's suicide. I had to get away from home.

September couldn't come soon enough that year. I was relieved to get to travel across town to Boston Latin. After school I'd travel downtown to kill time so I wouldn't have to go back to Southie so soon. I spent hours at Strawberries looking at records. Disco was on its way out, and bands like Cameo and Parliament were filling the void with funk, while Rapper's Delight was blaring out of car windows all over town, and all the talk was about the brand-new style, rap. Strawberries had it all, even a small bin for Punk/New Wave — about twenty-five or thirty records — and that's where I could get in my best people-watching.

Occasionally, freaky-looking people hovered around this skimpy stack of records, wearing striped shirts, razor-shorn hair, formerly flared pants pegged tightly at the bottom with safety pins, and flat-footed Converse or generic "bobos," as we called the $1.49 sneakers Ma often tried to make us wear. These people seemed to be wearing their cheap bobos on purpose. I'd seen the news reports about the Sex Pistols' American tour and the suicide of Sid Vicious. The news talked about Sex Pistols fans spitting on each other, vomiting, pissing, and strangling each other, all as some sort of dance. I wanted nothing to do with all of that. I figured these people must have had no problems in their lives to go looking for trouble that way. Once I'd seen Davey after his jump from the roof, I'd seen ugly enough. I didn't need to go looking for more.

But the people looking through the Punk/New Wave bins — usually about five or ten years older than I was — didn't look violent. It was everyone else who was getting ugly in response to their looks. One day I followed one of them out of Strawberries to see what people would do to him. He looked like something out of *The Addams Family,* a real ghoul, with a black pinstripe suit too small for him, a dog collar, and hair that shot out like black rays in all directions. He seemed to enjoy the raucous laughter and insults hurled at him in the streets of downtown Boston. People screamed, "Freak!" "Faggot!" and the names of the more popular New Wave bands that appeared on *Don Kirshner's Rock Concert* late on Saturday nights, like Devo or Blondie. Black people on the street just cleared a path and shrugged to each other, as if this must be some white thing they wouldn't understand. But the white jocks got aggressive, as if the freak had insulted them personally and they had to fight him to defend their honor. He just gave them the finger and barreled through the crowd with a hunched walk that was as outlandish as his getup. He told people to fuck off, but he looked energized, as if he was enjoying every minute of the attention, as if it was his accepted role in life, his duty even, to piss people off. When someone threw a can of Coke at his arm, he simply wiped off the drips and kept walking. He nonchalantly gave the finger, but to no one in particular, just raised it in the air as if he meant it for the whole world. I was wearing beige pleated pants and an alligator shirt, and like every other white person walking down the street I had a feathered blow cut like Tony Manero from *Saturday Night Fever*. If anything, I looked like the ugly people hurling insults and wanting to get violent. It would have been worse for the freak, though, if he walked through Southie. He might not get out alive.

The whole spectacle thrilled me. I admired the freak in a way, and went back into Strawberries to buy a Sex Pistols album. I felt embarrassed, though, not because of the name of the group, but because I was buying the album even though I looked "normal." The cashiers at Strawberries were know-it-alls about music. "Yeah, man, the guitar was wicked tight" was the most repeated refrain behind the cash register. Everything was about being "tight" or "powerful" as they looked down their noses at customers' purchases and carried on about how they preferred some band's "early" recording to the later ones. The New Waver at the cash register wore a huge feather in one ear and was dissecting every song by some band called the Talking Heads. "Eno's a genius, an absolute genius," he said, without giving any clues to who Eno was. This guy would definitely look down his nose at me and my year-old Sex Pistols album, like I was a Johnny-come-lately who couldn't possibly live up to what was inside the Day-Glo pink and green album cover. So I put it between my Latin book, *Veni, Vidi, Vici,* and my massive Ancient Civilizations book and walked out the front door.

Back in Southie after dark, I took my usual route into the maze of Old Colony: through darkened courtyards, ducking under abandoned clotheslines from the time when people were trusting enough to hang their laundry outside, down the steps leading to the rear entrance of 8 Patterson, past the secretive voices of my sister Kathy and her friends getting high in the cellar, then a nimble jump over a huge polluted puddle — as kids we called it "polio water" — and into the dark hallway. If I could get past the polio water without stepping in it and didn't have to climb over any teenagers hanging out on the stairs or some mother's boyfriend camping out for the night, the rest of the coast was clear. But no matter what happened on this long route, it was better than having to make the ladies on the front stoop get up to let me pass. After Davey's death, I couldn't stand their sudden hush in my presence.

Once in the apartment I walked straight down the long hallway to my room at the back. I wanted to avoid anyone at home who might be awake — Ma or my older brothers and sisters. I knew they would think I was some kind of weirdo carrying a record that said THE SEX PISTOLS on the cover. In my room I stared at the album's title: *Never Mind the Bollocks.* From being around the Irish all my life I knew that "bollocks" meant balls or was a name for someone you considered an idiot or an asshole, or else it meant just plain "bullshit." I wondered which one the band meant. Kevin had given me a record player he'd swiped off the back of a truck. He couldn't sell it on the street because the plastic cover had broken off in the heist. Putting the needle on the record, I was distracted by a fight breaking out below my bedroom window.

"You like fuckin' my man, dontcha, Cookie!" Betty downstairs was yelling up to a neighbor across the street. "Because you want more babies! 'Cause you're the mothering kind. Ain't that right, Cookie!" Everyone knew that for Betty's husband Cookie was old news. These days he was messing around with Jeanie Gallagher, who was watching it all innocently from her window. But Betty had a baseball bat, and everyone was coming out to see what she would do with it. "'Cause you want more fuckin' money from the welfare! Ain't that right, Cookie?"

Then, in an instant of crashing guitar and a bloodcurdling voice that I could barely understand, the world of Old Colony Project began to crumble around me. Once and for all. It was terrifying and beautiful. Johnny Rotten's voice — whatever he was saying — fucked it all back out the window, every single thing I'd known, my whole life. I understood what "Never Mind the Bollocks" meant. As the album progressed from "Anarchy in the U.K." to "Belsen Was a Gas," ugly was beautiful and beautiful was ugly, all authority was mocked. The world around me was made weak and powerless by the most hideous and destructive voice I'd ever heard. In the collapse, a knot in my stomach — one I didn't even know I had — came undone. It was as if the voice was my own, and I'd rediscovered it in the rubble around me. The most important word I could make out upon the first listen was "destroy." I'd often heard adults and commentators on TV saying how music like this could destroy kids' lives. Staring at the neon album cover's kidnap-letter style, for once I thought they might be right. But to me that didn't feel like such a bad thing.

WHEN I CAME OUT of the bathroom, everyone in my family burst into laughter. "Who fucked up your head?" Kevin asked, like he was ready to give my barber a beating. I had chopped my hair into random near-bald spots and spiky clumps. I'd cut it without looking in the mirror, thinking that would be the best way to avoid a hair "style." Ma said I looked like I'd just escaped from Mass Mental. "That's that Sex Pistols shit I saw in his room," Kathy said. I didn't respond; I just gave them all dirty looks and slipped out the door with my books under my arm. The whole way to school I was yelled at by every group of kids I passed, from the streets of Southie, where most people shouted "Losah!" all the way across town on the Red Line and the Green Line, where some people moved away to get a look from a distance. I felt superior, in a way, like I'd been initiated into something that no one else got. The feathered haircuts that were so popular in 1979, which made people look as if they had wings sculpted to their heads, now looked absurd to me. I said nothing to any of the taunts from the winged crowd. When I walked into homeroom ten minutes late, the whole class exploded into fits of laughter. I felt pure exhilaration as I sat at my desk in the shadow of Mr. Tedeschi and deliberately ignored his sigh of jaded disapproval.

I was sent to Mr. Flaherty in Guidance for my constant tardiness the first few weeks of school. I was usually late because I took the subway through downtown so I wouldn't have to ride the Southie-to-Latin school bus. I had been the only one in my class at Saint Augustine's accepted to Boston Latin for seventh grade the previous year. Most of the kids on the bus were from City Point — only a few were from the Lower End of Southie, as I was. So I didn't know anyone, and to me the kids from the Point, with their pink cheeks and Irish knit sweaters, looked and acted like rich kids. They weren't really rich — they just had fathers and lived in houses instead of projects. But they usually kept their distance from us "project rats," and after a few times of being the only one picked up near the project and getting on the bus to abrupt silence, I was done with them.

When Mr. Flaherty asked me why I was late every day, I didn't know how to explain my complicated routes or the geography of Southie's City Point versus the Lower End. Instead I told him it was because there were problems at home, that my oldest brother had killed himself just over a month before. I wasn't looking for sympathy. I just thought that mentioning suicide would make him give up on the idea of lecturing me, and he'd send me back to class. But he said Davey's suicide was no excuse. "You need to get on with your life," he said, leaning back and folding his hands on his crossed leg. I wasn't even thinking of Davey or feeling bad about him that day. But when Mr. Flaherty said that I felt myself tense up. I was pissed off for Davey, that he should be forgotten so easily. But I didn't say anything. All the guidance counselors were pretty ancient, especially Mr. Flaherty, with his polyester suit, bow tie, and dyed orange hair. I let him lecture me for as long as he needed to, about how difficult his life was as a kid in the Depression, how hard he worked to get an education. "You can't sit around feeling sorry for yourself," he said, and I started to burn up with rage. I wanted to get out of there. The worst thing you could be accused of in my house was sitting around feeling sorry for yourself. When the bell for first period rang, I jumped up and told Mr. Flaherty I didn't feel sorry for myself and that I wouldn't be late again.

"Fuckin' weirdo," someone said in the hall. I was reminded again how butchered my hair looked compared to all the Barry Manilows and Farrah Fawcetts walking by. Mr. Flaherty hadn't even noticed my head, and I'd almost forgotten all about it. I tossed aside his comment about self-pity. I had been feeling really tired, always worn out, since the day Davey had killed himself. But today I felt alive. And everything felt new.

I was starting to think that the punishment for being late, forty minutes after school in detention, was not a bad deal. In the mornings I got to take the subways and see people coming from and going to all ends of the city, and after school I spent the extra period with an assortment of Latin's outcasts: a few rock 'n' roll stoners with shag haircuts and dingy KISS shirts; the sulking, angry black kid, Trey, who wore his laces undone and who sat pushed away from his desk, looking like he wanted nothing to do with any of us; Keith, a black rock 'n' roll kid whose tight jeans and Led Zeppelin shirt made Trey shake his head in disgust; a pretty girl all in black from my English class, who came into detention bundled up in a trench coat and a beret, looking like a terrorist and talking to no one; and a tall, lanky senior named Ginny, a punk rocker who walked pigeon-toed in pointed men's shoes and wore huge sweatshirts with sleeves that hung down to her knees. You always knew Ginny was coming into the detention room when you saw people nudge each other and laugh. This became the school period I most looked forward to, especially after I'd chopped my hair up and Ginny started to look at me with recognition. Before long she was telling me all about the bands she was seeing around town, at the Rathskeller — the Rat — and Cantone's. She talked to me like I knew about all the local bands, and I pretended I did.

Every day after detention I still had to kill hours and hours before going back to the project to sleep. I started loitering in

High Society, a New Wave clothes store on fancy Newbury Street that sold pointy shoes, Jetsons-style vinyl spacesuits, checkered pants, skinny ties, wraparound sunglasses, and badges with the names of bands like the Weirdos or pictures of David Bowie as space alien Ziggy Stardust. I never had more than a couple of bucks, but it didn't cost anything to hang around and listen to the records the shopkeepers were playing. I lingered at the glass case at the front of the store, pretending to look at the wraparound glasses and badges, so I could study the names on the album covers leaning against the record player: New York Dolls, the Talking Heads, Teenage Jesus and the Jerks. I had seen Blondie late at night on *Don Kirshner's Rock Concert,* and Elvis Costello on *Saturday Night Live,* but I didn't know most of these groups, and I didn't want to reveal my ignorance by being too obvious about it.

My first afternoon there I was just about to leave the store when one of the clerks took down a Patti Smith record that was propped on a fireplace mantel left over from the days when the shop had been an apartment. I had seen Patti Smith a couple years earlier, on the Saturday morning TV show *Kids Are People Too.* She wore an oversized man's blazer, and her gaunt face made her look something like Jesus on the cross. She sang Debby Boone's "You Light Up My Life" surrounded by an audience of entranced eight-year-olds. The show host had announced her as a "punk poet" and "the female Mick Jagger." As a kid I hadn't been into rock 'n' roll. All we ever listened to in Southie was soul or disco, even though the neighborhood wasn't safe for black people — or anyone else different from us — after the busing riots. Still, everyone knew who Mick Jagger was — especially after the Rolling Stones' "Miss You" became a disco hit. If Patti Smith was his female counterpart I was surprised I'd never heard of her. Seeing her on TV that Saturday morning gave me the willies, and I couldn't get her blank stare out of my head all day. I was probably eleven and couldn't believe she was on a show for kids younger than me, singing the worst soft-rock song ever but turning it into an intense dirge with her deep and ominous voice. The show's host asked her, "Are you punk rock?" She simply answered, "No," her blank stare unmoved by the host's enthusiasm. "Well, we think you're punk rock, right, kids?" the apple-cheeked host shouted, to the cheers of dozens of eight-year-olds screaming, "Yeah!" I had no idea what was going on. Punk rock? And the Debby Boone song? And that frightening gaze!

Here was that face again on the cover of an album the rockers at High Society were just opening. In the photo she wore a white, crisply pressed man's shirt and a black skinny tie. She looked like neither a man nor a woman. I had to stick around, looking through a rack of crazy polka-dot shirts, just so I could hear a song on the album. And as soon as it began it scared the shit out of me. *Jesus died for somebody's sins, but not mine . . .*

The sacrilegious mention of Jesus was enough to make my hair stand on end. I wanted more. Beyond that, I felt like I was being pulled into the singer's world, which I imagined was dangerous. And that made my heart really race. That face, and her stare. It wasn't a frightened look at all; it was more like someone who'd come down from the mountain after seeing the Burning Bush. I didn't want to be drawn in too far, but I stayed, listening to the slow-singing voice become deeper and even slower, almost to the point of talking the line *My sins my own, they belong to me . . .*

I was glued to every word, lingering on phrases and thinking I was hearing things I shouldn't hear. The language was familiar, as if from Catholic school and catechism. Sometimes she even reminded me of Davey's darker days of hating and loving God. But the familiar words were being swept into a heap and set on fire — for good or bad, it didn't matter. She was just doing it. She was saying things I'd never heard anyone say. It was hard to tell whether she was religious or antireligious. I hadn't been feeling too religious since Davey died. But even though I was pissed off at any God there might be, I could never curse God. Still, it did feel good to listen to someone else getting it all out. Then she broke into a different kind of familiarity, with the chorus taken from the oldies song "Gloria," but in a louder and faster version. I stayed at High Society for another half-hour just to listen to more of the album. I tried to be inconspicuous, but I was the only customer in the store, and the rocker clerks occasionally stared at me curiously from between racks of spacesuits that I had no intention of buying.

I overheard one of them call Patti Smith's voice abrasive. That did seem a good word to describe what I was hearing. But it was the cleansing kind of abrasive. "Scouring" made even more sense, like Ajax. Most of the words were lost on me, references to poets and figures from the Bible. But regardless of the meaning of the words, it seemed dangerous to open up to someone who said she wanted to be "outside of society." The voice, the blasphemies — it all seemed so brave. Not just blasphemy against God but against everything she must have come from — wherever that was — and the desire to break out of that world. Her manic recitations reminded me of some of the inmates I'd been preoccupied with during visits to see Davey at Mass Mental when I was a kid. Patti Smith didn't seem trapped in an illness or in a hospital, but it did seem like she'd escaped from somewhere.

After visiting High Society for a few days in a row, I knew I had to buy something, so I went for the cheapest thing I could find: a one-dollar badge that said B-52'S. I knew by then that the B-52's were a band. After that I felt I had to buy at least a badge when I showed up at the store, so before long I had a collection. I had badges for all the bands I was hearing there, like the Clash and the Ramones, and some of the badges with sayings, like NO ONE IS INNOCENT, with a picture of Sid Vicious giving the two-fingered British hand gesture for "fuck off." My favorite was the badge that said IN ORDER TO CREATE, YOU MUST DESTROY. The saying didn't really make sense to me, but I was running out of one-dollar buttons to buy and was afraid I'd have to move on to the flashy skinny ties. One day I splurged and got ten-dollar wraparound sunglasses, which I might wear downtown but never into Southie. If I wore them there, I imagined that even my older brothers would want to give me a beating.

At the welfare office Ma got me an application for a part-time job through Youth Enrichment Services. Unlike the summer jobs we always got through the antipoverty program ABCD, the jobs from YES were year-round. Most of the ABCD jobs were with teams of kids sweeping glass and cutting weeds in Southie's three housing projects. I lucked out with YES, though, getting placed at the Children's Museum, just over the bridge from Southie — a good excuse to be gone from home a lot. And it was an easy job, with hippie bosses who didn't care about dress codes. My supervisors for the chain-gang jobs in the projects had been Southie guys who liked being bosses a little too much. They almost always carried a clipboard and wrote god-knows-what while watching us sweep. "You think you're King Shit," Kevin told our supervisor one year, "just because you live in the Point." When Kevin heard he'd been docked a whole week's pay for that remark, he slammed down his broom for good, throwing it into a gutter filled with polio water. I wasn't one to talk up like that — some of our neighbors had even nicknamed me "the quiet one" among the MacDonalds. I stopped to watch Kevin in admiration as he took off with a resolute stomp through the courtyard. But I got back to my weed-whacking when King Shit barked at me, "You got something to say too?"

Kevin said he'd heard that King Shit originally came from Old Colony but his family had moved to City Point. "Them are the worst kind," he assured me, shaking his head, "ex-project rats!" We were better versed in the neighborhood's turflines than in anything we learned in school. But to me it was all becoming the same, whether lace-curtain City Point, the shabby row houses crowding the West Side, or the hard dirt and concrete courtyards of the three projects. It was all Southie. And its borders were starting to feel like a noose closing in on me.

I looked forward to going straight from school to the Children's Museum, perfectly located in the no man's land among the abandoned warehouses and factories on Southie's perimeter.

At work all I had to do was hang out at the exhibits and make sure kids didn't break things or cut in line. My bosses gave me a quick lesson in using chopsticks, and when I became a chopstick expert on the first try, they assigned me to the Japanese house. I'd never thought work could be as easy as this, sitting on the floor of a house made of bamboo and rice paper — shipped piece by piece from Japan — awaiting my next student, chopsticks in hand. Most of the time I sat there alone, though, since school groups were the main visitors to the Japanese house, and I worked the after-school hours. Passing the time by imagining I lived in the Japanese house was fun for about two weeks.

But after a while the silence made me nervous, and I asked to be moved to the Native American wigwam. I sat in the dark hut, usually wearing my wraparound sunglasses, dog collar, and army surplus clothes, waiting for visitors — who were always shocked to see a person take form once their eyes adjusted to the dark. Little kids would run into the wigwam to dance in circles, cupping their hands over their mouths and relentlessly droning *wawawawa*. The job description for the wigwam post included teaching the kids that it was not called a "tepee" and that Native Americans never really did that thing with the cupped hand over the mouth. But I got sick of all the rich kids with Pilgrimlike bowl haircuts shouting "Look, Mom, it's a tepee!" followed by the predictable rain dance. So I asked to be assigned to the play-space, a free-for-all area where toddlers ran wild and threw wooden blocks at each other's heads. Nobody wanted to be assigned there. But Seamus and Stevie had given me experience with that age group, and it felt normal to have a little life going on around me. And even if these kids were rich they weren't talking yet, other than in meaningless gabble. So it became my favorite post.

The only problem at work was, you were supposed to be sixteen to get a job through YES. I was thirteen. But Ma always got us over that hurdle by giving each kid the birth certificate and Social Security card of the next one up in the family. Kevin had a work ID for "Frank MacDonald," Frank became "Joseph," and so on, allowing each of us to get summer jobs before we were old enough. Ma had given me Kevin's birth certificate to use, so I had to learn to answer to "Kevin" at the Children's Museum. That was easy enough, but when I went home to Old Colony, I'd jump out of bed whenever someone hollered "Kevin!" up to our windows, looking for some stolen Calvin Kleins or a dime bag. I was unsure of my own name sometimes, and I felt like an imposter at work, but it was worth any amount of confusion to make three dollars and sixty-five cents an hour: about a hundred dollars every two weeks. From the Children's Museum it was only a short walk to the ancient wooden escalator at South Station, an easy sneak-in point on the MBTA, so I could always get home for free. And on payday I'd use the escalator entrance to go to the record stores. Ma didn't want any of my check, so I could have paid the fare, but I wanted to spend it all on records.

Coming out of High Society, wearing a Sex Pistols T-shirt with PRETTY VACANT scrawled on it, wraparounds, and a badge I'd just bought that said I'M A MESS, I saw the ghoulish guy from Strawberries across the street. He had on the same too-small pinstripe suit and the dog collar. He was shouting at a couple heading into High Society wearing spacesuits and carrying huge Fiorucci shopping bags. "New Wave fuckwads!" he screamed. "Die!" He muttered to himself that High Society should be blown up. It was a warm day in September, and the B-52's "Rock Lobster" blasted from High Society's open windows, pissing off Ghoulish Guy even more, making him scream at onlookers that the B-52's sucked shit.

I thought he was shouting at me until I realized he hadn't even seen me come out of the store. I would have thought High

Society was his kind of place, since he looked so weird. New Wave? All I knew was that all of it was worlds away from Southie. And I was thinking I *liked* the B-52's. Ghoulish Guy disappeared into a dimly lit shop in an apartment building across the street from High Society. It was a comic-book store, but the cardboard sign taped to the window said IMPORT RECORDS. A great racket blared from the open windows: jittery guitar, violent pounding drums, and the whiny voice of someone who couldn't sing and didn't seem to care.

I walked by the store five times before I got up the guts to go in and investigate. I didn't know much about bands beyond the Sex Pistols and the Ramones, and I was afraid I'd get a quiz upon entering. The people I'd spied going into the store looked like they lived and breathed the music blasting out the windows. Some were dressed like crazy people, others were spooky-looking, like Ghoulish Guy. A few wore dirty, wrinkled clothes and maybe one weird thing, like bobo sneakers or an oversized dress shirt, which was enough to get stares and judgmental headshakes from passers-by.

The store was cluttered with rows of dusty cardboard boxes labeled IMPORT and filled with 45s. Flipping through, I saw that most were from England. The S bin had the Sex Pistols but also lots of bands I'd never heard of, like Slaughter and the Dogs, the Stains, and the Slits. And all the talk in the store was about a new record from the Gang of Four. I got the sense, from nearly every name I read, that none of this stuff was meant to be popular. How many people would want to answer "Who's your favorite band?" with "The Buzzcocks"? Catching sight of the 45 on the ramshackle turntable, I realized that's what had been spewing out the window when I walked in. I knew I had stumbled into the center of the universe I wanted to be in, so I took note of everything I saw and heard, trying not to be identified as an outsider. I caught on quickly that the song was called "Boredom," because that was the most repeated word, and there were only a handful of words in the first place. The singer with the off-key whiny voice wailed, boredom, boredom, boredom. As simple as that. The song was so simple, it seemed ridiculous that *everyone* hadn't written a song about boredom. Anyone could do it. And I could relate to it. I was bored all the time, wandering Boston trying to kill time. It was either that or go back to the project, with the same old fights, same old wheeling and dealing on the corner, same old fears about the bigger world. I liked riding the subways, but that was getting boring too. I had to admit to myself, *I'm totally fucking bored!*

Ghoulish Guy was bopping his nest of hair, which looked like it had exploded that morning. It was ratted in all directions except in back, which was oddly flat — as if he didn't bother with the back of his head because he couldn't see it. He flailed his arms and convulsed in a dance that didn't seem safe in such a small shop. Then he made a sudden spastic movement that looked like a cross between playing air guitar and getting punched in the stomach. I watched him out of the corner of my eye so I could protect myself if a limb came my way. He knew all the words to the chorus — the one word to the chorus, boredom — and sang it like he was pissed off about being bored. But I was just bored of being bored. I guessed there were many ways you could be bored. Good thing the song was less than three minutes long, because even *it* was getting boring.

I spent a good two hours in the store and was amazed at how many songs were about being bored, or everything being stupid, or needing to escape this world or smash it all up.

"Yeah! Iggy and the Stooges!" Ghoulish Guy shouted. "The only true punk band!" *'Cause I'm the world's forgotten boy. The one who's searching, and searching to destroy.* I was getting all the lyrics from Ghoulish Guy's singalong, each line followed by that punch-in-the-stomach air guitar. He asked the clerk if they carried the Soft Boys' "I Wanna Destroy You." A lot of the songs seemed to be about destroying. Some of them just said that everything was screwed up. It felt good that someone was taking notice. It made me feel normal. I was taking it all in, not missing a word in the songs or in the comments of people in the store. The jacket of each record being played was set on the mantel next to the turntable. Richard Hell and the Voidoids came on next, convulsing some words about belonging to the blank generation. Most rock 'n' roll songs were about love and romance. The R&B and funk I'd grown up on was grounded in everyday city life, but a lot of the newer disco was about nothing more than escaping to the dance floor. The music I was hearing now was about the side of life no one wanted to talk about, and just telling the truth about that, like the next single on the turntable, "Nervous Breakdown."

> I'm about
> To have a nervous breakdown
> My head really hurts
> If I don't find a way out of here
> I'm gonna go berserk 'cuz
> I'm crazy and I'm hurt
> Head on my shoulders
> It's going . . . berserk

I wanted to buy the Black Flag single, but I also wanted to stick around and listen to more records. Ghoulish Guy lingered in the store too. The place felt like a hangout, where no one was pressured to buy. People flipped through records and talked about bands all afternoon. Even with eight people in the tiny room it felt packed. Ghoulish Guy flaunted his knowledge of the music, asking about records the store didn't have yet. He called the music "underground," not punk or New Wave. I noticed that nothing in the store mentioned punk or New Wave. I didn't dare open my mouth to ask any questions. When someone put on the Patti Smith album I wanted to buy, Ghoulish Guy said, "C'mon, man. It's 1979 already. This hippie shit is boring." He had an opinion about everything, and later I overheard him carrying on about the Clash being sellouts and too trendy for him. "Next thing you know, the fucking jocks will be chanting along to them," he said. I was just getting into the Clash, and was excited that the store was playing something I actually knew.

I flipped through the bins, pretending to know what I was looking at. When Ghoulish Guy started looking through the bin next to me, I moved away so he couldn't strike up a conversation and expose my ignorance. He was staring at the Damned record in his hand like he was dying to discuss it. "If this is anything like their lame album last year . . ." he muttered to himself. I saw one song title on the album cover, "I Just Can't Be Happy Today," and figured Ghoulish was in for a treat. I moved to the other side of the shop — probably the bedroom when the shop had been an apartment — and came upon the mostly British magazines and newspapers: *New Musical Express, Sounds, Melody Maker.* There were some Xeroxed Boston "fanzines" with photos of local people in a variety of freakish styles: girls in knee socks, miniskirts, men's shoes, pigtails, and eyes blackened like a raccoon's; guys with chopped-up hair and high-water pants like the patients I'd seen when I visited Davey at Mass Mental years before. Some had leather jackets and shaggy exploded hair, but most were much less identifiable as any kind of "rockers." In Southie a person dressed like that would be considered "a retard," or "a freak show" and "a fuckin' losah," which in Southie was as bad as being a communist or a liberal. What thrilled me was that these people looked like they wouldn't mind being called freak shows, or even communists. They were flaunting that they weren't like everyone else or even like each other.

After spending hours at Newbury Comics I bought the English paper *NME* and the Boston fanzine *Killer Children.* I wanted to go home, lock myself in my back room, and study it all. But I never looked forward to the trip through the neighborhood, where the basement hangouts of Old Colony were starting to smell like angel dust, and street-corner conversation was all about this one sucker punching that one. Walking back down Newbury Street toward the T stop, I felt like everyone I passed — businesspeople, college jocks, meter maids, and the done-up Back Bay women — knew nothing of the new secret world I'd discovered, where each person could be in charge of who he was and stand up to what's "normal."

Out of nowhere Ghoulish Guy appeared next to me, talking away as if we were allies against all the people he pushed past on the street, "fucking suits, fucking jocks." Then he saw another New Waver, who to me looked basically like him, except with newer designer versions of what he wore. My dark friend yelled at him, "Take the hog!" It was like New Wavers were a threat to this secret world I'd witnessed in the tiny vault of the record store. Then Ghoulish Guy ranted about the last Stranglers album versus the early Stranglers. I'd never heard of the Stranglers. I just nodded in case he was talking to me, and kept walking. He always seemed to be griping, whether anyone was listening or not. He mentioned his purchase, the album by the Damned, looking at it like it was going to be a big disappointment. I had never seen anyone so skeptical about everything, so hopeless, even about all this music I was jumping out of my skin for. "Same old shit," he said more than once, about anything from the direction the Stranglers were going in to the jocks we were approaching in front of Daisy Buchanan's Pub.

"Faggot!" someone yelled from a passing car, which made him grab his crotch and yell back, "Suck this!" When someone shouted "Rock Lobster," the B-52's song, he held his middle finger up in the air as if at the whole world. "All it takes is one trendy New Wave group like the B-52's, and suddenly every one of them thinks they know what you're into." I just nodded, thinking *At least he doesn't think I'm one of "them."* But I was worried that I could get into a fight by hanging out near someone dressed like him. "Freak!" someone screamed from the jock bar, Daisy Buchanan's. The whole crowd inside poured out to get a good laugh at him.

"Okay, um, I'll see you later," I said nervously. Ghoulish Guy continued to gripe about this and that, looking straight ahead, determined to clear a path of destruction through the world of "normal people" he despised. "You going to see the Dead Boys if they tour again?" he asked, stopping to chitchat in spite of all hell breaking loose around us. "Definitely!" I said abruptly, looking for an escape from the riled crowd approaching us. *Who the fuck are the Dead Boys?* was what I was thinking as I inched toward the curb. *And why would a band call itself that?* Or even the Stranglers or the Damned, the other two bands he talked about. I knew too many real dead boys in Southie, had heard rumors of a few strangled people, and I was afraid that I knew more than a few of the damned, so the names irked me a little. But I guessed that was the point. It seemed like every band name I was hearing was meant to mess with everything I'd accepted as right and wrong, good taste and bad taste, discussable and beyond the pale.

Ghoulish Guy shook my hand and told me his name was Bob. *Such a normal name for such a weird guy,* I thought. I would have guessed he had a punk name, something like "Vic Demised." He stumbled off awkwardly, hunched over, adding to the freakish spectacle. The crowd of jocks outside Daisy Buchanan's cleared a path for him, nudging each other and laughing hysterically. No one wanted to *not* notice him. They all looked desperate to be in on the joke. Ghoulish Bob brought out the worst in everyone, it seemed, then celebrated his accomplishment by pointing out to them that they were "dumb fucks" and should go back to the caves they came from. The last I saw of him that afternoon, he was being chased by a mob of beefy guys with Red Sox hats.

All I had was messed-up hair and a Sex Pistols T-shirt, so I didn't think I was in danger. But when a bottle smashed at my feet, I bolted the rest of the way to the train station.

Last-period English class made me feel trapped. Mr. Nolan had an uncontrollable nervous gulp, and he'd sometimes get stuck on a swallow, like a broken record. Time stood still during his battle. It made me want to jump out of my skin, seeing him stuck that way, as he tried to distract us by pointing to the sentence he was diagramming on the blackboard. He looked like he was in hell. Panic would overtake his face, and he'd force the gulp deeper and deeper until he freed himself. When he finally came up for air, his posh mannerisms, which everyone made fun of, lightened everything up. He tossed back his layered Bee Gees hair and gave the back of his head a maintenance pat-down. I took a deep breath before counting down to the next time his voice would hesitate and he'd be ambushed again. I looked forward to detention during last period, and watching the clock only made it tick slower.

The girl in black sat next to me. She looked as uninterested in prepositional phrases as I was, and she nonchalantly scribbled a notch in her notebook every time Mr. Nolan took a gulp, like it was her job. During one of the multi-gulps, a panic that lasted a good ten seconds, she seemed to be debating whether that one was worth one notch or two. *I'd give it a three,* I thought. That's when she caught me staring at her notebook and pulled it closer to her, hiding the private count with her left arm. I didn't know what she was all about, why she always wore black. She carried around *The Flowers of Evil,* by Charles Baudelaire. And on Declamation Day, when everyone at Latin was expected to recite a favorite poem or speech from memory, her piece was by Arthur Rimbaud. She explained to the class that he was a French Romantic writing in the mid-nineteenth century. I had no idea what a French Romantic was, but his portrait on the cover of the book — in a disheveled suit and uncombed hair — made him look like Richard Hell or Johnny Rotten. Her clothes and intense expression looked sort of like a punk rock thing too, but she wasn't really all that punked out — not like Bob. The Patti Smith button on her lapel might have identified her as punk — punk bands in fanzines often mentioned Patti Smith as an influence, along with other strange people who came before punk, like Bowie or the Velvet Underground, but I'd learned that Patti Smith appealed to oddballs of every stripe. This girl had an old-fashioned hairdo, beautiful shiny black waves like the women in movies from the 1940s. Her clothes were like the clothes in those movies too, except that hers were all black. The only other people I saw wearing all black in Boston were Greek widows or Catholic priests. I couldn't figure her out. So I passed her a note during one of Mr. Nolan's extended gulps.

Are you New Wave? I wrote.

No. I am No Wave!!! she scribbled angrily.

I thought that was a good one, but I wanted her to elaborate. *What do you mean?*

She scrawled abruptly and impatiently, *I am not into labels!*

Wow, I thought. *That was wicked cool.* To me, she was one-up on the punk bands that were declaring in fanzines that they were "anti-art" or "anti-fashion."

What is your name? I wrote.

SIOUXSIE, she spelled out in capital letters.

"See-oox-see," I mouthed, examining the scrap of paper in my hand. *Whoa,* I muttered.

"What *are* you?" I whispered to her. That's how we asked about ethnic background in Boston — one of the first things we asked about anyone. She was olive-skinned and she had a strange name. She grabbed back the piece of paper with her name, which I was still studying, and scribbled in big letters *AN ANARCHIST.*

My jaw dropped. I looked at her in recognition. I had been dying to find out what "anarchy" really meant ever since I'd first heard the word in a Sex Pistols song. But I didn't dare ask. Instead I wrote back, *Just like Johnny Rotten,* hoping she'd identify me as someone from her exclusive underground world. *It's Lydon, Johnny Lydon,* she wrote back, shooting me down for being a year behind on the Sex Pistols breakup. I had read all about Johnny Rotten recently moving on from his Sex Pistols past and going back to his birth name. But before I could respond, she grabbed the paper again and wrote *PUNK IS DEAD! GET OVER IT!*

Punk is dead? Fuck it, I thought. *I'm gonna ask some ques-*

tions here. Pushing aside the scrap of paper in front of me that said *GET OVER IT,* I asked out loud, "What's an anarchist?"

"Mr. [gulp] MacDonald," Mr. Nolan said, after looking at his list of student names, "when do we use a semicolon?" I was glad he'd escaped with only one gulp, but I couldn't answer the question. "Misdemeanor mark!" he said without hesitation. He scratched a note on the roster. "Remedios," Mr. Nolan continued, addressing the girl in black — who had apparently lied about her name being Siouxsie — "what is a prepositional phrase?"

She knew the answer, even though she must have had about thirty notches on her notebook, one for each of Mr. Nolan's gulps, and had been paying no more attention than I had. I was pissed off now. Not because she knew the answer to Mr. Nolan's question, but because she'd lied to me about her name. She must have thought I was some kind of idiot, I thought. This was my first misdemeanor mark. It took only seven marks to fail in conduct at Latin School, but I didn't really care much about that. I had always been the goody two-shoes in my family, and it was about time I received a blotch on my report card. I was determined, though, to find out what an anarchist was and to show the girl in black — Remedios, an even stranger name than Siouxsie — that I wasn't one of the normal people.

Everywhere I turned I was picking up information from the underground music world. The blasphemous songs and ugly clothes that enraged passers-by were my private obsession. Ma asked me why I had stopped hanging out with my friends in Old Colony, and I didn't really have an answer. We had nothing in common, I guessed.

I started to go home only after dark, usually after working at the Children's Museum or spending hours on Newbury Street, and I'd go straight down the long hallway to my room without talking to anyone in my family. Johnny was away serving in the Navy SEALs, Joe had recently disappeared into the air force, and Kathy and Kevin were always out. Frankie often came over to eat and watch TV with Ma and the little kids, but I avoided going into the kitchen or parlor until everyone had gone to bed. "Mike, sit down for God's sake," Ma would shout at me as I made a beeline for my stereo, but I paid no attention.

Late one night I came across a fuzzy-sounding radio station playing the Buzzcocks' "Boredom." I couldn't believe it. The signal was at the very far end of the dial, where there were hardly any stations. I began to listen to the show *The Nite Club*, religiously every night from eight to eleven. My radio became the only thing I looked forward to in Old Colony Project. I usually couldn't get to sleep until very late, when I was completely exhausted from hours of listening to music and reading British music newspapers.

Alone in my room I began to hear some of the groups I was reading about. By now I knew dozens of songs by bands like the Stranglers, the Damned, and the Dead Boys, whose song "Sonic Reducer" made me cue up my cassette recorder every night. Even so, I always missed the first few lines of the song. I decided one night to spend the whole three hours of *The Nite Club* with my fingers on PAUSE, RECORD, and PLAY, to finally tape the song from start to finish. I had nothing else to do except Latin homework.

I'd bought one ninety-minute cassette and filled it with songs, recording over the ones I was sick of whenever I needed space for something new. Copies of *New Musical Express* — NME — were strewn all over my floor, and my walls were becoming covered with pictures of bands, vampires, and legendary people who looked like they had landed on the wrong planet. Crumpled aluminum foil and cool-looking trash from the streets surrounded photos of Samuel Beckett with his stark expression or Maria Callas opening her mouth and eyes wide as if she was either screaming in terror or hitting a high note.

"Mother of Christ!" Ma yelled when she walked in on me covering my windows with black cloth. She asked if I thought I might be having a nervous breakdown. When I calmly answered no, she yelled back down the hallway, "Well then, open those goddamn windows! It's like a friggin' tomb back there."

But to me, entering my room felt like entering into a world that only I needed to get, one that I controlled entirely. And most nights I kept the windows closed despite the project radiators' constant dry heat. That way I could prevent the chaos on the streets from pouring in and invading the world I'd created. And with my windows covered in black cloth, I could sometimes forget even in daytime that I was in Southie.

It was from here that I could read up on all the bands I was taping from the radio. A lot of these people were in their early twenties — almost a decade older than me. In interviews the British bands talked about things I didn't understand and had to look up, like the "status quo" in Britain, and how they wished to destroy everything that previous generations had created, whether the laziness of the stoned hippies or the seventies glam notion of the rock star. In most of the interviews I read, English punks insisted they weren't really musicians or artists at all, just bored kids on the dole. Some were against drugs, while others bragged about getting "pissed" drunk. But they encouraged everyone to make up his own mind, and to get up and do something — anything — to change the world. Some of the British phrases in *NME* were like Irish ones, so once in a while I'd come out of my room to ask Ma about things like "the dole" and "council housing." I was surprised to realize that a lot of the British punks had grown up on welfare and in the projects, like me. The American bands like Patti Smith, Television, and Richard Hell had escaped from suburban towns in New Jersey or Ohio to CBGB, New York's East Village club that was a notorious mecca for underground music. In Southie I was on my own, since I couldn't imagine my neighbors going against the grain like this.

I was learning more vocabulary and history and social studies through the music than in school. Patti Smith pointed me to William Blake, Jackson Pollock, and the Beat writers. When I read that a Cure song was about Camus's book *The Stranger,* I read it in two days, faster than I'd ever read anything assigned by my teachers. X-Ray Spex's seventeen-year-old Poly Styrene sang about people shopping too much, about the environment, about an increasingly plastic world. I had to look up words like "consumerism." Johnny Lydon — or Rotten, as I still preferred to call him — with his new band, Public Image Ltd., continued to knock everything.

One of the only Saturdays I stayed home to watch TV on the couch with my family, I happened to catch him on Dick Clark's *American Bandstand*. Rotten refused to lip-synch, and, pushing confused audience members onto the stage, caused chaos on live TV. Ma's only comment was that Johnny Rotten looked Irish. Frankie said, "Why are we watching this shit?" and changed the channel.

Where Johnny Rotten continued on his rampage to tear it all down, the Clash gave me political ideas to look up, as they sang about class, racism, and the need to question everything. I felt that I was at the center of something that had never happened before, a completely new era when each person could invent a whole new existence, new ways of looking at things, aesthetically, politically, and personally. And that this would change the world for sure.

Whenever someone in Southie died, the whole neighborhood got together to throw a "time" to raise money for the burial. A time was one of those neighborhood traditions that made you feel you were part of one big family. I couldn't believe they were doing it for Davey, since he'd committed suicide. The priests at Saint Augustine's had been good enough to sneak Davey through with a Catholic funeral. They said nothing in the Mass about heaven or hell, which was a relief, but I knew it was the biggest thing on everyone's mind.

Sister Peggy from Saint Augustine's School had been the only one to break the silence about Davey's death. She was everyone's favorite nun, known for her fluorescent beach hats and for making us all get up in music class to dance the hully gully.

She called me soon after Davey jumped to tell me that she too had once wanted to die. "Desperately! Oh, I was bad," she said, her voice dropping low. "One time I even lay on the railroad track for an hour before realizing my friggin' train wasn't coming that day." Sister Peggy laughed nervously but got serious again as she told me that someday, when I was able to, I should try to forgive Davey, that most people didn't have a clue about the pain he was in when he made that awful decision, "but I sure as hell do." As sad as it was to picture Sister Peggy on a train track, I hung up the phone feeling that Davey was not so alone, and neither was I.

Now, two months later, with no talk about the bloody scene we'd all witnessed in August, I figured everyone but Sister Peggy had moved on. The chorus of that season's hit song said it best: *Leave your cares behind, these are the good times.* And who would ever want to argue with that?

But Southie was coming together to remember Davey, by organizing a time that would pay the entire bill at Jackie O'Brien's funeral parlor. I was startled to see the flyers up at every corner store for Davey's time at the Social Club. Since I no longer wanted anything to do with Southie, it was almost too much to bear.

Even I had been thinking less about Davey. At first, after his funeral, I gathered the Mass cards people gave us and placed them around a large table. Most of them had sketches of Jesus with rays coming from his palms, reminding me of Davey's obsession with Christ's stigmata, which he'd sometimes thought he had during his sicker periods. I surrounded the Mass cards with mementos, like a Polaroid someone had taken of Davey the night before he jumped. The picture was shot at Jolly Donuts, and Davey's face was whited out like a ghost's from the glare of the flash. You knew it was him, though, by the crown of curls and the nervous way he faced the camera and waved. My memorial to Davey had dominated my bedroom before my punk cutouts took over and turned my room into a giant shrine to a madness I could control. Lately the neglected memorial had gotten dusty, and some of the cards had curled and fallen over. Part of the table was taken up by my stereo and piles of old disco cassettes I'd found and taped over with songs from *The Nite Club*. I was ashamed to think that I'd moved on while the neighbors I'd begun to hate were dressing the Social Club in green balloons, shamrocks, and IN MEMORY OF DAVEY MACDONALD posters.

All of Southie came out for Davey's time. I made an effort to deal with my brothers and sisters for the night, even combing my tangled, spiky hair flat to cover the bald spots I'd shaved. Kevin warned that I'd better dress normal or he was going to beat the fuck out of me. Most of my clothes were torn or spray-painted old men's clothes I'd rummaged from Grandpa's closet and thrift shops. But I found a suit from a couple of years earlier in a pile in the clothes room. The same people who would have been horrified to see the clothes I usually wore didn't bat an eye at the too-small pale blue polyester suit with a fake napkin sewn into the chest pocket. I couldn't button the pants and was afraid they'd fall, so I sat in a chair all evening and resisted all the attempts by neighbors and former friends to drag me up by the arm every time one of the current disco anthems came on. As I watched the constant trips to the bathroom, I realized that half the crowd was probably snorting coke. Kathy showed up late with a gang of girls Kevin called "dust mops" because they were always high on angel dust. Ma got into an argument with Kathy after asking her too many questions about this friend and that friend. But for the most part everyone got along that night.

Ma was partying on the dance floor with her new boyfriend, Jitterbug Joe. Jitterbug had been homeless, but Ma got him all cleaned up. She said she liked going out dancing with him — he was once known for his moves on dance floors from Southie to Dorchester. But Grandpa knew him from when Jitterbug looked for day jobs on the Southie docks, where Grandpa worked as a longshoreman. He said Jitterbug was a bum, and that after cleaning up his act he just looked like a rat that had taken a bath. Grandpa wouldn't honor Jitterbug with his dance floor name, and would only call him Bedbug Joe, each time scowling and scratching his head, no matter how many times someone corrected him.

I felt weighed down, reminded of the sadness of Davey's life and death, and the disco made it all the more depressing. When "Boogie Wonderland" came on, I remembered liking that beat growing up, but now it all seemed like lies. Disco and funk to me were about the bass, so I'd never actually listened closely to the lyrics of the songs. I looked around and realized that I was the only one who was really listening that night.

> The mirror stares you in the face and says
> Baby, uh uh it don't work
> You say your prayers though you don't care
> You dance and shake the hurt
> Dance boogie wonderland.

Frankie came to the time surrounded by some of the guys from McDonough's Gym and their older fans, the gangsters who ran Southie. Frankie was known for staying straight, but a lot of the guys from the gym were whispered to be pushing the dust and coke on the street. I wanted a strong drink so I could get dizzy and stop analyzing everything. But if there was one thing I hated the sight of, especially in Southie, it was alcohol. I stayed sober and felt superior to all the people so easily sucked in by drink, pills, and a beat that betrayed them. It was nice of Southie to pay for the funeral with a time. But I missed Davey's crazy talk and preaching about "the truth" more than ever.

Right in the middle of "Boogie Wonderland" Kevin ordered the disc jockey to stop. He swayed drunk and grabbed the mike. When he had everyone's attention, he shouted, "Let's hear it for Disco Davey!" All the young people burst into applause, as they would for anything Kevin might say. But the older people shook their heads at his disrespect for the dead. He was about to say more, when Ann Daly from across the street slapped him in the face. Kathy went to grab her by the hair, ready for a brawl, but Ma stopped her. Ann was one of the time's organizers. She just didn't get what Kevin was trying to do. Nor did the crowd still cheering for "Disco Davey." I was shocked that Kevin had thought of something so brilliant. What did any of this dusted-out disco party have to do with Davey, who would have seen only "the end of time" playing out around him here? For a moment I felt like Kevin was thinking the same thing that night. But he left the party with his gang of friends, and since we never really talked about Davey, I knew I'd never find out.

Ma told the disc jockey to carry on. He announced "We Are Family" as the last song of the night and, as if on cue, the whole hall jumped up except me. Girls ran to the dance floor, shrieking that the song was their favorite, claiming it like no one had ever claimed it before. And stoned guys staggered behind them agreeing that the song was "fuckin' pissa." *All of the people around us they say / Can they be that close.* My sister Mary tried to pull me up. "Nah, I hate this song," I said. "Fuckin' weirdo," Kathy muttered, walking by me on the way to the dance floor. She was always grouchy and looking for a fistfight these days. *Just let me state for the record / We're giving love in a family dose.*

Getting ready for Davey's time, I had felt some nostalgia for Southie's closeness. But now — completely sober and wearing a too-small polyester suit from my disco days — I was a little sick to see the neighborhood sing along like one big family. *High hopes we have for the future / And our goal's in sight / No we don't get depressed / Here's what we call our golden rule.*

I knew everyone in the neighborhood was so lit from Davey's time that it would be a wild night in Old Colony, and I couldn't wait to get back to my room with its sealed and blackened windows.

THE WHOLE TRAIN was staring at me, but I pretended not to notice. I'd been having insomnia and couldn't get to sleep the night before, and now I was late for school. An older black woman standing next to me leaned back and gasped, like I was the devil himself. I was wearing spray-painted black-and-white-checkered pants and black pointy shoes that even the homeless guys at Andrew Station had commented on. "Jeez, I coulda used them last night," one said, telling me that the rats were as big as cats in the station overnight. Now the woman next to me started beating on my back with her fists. I didn't think it would really come to this, strangers getting violent over the way I looked. I pulled away from her, just as she raised her foot to stomp on the cockroach she'd beaten off my back. She crushed it until she was sure it was dead, and looked at me with satisfaction. I saw the dead cockroach but didn't acknowledge any of it. I ignored the woman's pride in her roach-stomping skills and the chuckles of some of the other kids on the train, and slipped off at the next stop.

The doorway of my homeroom was filled with kids clambering over each other to get a look at me. I was at my desk working on the previous night's homework, pretending not to notice all the commotion. My homeroom teacher, Mr. Tedeschi, leaned against the wall with arms folded, shaking his head in disdain at my "looking for attention." I shrugged, glancing over at the black kids filing in to take their seats. None of them cared about my pink hair, which I'd meant to dye blood red. When the human pyramid in the doorway turned into a pig pile at Mr. Tedeschi's feet, he said he'd had enough and told me to go to the school nurse. "To get your head examined," he shouted after me, hoping and failing to get a laugh from the dispersing crowd.

The school nurse was on the phone but couldn't contain her look of disgust. She cupped her hand over the receiver, as if the person on the other end might hear her thoughts, and waved urgently for me to lie down on the green vinyl bed. Nurse Feely was always chirpy in a nervous way. Whenever I went to the nurse's office, faking symptoms and hoping to be sent home, she'd tell me repeatedly that I was going to be fine. But she was clearly so concerned about me — even without the slightest temperature — that she'd keep me all day for observation instead of sending me home. I'd given up on faking sick, and I avoided her concern like the plague. Now I lay down on the rock-hard green vinyl bed, folded my hands on top of my stomach, and kept perfectly still to avoid making crunchy vinyl noises. I glanced sideways at Nurse Feely on the phone, not moving my head, and wondered what she could do for someone with pink hair anyway. Her face told me she didn't know exactly what I was doing there, and she cupped the receiver again as if to keep her perplexed thoughts from the person she was talking to.

"Woohoo! . . . Oh boy! . . . What have we got here?" she asked as soon as she'd hung up. She walked to the far end of the room to study me from a safe distance while trying to look upbeat and unfazed. Then she began to pace, massaging her hands and looking worried about our predicament. "It's really no big deal," I said, shrugging. "I don't know why I was sent here." She walked over to me slowly, then bent forward, looking into my eyes like she was looking into a new neighbor's windows, trying to snoop without offending. "So, ah, I never saw this before," she said, throwing up her hands and letting out a sigh. "This pink hair thing . . . does, um, your mother do this? Is this a family thing? What is it?" She backed up again.

I laughed at the idea of my mother having electric pink hair but found the "What is it?" question really difficult and decided to sit up. I could explain that it was punk rock or New Wave or whatever and hope that she had seen some report on *20/20* about Johnny Rotten or Sid Vicious. By now I wasn't too keen on those labels and didn't consider myself part of a club. But I figured she wouldn't get *I'm not into labels, Nurse Feely.* I could tell her that I'd dyed my hair to fuck with people's heads and force them to rethink their ideas about what's "normal." But then the jig would be up. Everyone would be over it and I'd never be able to cause a ruckus in school again. So I said nothing and just lay back down, thinking that the psychiatrist's couch added to the psychotic image I was going for.

Just then the cranky older nurse, Nurse Lafferty, came in, flustered because she was late. At first she paid no attention to me as she ran around hanging up her coat, patting her vaguely bluish perm into place, and stopping to adjust her skirt and blouse before the mirror. She was in her sixties and was known for being a tough cookie from Southie. She had no interest in studying your symptoms all day the way Nurse Feely did and would send you home as soon as you complained of the slightest stomachache. The trick was to get her instead of Nurse Feely, but unlike Nurse Lafferty, Nurse Feely was never late or absent.

While Nurse Feely paced at the far end of the room, creaking up and down on the warped floorboards, wondering what to ask me next, Nurse Lafferty suddenly did a double take at me on the psych bed and bellowed, "What the Christ is this? Oh shit, is it Halloween again?" She got a kick out of that one, slapping her thigh after lifting herself onto the desk and then swinging her legs like a little kid. Nurse Feely approached me gently, almost tiptoeing in her loafers, and asked whether I had brothers and sisters and whether they dyed their hair pink too. "Yeah, what are they, a bunch of friggin' hippies?" Nurse Lafferty added, using the back of her hand like she was saying "friggin'" only for my ears. Then she slapped her other thigh, like she had just told another good one. She crossed her legs so she could grab a high heel and shake something out of it, muttering that "some goddamn thing" had been pinching her foot all morning. She hit the back of the shoe like it was a ketchup bottle. Nurse Feely kept trying the gentle approach. "I mean, is this some kind of family thing, or religious thing?" I sat up to laugh and couldn't control myself. I was thinking about my family all lined up for Communion at Saint Augustine's Church with pink hair. Maybe my eyes were watery from laughing because Nurse Feely did the staring-in-the-neighbor's-window thing again and told Nurse Lafferty I might be on drugs. "We should check him out," she said, sounding more decisive. She went to get the blood pressure cuff from behind a screen.

"Drugs?" I said, stunned. "I hate drugs," I told her. "Idiots do drugs. Normal people do drugs."

"Um, *normal* people?" she asked. "Don't you think you're a . . . normal person?" I didn't want to answer that one because I thought it sounded like a trick question, so there was a long silence as she waited.

"Do you think he should see the psychiatrist?" she asked Nurse Lafferty.

"Psychiatrist?" I yelled.

"Well, I just don't know. Why did you do this?" she asked again.

"I don't know," I snapped back. "I just felt like it." Which was the truth. "I guess I was bored. Who knows? Who cares?" I said, standing now, just wanting to get out of there.

"Oh, leave the kid alone. I think it's kinda cute," Nurse Lafferty said, hopping off the desk, coming over and moving my chin to the left to look at me from another angle. She fixed one of the pink spikes of hair. She was cracking up again, and I started laughing with her, until we both spotted the headmaster, Mr. Contompasis, striding into the nurses' office and glaring at me.

Mr. Contompasis always looked angry and unimpressed, if not downright ashamed, of the Boston Latin youth of today. He and many of the ancient teachers often took time in class to remind us of the school's prestigious history as the first public school in America, as a preparatory for Harvard University, and as the alma mater of Samuel Adams, Cotton Mather, and John Hancock, whose portraits hung in the auditorium, along with that of Benjamin Franklin, who had been a Latin dropout. But they never mentioned that. I noticed Mr. Contompasis's pale green double-knit suit with tight flared pants. His Captain Kangaroo–style helmet hair only added to the wonder of it all. And I thought how relative "normal" really was.

I came out of my ten-second daydream when my ally, Nurse Lafferty, suddenly turned on me. She posed the question to Mr. Contompasis, "I mean, what kind of a goddamn fool would do the like of this?" Then Nurse Feely blurted, "I think he's on drugs!" and pointed at me like she was tattletaling. She moved to the other side of Mr. Contompasis, as if for safety. "Goddamn foolishness, that's all it is," Nurse Lafferty said, reaching up to grab me by the hair and walking me over to the sink in the corner of the room. She threw on the faucet, pushed my head beneath a gush of cold water, and rubbed soap all over my hair. Between deafening torrents of water over my ears I could hear more hostile rants about foolishness and attention-getting. I could see Nurse Feely in the background wringing her hands and probably still talking about drugs. Mr. Contompasis, his arms folded, continued to look angry and unimpressed, if not downright ashamed.

Finally, sick of it all, I spat out through the gush of water, "It doesn't just wash out!"

Ma had gone to bed early in the evening, so I stayed up with Seamus and Stevie. I looked forward all week to Saturday night, when *Don Kirshner's Rock Concert* was on. Mostly the show featured the more popular rock bands like the Eagles, Electric Light Orchestra, or Foghat, which were torture to me. But I suffered through them to catch the new music from groups like the Pretenders or even, lately, the Clash.

Johnny called from some undisclosed location with the SEALs, but as usual on a Saturday night no one else was home to talk to him. Frankie was out cruising in his new Lincoln Continental that he'd bought from working in the carpenters' union. I could see Kathy's silhouette — ponytail pulled high — on the rooftop across the street, drinking with Tisha and a gang of boys. No one ever knew where Kevin was, but I told Johnny he seemed to be doing better than anyone else in the family, always throwing me a twenty and coming home once in a while with a box of Calvin Klein jeans from the back of some truck. After giving Johnny all the updates, I sat on the couch answering Seamus and Stevie's questions about why I was wearing a dog collar and why my hair was blackened with shoe polish.

The kids fell asleep just before *Saturday Night Live.* Patterson Way always got livelier right about then. I looked down at all the usual arguments breaking out below and the oaths of allegiance among drunken teenagers teetering arm in arm through the courtyards. I caught a glimpse of Kathy running across the roof, and when I saw the cop car below I figured someone must have called about the kids drinking up there — probably Ann Daly, who Kathy always blamed for ruining her night.

Soon the noise outside got worse, and I wondered how I'd landed in a place like this. I had the urgent need to get out of Old Colony for one of my lone night walks. Our apartment was bigger than most in the projects — ten rooms — because the housing authority had given us a "breakthrough." When there were too many kids for one apartment, they broke down the wall to the next-door apartment, so we had two parlors, two bathrooms, and two kitchens. Still, it felt small — not just the apartment but the entire housing project and Southie itself.

No matter how many walls we broke down it wouldn't have been big enough. Lately I couldn't get to sleep before three or four in the morning — even after Kevin and Kathy had gone to bed, Frankie's lights were out across the way, and the streets had quieted down. Some nights I was up until the sun rose. At that time the only person still going strong on Patterson Way was Al next door, who sat up drinking beer in his window and dancing with whatever woman he'd invited up for the night. Wandering the confines of our apartment, I felt trapped. "Jesus, you're like a goddamn ghost," Ma would say whenever I startled her on her way to the bathroom. She said I must have anxiety. But ever since Ma had studied psychology at Suffolk University, I'd learned to dodge her diagnoses by pretending not to hear them and changing the subject.

I'd begun to sneak out of the house so I could walk all over and not be scrutinized for being up so late. My walks were sometimes the only way I could get tired enough to sleep. Our breakthrough apartment's door led to the hallway at the bottom of the staircase to the roof. I'd perfected opening and closing that heavy steel door silently. It creaked, but I erased the noise by lifting up on the knob and moving the door slowly. Getting out seemed to take forever, and sneaking back in later on, I had to be just as careful.

Now, with Seamus and Stevie fast asleep on the couch, I was anxious to get out and walk across the Broadway Bridge into the bigger world. I didn't want to wait any longer for Don Kirshner to come on. So I carried the little kids to bed, thinking I'd make a clean getaway. And that's when Ma woke up.

"Thank God, I finally got a message from him," she said, walking into the parlor. Ma said she'd had a beautiful dream about Davey. I was caught off guard. I hadn't thought of Davey much since his time at the Social Club. Ma's voice sounded like happiness trying to break through, and I wished it would hurry. I was used to Ma being the strong one, showing off her biceps between sets on her accordion and bragging to Frankie's boxing friends that she could knock out any guy. It was too much to see her falling apart amid the happy words and the tears that fell away from her hand as she wiped her face. Once, when I was a kid, Ma told me that when adults were sick with the flu, they didn't throw up the way kids do. I'd come to assume that it was the same thing with crying. "Their tears just dry up," I once told Kevin, referring to all adults, when he asked me if I thought Ma ever cried. I had seen her cry once, over Patrick, the three-week-old baby who'd died before I was born, but that wasn't something I wanted to remember or talk to Kevin about.

I didn't want to hear any of Ma's dream or see her tears, even though she said she was happy about the message. But once she started I had no choice.

"First I saw only his face, no body," she said, swallowing and taking on a voice that was calm but sounded like she had a cold. "His face came closer and closer, out of this empty place." She sat down on the couch, and I felt trapped because it wasn't like me and Ma to sit and have a talk. "His face got bigger the closer it came, until I could see that his eyes were clear, his sickness was gone." Ma always said she could tell how Davey was doing — whether he was getting bad, plunging into schizophrenic delusions — just by looking at his eyes. "Not since before the breakdown had I seen his eyes looking so clear," she said. She suddenly sounded amazed, like Davey really *had* visited her. "I said to him, 'Davey, you're all better!'" Ma's voice broke when she exclaimed for me just like she had to Davey in the dream.

She said the scene changed, and the two of them were walking down Salem Street in the North End. Ma explained that she and Davey once spent a day wandering the narrow streets of the North End at Saint Anthony's Feast, buying lasagna — "Lasagna was Davey's favorite," she added. I didn't want to hear any more, but she continued. She said they had talked about everyday things that day. "None of his crazy talk about angels and demons," she added. She said that it had been their best day ever — and probably their only good full day, since

Davey ran away from home years before and had the break-down at fourteen. "That day in the North End seemed to last forever," she said. "And the dream felt the exact same way!"

I didn't know what to do. Ma was looking out the window at the roof across the street where Davey made the last decision of his life. Even though Sister Peggy said he must have been in so much pain to want to end it that way, anytime I thought about what he did I could only be mad at him. But imagining Ma's dream about their one great day, about Davey when he looked well — or about the fact that Davey, like anyone else, had a favorite food — made me want to jump out of my skin. I couldn't be mad at Davey now, thinking how happy he must have been eating lasagna in the North End, even though I'd learned in the months since his death that it felt a lot better to be pissed off than to be sad. I imagined him on the day Ma was describing, rocking back and forth as he did whenever he was enjoying something, whether food, a funny story, or a cigarette to collect his thoughts.

"Then the scene changed one last time," Ma said. "He be-came a baby, just like I remember him, with those intelligent and worried big brown eyes he had as a kid. I put him into the crib, pulled up the sides of it, and said, 'There, now you won't be getting away from me.' He was screaming crying — a baby, shouting, 'I want to go home. I want to go home.' I told him, 'Now, Davey, you won't be going anywhere, you're staying with me where you belong.' I turned to walk away, and no sooner than that, I looked back to see that he was gone." Ma couldn't talk for a second. Then she caught her breath. "All his clothes were left behind," she said. "A tiny heap of baby clothes."

Ma wiped her face of any wetness, like she was done. "Thank God I finally got a message from him," she repeated. Ma and I sat for a moment, not talking. I wouldn't ask about the spe-cifics of the dream, but finally questioned, "How could it be a message?" challenging Ma's assertion that something super-natural had happened, but at the same time wishing it true. As soon as she spoke, though, I was already blocking her out, catching only fragments about souls and the afterlife. I wasn't doing it on purpose. I was just fixated on getting out of the house and plotting how to slip away before I'd have to hear the story again.

It was almost midnight when Ma finally went back to bed. I closed my bedroom door loud enough for her to hear. Then I walked quietly — carrying my shoes — toward the door of the breakthrough apartment. I turned the knob without a sound, crept down the metal hallway stairs in my socks, and darted out the back door of our building. The only remaining obstacle was getting through the project without being caught up in the chaos of Patterson Way or being called over by someone who wanted to tell me how much they loved my whole family and what tough sonsabitches my older brothers were. So I followed elaborate routes through back courtyards and over rooftops to get to the outer edge of Old Colony without being seen.

Beyond the project, I walked through the dark streets of what had once been an industrial area but was now abandoned buildings and storage warehouses. There wasn't a soul in this part of Southie all the way to the Broadway Bridge, which led out of the neighborhood to a stretch of warehouses on the other side — a no man's land that buffered our neighborhood from the bigger world and the tall buildings of downtown Boston. I saw the scattered figures of the guys who hung out all day on Broadway's wino wall making their way across the bridge for overnight shelter at the Pine Street Inn. I was think-ing about Ma's dream still. I couldn't shake it, and now with Pine Street in view I was reminded of Davey's stories about the shelter and all the characters he knew there. Many were friends from his days at Mass Mental, before they were all "let loose to roam the earth," as Davey said, referring to the state's decision to downsize its mental hospitals and "deinstitutionalize" the inmates. He said they were all freed from places like Mass Mental to go live in homeless shelters. And those were the lucky ones who got a bed: a lot of Davey's friends seemed to be living in the subways or in jail. Davey worried a lot about his friends in the street. "Poor bastards" he called the mentally ill, looking down and shaking his head when he thought about them. Sometimes his worries kept him up late pacing the floors until everyone went to bed. Then he'd raid the fridge and take food to his friends. One time I caught him, and he said I'd probably go to hell if I told on him, since the homeless were "the least of my brothers." He always said the mentally ill in particular were the bottom of the barrel, below blacks or anyone else. Davey seemed more connected to the people at Pine Street than to anyone in Old Colony Project, or even to any of us.

The yellow brick watchtower on top of the Pine Street Inn was like the ones I'd seen in art books, the only defense for an Italian village in medieval times. The turret in the sky was lit, and a crowd milled around in the darkness below it. I wondered how often Davey had crossed the bridge I was crossing and had seen the same city landscape beyond Broadway. I was beginning to think Ma was right about me being a ghost. I was feeling more and more like one, like I was observing it all from another place. And I wondered if this was what it was like to be dead.

Some of the homeless guys en route to the shelter had stopped on the bridge and were sprawled out on the sidewalk. As usual during my walks I just stepped over the bodies, careful not to wake anyone up.

All the lights were out on the bridge. I almost stepped on someone — but I only realized it when he grabbed my leg and wouldn't let go. Passing truck lights shone on him — a man with flaming red hair and a nappy beard that was even redder. When he looked up at me, I couldn't tell if he wanted to murder me or if he just had that kind of face. It was so red it looked on fire, and his hair was matted into points that formed a crown of flames. But scariest of all were his baby blue eyes set in a weathered face whose deep cracks formed a series of fierce V's. He reached his hand up, and once I realized what he wanted, I pulled him up and leaned him against a concrete barrier. The bridge was full of these barriers, which looked like they'd been abandoned by road workers long ago, halfway through a job. He couldn't fix his gaze on anything and fell onto the sidewalk again. So we started all over.

He reeked of yesterday's whiskey and piss. I wanted him to steady himself so I could move on. "Christ Almighty!" he said, looking at my long black pointy shoes, "where'd you get those gunboats?" When he asked me where the Pine Street Inn was, I was glad I could simply point to the tower in the sky and be done with him. I figured he was just making small talk before asking me for money I didn't have, so I began to walk on. He asked if I could take him to the inn, since he couldn't walk. I told him not to move, and that I'd look for someone at Pine Street to come get him. "Where the fuck am I gonna go?" he asked. He said the police were kicking everyone off Broadway at night and he was lucky to have gotten this far. "Well, not *everyone,*" he added, "just handsome devils like me." That cracked him up, and he fell on the ground again, where I figured he was safer for now.

I had to walk down a dark alley with one working street light to get to the back of the shelter, where there might be a bell. I shook some coins to clear my path of any rats ahead of me. I saw the dark silhouette of someone pissing, then the silhouettes of two girls in short skirts and pointy heels smoking cigarettes on the hood of an abandoned car. More shadowy figures with jagged haircuts crossed the alleyway and disappeared into a warehouse. Farther down the alley I saw staircases full of freaks of every kind: girls with rag-doll hair, black lipstick, and dog collars; guys with fifties haircuts and thrift-shop highwater pants, or matted spiked hair and leather jackets. What I thought was an alley — narrow, abandoned, pitch dark — actually had a street sign. For a couple months I'd seen "Thayer Street" on the handwritten band flyers around town advertising parties at the loft of a guy named Steve Stain, who fronted a band called the Stains. The street was lined with deserted warehouses, but every time the door of one building opened, loud music and the chattering of a crowd spilled onto the street. I couldn't believe all this was secretly going on just over the bridge from Southie. I was about a mile from the confines of home, but a world away.

Then I saw Ghoulish Bob come tumbling out of the party, ass over ears. He landed on his rear end but stood up without missing a beat, like he was used to getting tossed into gutters. So he suffered abuse not only in the "normal" world but even in this underground world of outsiders. He came over to talk as if nothing had happened, but with that look on his face like he was about to gripe. He still had on the pinstripe suit. A girl ran down the stairs after him, asking if he was okay, and Bob didn't even have to tell me her name — I knew who she was from reading local music fanzines. Rita Ratt seemed to show up in a lot of stories and pictures in the Xeroxed pamphlets that gave the rundown on who was seen at what show in Boston. She did the hair-raising screams for Unnatural Axe's song "They Saved Hitler's Brain." Like Bob, Rita looked like one of the Damned, with slicked-back orange hair and black circles smudged around her eyes like a dead person.

The scattered cliques along the alley came out of the shadows to funnel back into the warehouse. Bob said Mission of Burma was on next, but he was going to skip out on "this art-fag scene," as if he hadn't just been kicked out of the scene by art fags, who packed a good wallop by the look of the swelling on his cheek. Rita Ratt pulled a Magic Marker out of her pocket to draw an admission stamp on my hand. She told me she was an artist and could draw like da Vinci, but the stamp she was forging was just a big fat X. I thought she was pulling my leg; the mark was too simple to possibly be an admission stamp. She said it would save me the three bucks, which was a good thing because I didn't have three bucks. I was only out for my usual midnight walk, and here I was going to see Mission of Burma! Bob walked off into the darkness of Harrison Ave., and I thought of how Ma had always called Harrison Ave.

"Skid Row," lined as it was with alcoholics. But now, right next to Skid Row, I was at the center of the only world that mattered to me.

Inside the loft Rita Ratt screamed to me, "Where you from?" and I pretended I couldn't hear her. I knew better than to tell anyone here I was from racist, backward Southie. That'd be the end of any welcomes. The entire floor was one big open room with bare walls, exposed pipes and wires, and rickety floors. It was so crowded that some people were sitting on the windowsills of the huge open windows. I couldn't believe the hand stamp had worked, and there was no need for an ID. A lot of people in the room looked anywhere from nineteen to twenty-five, but I was only thirteen. I liked to think Grandpa's long black overcoat made me look older, but here my age didn't even matter since it wasn't a legal club. I had never imagined a place like this, somewhere I could escape to on late nights from now on instead of taking my solitary ghost walks.

Mission of Burma was on the stage — if you could call the corner of the room a stage — and the place was starting to feel like an oven. The chaotic din of melodies and crashing guitars bounced off the walls. The pounding drums, louder than anything else, cut through the din. Most people stood around the band completely still, just nodding their heads to the beat. Some danced spastically, and one guy rolled around on the floor like he was doing the Worm. He was pretty much ignored by the cooler people, who stood on the outskirts shaking a leg or bopping their heads. I'd only read about this scene and always figured it would be over and done with by the time I'd get to witness it for myself.

Later, when the cops pulled the plug on the bands and ordered everyone to go home, saying the place had no license for live music, I slipped away from the dispersing crowd. I was sweaty and happy. Mission of Burma was the only band I'd ever seen, other than Chic and Chaka Khan, in a concert I'd been to on my twelfth birthday with my girlfriend, chaperoned by her mother. When we left the concert hall we talked about what a great show they had put on. Now, leaving Thayer Street, I couldn't remember hearing any of the words to songs, couldn't say if the band members knew how to play their instruments. Still, I'd felt something great come through the trembling speakers that night. I knew that I'd discovered an incredibly secret world, one that made anything possible.

I headed toward the Broadway Bridge while everyone else went toward the opposite end of Thayer Street. Rita Ratt spotted me drifting away from the mob of punks and asked me where I was going. "Broadway Station," I yelled. "In Southie?" she screamed, and I saw a few people turn around. "You'll get killed over there. They don't like people like us!" "I'm gonna stay up and wait for the first train at Broadway," I lied, afraid to shout out that *home* was "over there." She came over to tell me that everyone was just pretending to be leaving, until the cops went away. Then they'd all come out of hiding and go back into the loft. "Stay here," she said. "It beats waiting up all night in the station." My lie had gotten me in deeper. It was after one in the morning, and now I'd have to find a place to hide until the cops left — anything to avoid telling the truth about why I *really* was walking toward Southie. Eventually everyone poured back inside and I was able to sneak away, but by then it was three A.M.

I walked back over the Broadway Bridge with my ears ringing from standing next to the amp. I came across the fiery guy. I'd forgotten all about him. He asked me for change and said nothing about having met me, or my promise to get help at Pine Street. I was beat, but I asked him if he wanted me to walk him over to the shelter. He said no, the sun would be up soon enough. Just then a carload of Southie kids threw a full bottle of beer and it smashed at his feet. "What the fuck you doing? That's my brother," I heard, followed by laughter. The car pulled over, and Kathy stuck her head out. "Mike, get the fuck in the car!" I looked at the fiery guy and apologized. "I gotta get home," I said, and jumped into the car.

Kathy's boyfriend, Timmy, was driving and the car was

packed, but most of the passengers were passed out. Kathy gave out to me for being out so late and said I'd have to climb into the apartment from the roof with her. "I left the top part of the window open," she said. Kathy and Kevin always snuck in and out of the house from the roof, but I told her I wasn't climbing in from any rooftop. "I left the door to the break-through open after Ma went to bed." Luckily, we were only a few blocks from home, because I couldn't take all the questions from Timmy about what I was doing over the bridge anyway, and why I looked like a weirdo. "Some punk rock shit," Kathy grumbled to him. "What's that?" he asked, and Kathy ex-plained about people who dressed in Halloween costumes and pissed on each other at concerts. "You're into that?" Timmy asked. "Yeah." I shrugged, too tired to explain something that none of them would get anyway.

I kept a list of upcoming shows and venues taped to my wall. Sometimes I even cued up a cassette to record the "concert re-port" on *The Nite Club*, in case the radio DJ rattled off the list of gigs too fast for me to catch everything. It was a cinch to get into Thayer Street and a few other warehouse lofts around the city, since there was no carding at the door. I wanted to use my weekly paycheck for records and music magazines, not cover charges, so I invested in a fat black marker. The hand stamp was usually an X or some other easy symbol the doorman came up with. In the worst case, they'd switch to a red X, and I'd have to identify the person with a red marker — someone who looked like the type with a backup plan. I was proud that I could always spot that sharp-looking schemer in the crowd — until I realized that half the people at any show came sup-plied with a few markers and the other half were "with the band." Eventually I wondered who was paying at all.

I still had to figure out how to get into the shows at bars, though, which had strict ID policies and more official doormen — usually a huge jock or thug who didn't know any of the clubgoers and stood in front of the entrance looking like a brick wall. I bought a smaller black pen for drawing their more complicated stamps, and then I'd rub it in to look like I'd been inside sweating. But I still had to get around the fact that I was only thirteen. I didn't know if I could pass for twenty, even with Grandpa's long black coat. Remedios, the girl in black at Latin School, passed notes to me in class about upcoming shows. She told me about Cantone's, a bar in the financial district with a huge picture window at one end that faced the stage head-on. The next night I walked there — the area was a ghost town at night — only to find a small group of underage kids in tattered clothes congregated around the rear picture window. Before long I became a regular at the window. The people inside never seemed to wonder at the group of heads peering in and wiping the fogged glass every few minutes to see better. Through the window I got to see local bands like Lou Miami and the Kozmetix, La Peste, and Unnatural Axe, whose song "They Saved Hitler's Brain" featured Rita Ratt's hellish shrieks. The sound was muffled from where I stood, but that didn't matter at all.

Then a miracle happened. My brother Frankie got a job as a bouncer at the Rathskeller. I'd never imagined someone from my family guarding access to the most important place in Boston for seeing underground bands. I showed up one Saturday when Mission of Burma was playing. I recognized the Southie boxers standing side by side and forming a brick wall before the front door, with their Tony Manero hair, Izod shirts buttoned to the neck, collars up, arms folded, legs apart and firmly planted. I went around to the rear of the building, and from the blackness of an unlit parking lot I spotted Frank at the back door of the Rat. I hadn't told him I'd be showing up and expecting admission and wasn't sure he'd let me in. But I immediately noticed how much more physically relaxed he was than his friends at the front entry, who looked like they were guarding the borders of Southie itself. Frankie carried himself with relaxed shoulders, arms to the side, but with clenched fists.

When I emerged from behind a dumpster, his fists lifted just a little until he saw it was me. "Mike!" he yelled in surprise. "What are you doing all the way out here?" I told him Kenmore Square wasn't that far, and I hung out in town a lot. But before I could finish my casual answer, he added, "What the fuck are you wearing?" I looked down at my plaid high-waters and quickly changed the subject to getting inside the Rat. I knew he couldn't say no to his own brother. But before telling me how to get down the back stairs and to the stage, he pulled me aside and told me not to let anyone know we were brothers. I gladly agreed.

From then on I practically lived at the Rat on weekends, seeing every local band. Frankie was there in the same club, but in a parallel world, and we hardly spoke. His crew of bouncers was known for happily beating up freaks, my friends. I was too embarrassed to tell any punks that my brother was one of the "Neanderthals" they talked about, and Frankie was too embarrassed to tell anyone I was his brother. One time, when I wore long johns under huge boxer shorts that reached my knees, and wingtip shoes rescued from Grandpa's garbage, Frankie said I looked like a mental patient and begged me to go home and change. He took me over past the dumpster to tell me I had a lot going for me and I shouldn't throw away my life like this, dressing like a freak. I wanted to tell him it was even weirder that everyone in Southie looked alike and dressed like him, with alligator shirts, collars up, and perfectly feathered hair. Frankie did seem different from the other tough guys, though. He had a strong silence and wasn't known to start fights, but everyone said God help anyone who crossed him. As he lectured me I actually felt bad for Frank for being one of the normal people who just didn't get it.

Still, we were brothers. And Frankie always let me into the Rat, as long as it was a weekend. I simply had to wait at a distance from the back door, near the dumpsters, until Frankie was alone. Then I'd appear out of nowhere, usually startling him into a boxing stance before he shook his head at my clothes and told me to get the fuck inside. When I caught a ride home with him, I had to meet him halfway down Commonwealth Ave., far from the Rat. He couldn't remind me often enough that we weren't related when we were at the Rat. And I couldn't have been more relieved.

The Saint Paddy's Day parade had come and gone, and the mobs on Southie's streets had funneled into the local barrooms. An eerie calm settled over the trash-strewn parade route. The muted sound of happy-go-lucky songs would blare only occasionally outside a tavern when brawlers erupted through the doors onto Dorchester Street. Having avoided the parade, I figured it was safe to leave the house again, until I realized Ma was playing the accordion for a few neighbors on the front stoop and drawing a crowd. She called up to the window, telling me to come down so she could play "Happy Birthday" for me. But I wanted nothing to do with Saint Patrick's Day or my fourteenth birthday. The Clash was in town, and that was all I cared about. Seamus and Steve were disappointed that I didn't stop to eat the pound cake they'd stuck a bunch of candles in for my birthday. I'd waited all day for the streets to die down and was afraid I'd be late for the show. I avoided Ma and the party on the stoop by taking the stairs to the roof, crossing rooftops, and exiting from a building on the outskirts of the project.

The way to the train station was littered with torn green garlands, broken beer bottles, and the occasional puke. In two places I stepped over blood. I thought back to the time when I looked forward to the fights on Saint Paddy's as much as the parade itself, when the stories and the blow-by-blow descriptions of fights with outsiders kept us all in stitches for days.

A few stragglers on Dorchester Street held on to a wall to feel their way to the next pub — never far away in Southie. They were all decked out in green and regained their composure just long enough to focus on my black clothes and say,

"What the fuck?" or "Where's the funeral?" One was sitting on the curb draped in green Hawaiian leis and wearing a huge button that said GOD MADE THE IRISH #1. He looked abandoned, like he was the only one who hadn't been told the parade was over and that everyone had gone to the bars. He looked up at me and said, "What, you're not Irish or something?"

A gang of small kids playing in their front yard ran toward me, shouting in unison, "Bum! Bum! Bum!" They'd been doing it every time I passed them on my way to and from the train station. Each kid leapt onto the chain-link fence and chanted louder and louder before quieting down to let one brave one ask me, "How come you look like a bum?" The question was always earnest. I got a kick out of the little gang, so I just laughed and gave them a different story each time: one day I was a chimney sweep, another day when I was wearing a dark suit I was an undertaker. But this time I was in too much of a hurry to stop and talk. I left them behind, their faces pressed up against the fence. The brave one, in a last-ditch effort, screamed once more, "Bum!"

I was going to walk to Broadway Station — a half-mile on — because the transit police had been cracking down on the secret entrance at Andrew Station. When I got to Andrew, though, it seemed like a ghost town. Because of the parade no cops were in sight. I lay on my back to crawl under the gap in the security fence. A couple of years before, I'd discovered that the fence at the station entrance could be lifted just enough to slide under it. It required a group effort. Usually one or, even better, two of my friends from Old Colony would hold the fence up with all their might while one by one the rest slid underneath on our backs, then helped the others through the passage. Then we were off for joy rides to Quincy, our backs usually black with dirt and gravel until I started carrying a scrap of cardboard to put under us in the slide. Without the older teenagers we never dared get off the train in other people's neighborhoods, unless it was Quincy, where all the ex-Southie people lived when they betrayed the neighborhood by moving out. Kevin said they all thought they were "high and mighty" when they made it to Quincy, so he and the other Southie kids didn't mind stealing bikes there. But for me it was enough just to get my friends to walk around in Quincy, where we wouldn't get jumped by blacks like in Dorchester or be given dirty looks by the rich liberals in Cambridge.

I didn't need cardboard to slide on these days, since I wore clothes that looked better dirty or torn. I undid a bondage strap from my pants when it got caught on a chain link and slid under the fence. When I got through to the other side, I heard a fight break out downstairs at the tracks. I peeked down and saw my old friends from Old Colony being kicked off the train. They yelled "nigger" at the conductor as he pulled out of the station. I didn't want them to see me, so I waited at the top of the steps, hidden from view, until they got on the next train. I was already late and was going to be later if I had to skip this train. So I raced down the steps and caught it two cars down from them. I knew they'd be getting off at the next Southie stop, Broadway, while I'd ride on to Park Street to see a band from England. To my old friends I might just as well be crossing the Atlantic Ocean.

The Orpheum Theater was packed. I'd never seen a show as big as this, since the bands I'd been seeing played in small venues. It looked so much like a typical big rock 'n' roll concert that at first I thought I was at the wrong show. Even more confusing, there was a Jamaican guy onstage singing and talking in rhyme and rhythm, with no band behind him — only a sound system booming heavy bass and drum. Everyone in the audience, with all their zippers and badges and bondage straps, looked like they were definitely there to see the Clash. They seemed confused by the Jamaican too. Whenever he spoke to introduce the next song people around me complained that they couldn't understand a word of what he said. I understood

all of it, though — it sounded like the downward-rolling cadence of Grandpa's Kerry brogue, with some of the same old-
fashioned words, like "vexed," and pronunciations like "wan,
two, tree." He even began sentences with "For," like someone from Shakespeare's days. And he pronounced it like
Grandpa too: "Far dey taak 'bot dis and dey taak 'bot dat."
Even though I understood the words, I was in the dark about
what he meant. Who was "talking about this and talking about
that"?

His words all had such weight, the way Davey's prophecies
did. The Jamaican spoke of a day coming when justice would
be done "far di suffrah and di downtrodden of Babylon." But
everyone around me just wanted to see the Clash. Only one
woman next to me — with a crewcut and Catwoman makeup
— approved, raising her fist and screaming "Legalize it!" She
interrupted the Jamaican guy halfway through his sentences,
which made me think she didn't really understand a word
of it either, but approved anyway. *Legalize what?* I wondered.
Maybe abortion, but that's already legal. I asked her who the
Jamaican was and she just shrugged and then screamed "Rasta-far-I!" in the middle of the Jamaican's hypnotic chant. He
stopped to tell one guy in leather not to be spitting at the stage.
I'd read in the British music magazines that bands from the
original English punk scene — those from the 1977 heyday —
were upset that their wider appeal brought out people who believed the press rumors about punk bands liking to be spat on.
And now here in Boston people in bondage gear were spitting
at a Jamaican singer.

"Sekkle dun! Sekkle dun!" he pleaded, his outstretched hand
motioning for calm. When the audience actually did settle
down, the beat dropped in a way that hit me in the gut. The
Jamaican's feet were planted in one spot, and his knees buckled on every other beat, with every thump of bass drum. Then,
in that downward-rolling cadence, he broke into lyrics: *We
got to break down de walls, down inna Babylon, that separate us . . .*

"I hate this shit," a familiar voice said over my shoulder. It was Bob. He told me that the Jamaican was Mikey Dread, who produced the Clash's album and sang on their new reggae-influenced songs. "I get a kick out of these bands over in London trying to kiss Jamaican ass," he said. "Wait'll they get robbed by them." He sounded like my Southie neighbors. I'd always thought everyone from better-off liberal families in the suburbs, especially out beyond Cambridge where Bob lived, didn't really think that way.

> . . . Solidarity down inna Babylon, will be our motto,
> 'cuz when da right time come down inna Babylon,
> dis ya battle will be hotter . . .

Wanting to change the subject with Bob, I tried to yell over the heavy bass, "He sounds like my grandfather!" But the song had ended abruptly. "Except for what he's talking about," I added. By the puzzled faces around me I knew no one cared about Mikey Dread or my grandfather. The silence didn't last long, though, replaced by the grumblings of a restless crowd. "What the fuck's he saying?" protested one guy with a dog collar and I DON'T GIVE A FUCK written on his zippered spandex shirt that looked meant for someone smaller, maybe a woman. He looked like he could be a lumberjack during the week but was trying out this punk thing on the weekends. He was getting angrier, said he didn't pay to see "some Jamaican shit." I tried to translate some of what the Jamaican was singing about and explained that my grandfather was from Kerry and sounded a bit like this Mikey Dread guy. When I got to the line about "solidarity in battle" the rebel Catwoman screamed "Woohoo" and raised her fist. Mikey Dread raised his fist back, relieved to see one fan out there. By now the crowd was booing and Mikey Dread pointed at her, dedicating the next one to his "sistren wit de bald 'ed."

"What'd he say?" she screamed at me.

"He said you got a bald head," I screamed back.

"What the fuck!" she protested.

"It just means short hair," I explained. "My grandfather would say you have a bald head too."

The beat dropped again and sent the reverberating bass through me. In spite of the rising jeers from the crowd, I loved this music. In my disco past — which I now kept secret — I'd been into heavy funk, and this seemed like a down-tempo version. The heaviness of it, echoing through my whole body, made everything else go away. Mikey Dread shouted, "Dub stylee!" into the mike, and the words repeated and traveled endlessly. Geeky-looking sound engineers on the side of the stage turned knobs, and the spacy effects poured out of the speakers. Layers of noise came crashing down as the line "break down de walls" ricocheted around the room, sometimes cut off in midsentence for no apparent reason. Most of it sounded like mistakes, but by the focused expression of the soundmen I knew it wasn't. The beat kept tripping over itself and starting again. Mikey Dread danced a slow-motion march, like he was trudging through the hardship he called Babylon. Then he seemed to rise above it all, breaking into a double-time trot with his eyes closed in meditation, staying in his own world and seeming oblivious to his audience. The music was like a random cutting and pasting of rhythms and melodies. Beats changed and crashed again before the chaos took flight and left an empty space of silence to be filled by the listeners' changing thoughts. *Break down de wa-wa-wa-wa-wa . . . seem to divide us, divide us, divide us.*

"Wake me up when it's over," Bob said. "I hate this dub bullshit." Then he took off into the crowd. Before long everyone was booing and throwing things. The only one enjoying it besides me was the Catwoman, who, like Mikey Dread now, was oblivious to the booing crowd, raising her fist and screaming "Rasta-far-I!" and "Legalize it!" She offered me a hit on her joint. I liked the smell of pot, but to me drugs were what normal people did, average people without much imagination. When I said that in Southie, they looked at me like I had two heads. But in the scene I was now hanging in it was another way of being different, and some thought it was pretty cool that I would take this individualism thing so far. Catwoman said my refusal was all well and good, but dub music sounded a lot better stoned. "That's why all the speed freaks are booing," she shouted. But I wasn't stoned and still I was elated by the sound. All music that made me feel like this — whether the Ramones or now dub — made me think this was how heroin might feel to others, but without having to give up control to a drug. The point of this new music world I'd found, and the whole reinvention of life, was to let yourself be a little bit different, a little bit out there in an out-of-control world. And who needed drugs to be a little bit out there?

Mikey Dread walked offstage amid heckles and the fading echoes of Babylon's walls crashing. The Clash walked him back onstage for an encore, to the ear-splitting cheers of the crowd. It was the same Jamaican beat, but it seemed the crowd could stomach it more from the Clash. Then the Clash's other friend, Pearl Harbour — of Pearl Harbour & the Explosions — came onstage with a fiddle to sing "Lose This Skin I'm Imprisoned In." I looked around for Bob to return and tell me this sucked. But he didn't show up until the Clash took to the stage again. He didn't look impressed by their appearance either, but from the moment they walked onstage I was starstruck. The days of rock stardom were supposed to be as dead as the Beatles, though. So I kept a lid on the thrill of it all and acted as uninterested as Bob until they broke into the first song, "Clash City Rockers." From that moment until the final song, "London's Burning," nothing else existed in the room. They did their earlier hard guitar songs, but also played rhythm and blues and more reggae rhythms. It was like they weren't part of any one type of music and were even rebelling against the whole punk thing.

I walked out of the Orpheum soaking wet, on a post-gig high that I was starting to know well. My ears were ringing with Clash songs as I walked all the way home. I could still feel the pounding bass and drums of the rocking reggae songs. I crossed the decrepit Broadway Bridge with its parade of home-less men making their way to the Pine Street Inn. *A lot of peo-ple won't get no justice tonight.* After passing a fistfight in front of the Quiet Man pub, I took Southie's back routes through dark alleys, where I wouldn't bump into the neighbors and friends who used to know me and thought they still did. Com-ing into Old Colony, I took my new route across the rooftops to avoid Kevin and his gang wheeling and dealing on the cor-ner of Patterson Way. *Remember to kick it over. No one will guide you through Armagideon time.*

Kevin was in the parlor explaining to everyone about the bar owner who was found in a body bag in his own car trunk. He said any fool would know it was a Whitey hit. "They say the guy was a snitch," Kevin said, "and Whitey got wind of it." No one ever asked how Whitey got wind of anything, but one thing was for sure, nothing could happen in Southie that our gangster boss Whitey Bulger didn't know. "Think about it," Kevin said. "If the guy was about to go on trial for murder, of course he's gonna become an informant on everything that goes on around here." Kevin was looking at me now and in-cluding me in the conversation. I pretended to ignore it as I sat eating my morning cereal out of the box. "And how do you think Whitey found out the guy was going state's evidence?" Kevin asked me, adding, "Mike, you're the smart one, you do the math!" When it came to the streets of Southie, Kevin al-ways got worked up over the details. After following his equa-tion, I came up with the answer, cops on Whitey's payroll, be-fore reminding myself that I didn't give a fuck about any of it. I just kept quiet. I was known for that in my family, and the neighbors still called me the quiet one. Like most of the neigh-borhood, Kevin always knew more than the papers, which had printed only a vague article about the man found in his own trunk. To me, though, it was all part of a really small world — one that I liked to imagine did not surround me.

I went into my room, back to the world where the only

sound that mattered was from my mixed tapes. I pressed PLAY and turned up Junior Murvin's original "Police and Thieves," about the good guys and the bad guys being the same guys in Jamaica's shanty towns, a song the Clash covered, applying the meaning to their own London. I got dressed fast, tucked a pile of books under my arm to look like I was going to school, and slipped out without interrupting Kevin's ongoing rant about this weekend's gangster killing in the small world of South Boston. Johnny Rotten was in town with his new band, Public Image Ltd., for their first-ever American gig. And I had to hook school to try to get into the show for free.

"Pineapple!" I heard Sculley yell to me from the Boston Public Library steps. Sculley was a friend of Remedios's who never went to school, and I'd heard she walked around town with PiL the previous day, so I joined her in the quest for free tickets to the show. As I crossed the street, Sculley screamed at all the passers-by who stared at her, the way Bob did, even though she couldn't have expected anything less than stares that morning. Besides looking like an intentional lunatic in a leopard coat, a slip, and white go-go boots, she had the unintended distinction of being a Korean Irish girl with freckles and orange hair. Her family had left the D Street Project right about the time of school desegregation and the riots that had sent anyone who wasn't white packing their bags. "Will you stop calling me that?" I asked in a hushed tone, reminding her that I hated the nickname Pineapple-head, which Remedios had given me the first time I went to school thinking I looked menacing with my butchered bed-head. It seemed like everyone on the music scene had cool nicknames, like Rita Ratt or Steve Stain, and I feared Remedios had branded me forever with Pineapple-head.

We walked over to the library's revolving doors to wait until nine o'clock, when we could get in, out of the cold. We both hung out at the library a lot, and we'd gotten to know the homeless gang that spent their days there. We'd made up names for all of them, since many were paranoid and wouldn't give the same name twice. Pippi showed up first, weaving in and out of traffic on Boylston Street, oblivious to the honking horns. Her childish face and Pippi Longstocking braids jutting from the sides of her head had inspired our nickname for her. Her gray beard made me guess she was about sixty-five. She always greeted us with a whispered conspiracy theory. Today it was "Hey, did you hear they took hot chocolate off the market?"

A woman named Felix busily arranged her painting supplies on the sidewalk. Felix covered Boston's grimiest sidewalks with ethereal scenes of punks, Rastas, skinheads, and angels, and the audience that gathered around her was Boston's most motley selection of homeless people and kids hooking school. Sculley and I knew Felix from shows at Thayer Street and the Rat. She looked almost anti-punk, though, in her psychedelic hippie smocks and church-lady hats piled high with plastic flowers and birds. "Jolliness" was the word she often repeated, like advice, while squatting on the littered sidewalk to smoke a cigarette and rocking back and forth like Davey.

Before long all the other regulars had showed up, and the library's front entrance looked more like the Pine Street Inn. There was Peter Pan, who looked straight out of *Leave It to Beaver* and always carried one book, *The Adventures of Peter Pan*. He would walk in circles as he looked up at the clouds and talked about Peter Pan, which I sometimes found disturbing. *But who am I to judge?* I thought. Growing up with Ma, who talked to pretty much every homeless person we passed in Southie and sometimes let them sleep on the couch, I was used to characters on the streets. A woman in her sixties named Mary showed up shouting obscenities at the businesspeople she was trying to hustle change from. I knew Scary Mary was originally from Southie, though she always said, "I ain't giving up no information to no one!" when I asked. I first guessed she was Southie when she addressed me affectionately as "douchebag." But I was certain of it when she asked if I had any change for a "spuckie" — Southie-talk for a submarine sandwich. "The purple lady" showed up right as the library was opening. She was middle-aged and as scary as Mary, but in a darker way. Her face was covered in purple nail polish and, in her black cape and hood, she looked like the Grim Reaper.

Most of our library acquaintances talked only to us, never to each other. Some were even hostile, glaring or talking behind each other's backs. When the purple lady came around the corner minutes before the library opened, Mary muttered about "the whore coming round the bend." Pippi never got into confrontations, but Mary and the purple lady seemed out for blood: Mary with her obscenities, and the purple lady with her silent stares from under the hood. To ease the mood we told Pippi that Johnny Rotten was in town, but she didn't know who he was, and when I told her the history of the Sex Pistols she just looked at me like I was crazy.

Going through the revolving doors, it was a relief to feel the blast of warm, dry library air. Peter Pan went through three revolutions before entering. He looked up at the library's gray concrete ceilings like he'd entered the Sistine Chapel. Purple lady pulled her hood lower and headed toward the bathrooms in the basement. Pippi headed to the young adult section. "Smell ya later," Scary Mary said to all of us, waddling toward the elevators.

We went to the third floor, where we could watch out the windows for Johnny Rotten, whom Sculley had followed the day before to the Lenox Hotel next door. It was too early for anyone in a band to be awake, so I lay down on a makeshift bed of three library chairs while Sculley kept watch. I started to daydream, imagining what it would be like to be from the faraway world of London, where legions of kids seemed to be taking over the streets.

Growing up in an Irish American family, I'd heard only bad things about the English. But a lot of the characters in England's early punk scene were from families that had immigrated to England, like London's dreaded Jamaicans. X-Ray Spex's Poly Styrene was of Somali background. The Slits' members were from Spain, France, and Germany. And Irish last names often lay buried underneath invented punk names. Johnny Rotten was a Lydon, and his parents were from Ireland. Generation X's Billy Idol's mother was from Cork. Unlike us "Irish" who lived in Southie and who'd never been to Ireland, people born in England seemed to call themselves English, even if they were of Irish blood. I wanted nothing to do with the whole Irish thing myself. But I still noticed when someone was from an Irish family or any background like mine. And I paid special attention when anyone like Johnny Rotten or the Clash's Paul Simenon mentioned growing up in a "council estate."

I was amazed, though, that white people from places like Old Colony would be so preoccupied in their songs and interviews with fighting racism. And even though they made a whole new white noise on stage, most of them listened to Jamaican music. After our busing riots five years earlier, when Southie's borders were fortified against both the blacks and the liberals of the outside world, it was shocking to read in the music papers that these English kids were talking about "class" and about what they had in common with the Jamaican immigrants in their housing estates. They said the "class system" instigated the racism in Britain. The English kids bragged about being from neighborhoods like mine, while I was only ashamed of Old Colony.

Southie pride had always seemed to be not only about race but also about being hostile to any outsiders, especially if they weren't Irish. Everyone in the projects thought it was better to be from the tough end of town, but no one admitted to being poor. Reading of these kids talking about class made me realize for the first time that I had grown up poor. All through my childhood we convinced ourselves that Old Colony Project was the greatest, the only place anyone would *choose* to be. But I no longer believed that we were in heaven on earth and that the outsiders were the bad guys. Reading about housing estates and class solidarity didn't make me any more comfortable in Old Colony. The maze of bricks and concrete I lived in still felt like a dead end. And learning that the people living in neighborhoods just like mine across the sea knew where they stood in the bigger scheme of things only made me daydream about being part of this faraway rebellion against all that was wrong with England.

The British music papers were also writing about the new Two Tone movement of black and white kids in 1950s suits reviving Jamaican ska on the streets of London, an intentional stand against racism. With my paychecks from the Children's Museum I was buying all the roots and dub music that bands like the Slits and the Clash referred to: Big Youth, Toots and the Maytals, King Tubby. Along with the reggae bands and dub sound systems, English punks were putting on concerts against racism and the rising National Front. *That could never happen here,* I thought. I guessed that was because we didn't have a "class system" here in America, where everyone could become whatever they wanted to become, as Mr. Flaherty at Latin said.

I woke up from a doze and glanced out the library window. "There he goes!" I said, watching the tracks being laid by the kid we called Disco Train. "Where?" Sculley yelled, pulling herself out of the nap she'd been taking, head on desk. She thought I was talking about Johnny Rotten. Sculley wasn't exactly disappointed, though, to see Disco Train passing on the street below our window. I saw his mouth let out his usual "Choo Choooooo," as he did his train shuffle down Boylston Street in a straight line, startling people into clearing a path. He was an ordinary-looking black teenager, but he thought he was a train and he carried a record with DISCO emblazoned on the cover, raising it to his ear, chugging along and snapping his fingers to an imagined beat. And the smile on his face was so big you had to believe he was really hearing it.

He was just another one of the many street characters around the library at Copley Square. Whenever Disco Train crossed our path we'd stop everything to watch him, completely entranced, until he disappeared in the distance. Felix often shouted, "Jolliness!" and wagged her finger at him, her gesture of approval. It was always a highlight to see him making tracks through the everyday drudgery of people going to and coming from jobs they seemed to hate. I sat in silence and wondered what it must be like for him, to be so filled with happiness, oblivious to the world he danced through.

As soon as Disco Train was gone, Johnny Rotten stumbled out of the Lenox Hotel. His hunchback walk, fluorescent orange hair, and deathly white skin were unmistakable. We jumped up to go talk to him, then looked at each other, thinking, *What do you say to someone whose job it is to be the biggest asshole in the world?* Until now I'd figured we'd hang out or go to lunch with him at Mug-N-Muffin, our favorite haunt. But we didn't even know him. By the time we made it out the revolving library doors, he was lurching down Boylston Street and clearing a path through people who hadn't a clue who he was and expressed disgust at the sickly sight of him. Crossing the street, he spotted us walking fast toward him and stopped in his tracks. He must have realized we knew who he was. But when we finally caught up with our friend, I saw that his wide-eyed stare was not his usual stark expression but a seething glare.

"Wouldja piss off!" he snarled in his cockney accent, which sounded almost unreal in Boston. We stopped, unsure what to do next, until we spotted his bandmates Martin Atkins and Jah Wobble walking toward us. As Johnny Rotten disappeared down a side street, we stopped them to talk. They were friendly and even asked for advice on getting around Boston, so I figured they'd be easier to work on for free tickets. And they were — we got on their guest list.

Having decided we were the band's welcoming committee in Boston, I hooked school again the next day so we could wait for them in the Lenox Hotel lobby. But as we approached the Lenox I heard a voice from behind me. "Mike, what the Christ are you doing out of school?" Ma, of all people, was in Copley, of all places! And with Jitterbug. Ma, with her big country-western hairdo and fringed cowboy jacket, was crossing the intersection carrying her acoustic guitar. Sculley asked, "Who's that cool-looking lady?" about my mother. Between being red-faced at getting caught hooking school and embarrassed that people — maybe even Johnny Rotten — would see me around my mother, I wanted to flee. When I told Ma why I wasn't in school, she cursed me out for only a minute before Jitterbug interrupted to ask who the hell Johnny Rotten was. Ma said he was a jackass who couldn't sing for shit. Ma went on her way with Jitterbug, saying she had to play guitar at a nearby soup kitchen. She yelled back that I had to pick up Seamus and Stevie from nursery school later that day. Sculley said afterward, "She looks wild for a mother," meaning it in a good way. I changed the subject, though.

The next two days I went to the Lenox Hotel only after school. Ma was onto my hooking and said she'd call Boston Latin. Each afternoon Johnny Rotten walked by us in the hotel lobby and told us to piss off, while we waited for his friendlier bandmates. I figured the concierge knew that the two fourteen-year-olds in oversized hobo clothes were not hotel guests, but he never asked questions as we slouched patiently on the plush couches and stared up at the fancy chandelier. Eventually the other band members — Wobble, Atkins, and Keith Levine — would come down and we'd have another great conversation about the lefts and rights they might take that day on their walks around Boston before radio interviews.

It didn't matter that Johnny Rotten was an asshole. I would have been disappointed if he were anything less, and a few times we followed him just to be as rotten as he. It was a thrill to meet characters from the faraway English music world I'd read so much about, which now seemed actually within reach.

Month after month, more great English bands came to Boston. Even though I was underage I was becoming an expert at getting in "by hook or by crook," as they said in Southie. The London bands that weren't big enough to headline at the Orpheum started to play at the ballroom of the Bradford Hotel, just a mile walk past the Broadway Bridge. The funding had dried up for youth service jobs at the Children's Museum, so I wasn't working anymore and usually had no money. Luckily, most of the bands I liked weren't very famous and still played in places where you could just walk in for the sound check, meet the band, and ask to be put on the guest list. They always put me on. It was embarrassing to ask, though; I was afraid they'd think I was a crazy fan. I had to let them know immediately that I didn't want an autograph, that I was just broke and wanted to see the show.

I'd found out how to get in free without bothering the band one time when I went to the Bradford after school for the Slits' sound check, planning to ask a band member to put me on the list or walk me in. I loitered in the lobby, not sure what anyone in the band looked like, though I figured they'd be easy enough to spot. I watched the door of the hotel, looking for British punk girls, probably in leather and zippers like the Clash. Then a taxi pulled up, blasting deadly dub bass lines that shook the glass doors of the lobby. A gang of teenage girls poured out. They looked strange, but nothing like any punks I'd ever seen. One, who was dressed like a ragamuffin straight out of a Dickens novel, led the pack, rubbing her throat and hitting high-pitched jarring notes. Instead of the punk look I was used to seeing at shows, she had clumpy dreadlocks spilling out from under a Hasidic Jewish top hat perched lopsided on her head. A white person with dreadlocks seemed unheard of. The few black people who had them got even more stares than punks.

And these kids were from the racially tense streets of London, where the National Front was stirring up racist attacks. So I figured she was asking for trouble back home. The other girls followed her, all in long, ragged hair tied up in ribbons and what looked like socks. I was floored by their presence, by their wild shrieks through the lobby, backed by the otherworldly dub music pumping from the boom box one of them carried. I didn't have the guts to say anything. But they knew I was there to see them, as they gave me dirty looks and cackled.

I followed them, creeping up the hotel stairs and always staying a flight behind. I entered the empty, dark ballroom to watch the sound check. Since there was a bar, I figured the show would be only for twenty and older. I hoped that no one would ask what I was doing there and that I could remain in the ballroom until after the doors opened for the show. I stood in the back wearing wraparound sunglasses, wishing that the room was as dark as it looked to me and that I was invisible to the bouncers. The band kept doing *testing-one-two-threes,* and no one ever asked who I was or what I was doing there.

The Slits' lead singer, Ari Up, was only seventeen herself. I'd read nearly everything there was to know about the group and all their friends. The Slits were some of the first kids to hang out around the Sex Pistols. Ari Up was fourteen then, and her mother was said to have supported a lot of the bands, buying instruments for those who couldn't afford them. Johnny Rotten and the Slits were at the forefront of the mixing of white punks and Jamaican immigrants, leading all the punks into *shebeens* — basement parties in black neighborhoods where they danced until daybreak to mesmerizing dub music. When I read about them in *New Musical Express,* I'd imagine I was right there among them, not like rock stars but rather like friends, at a Jamaican shebeen in London. Standing alone at the back of the auditorium, though, I started to feel like a stalker and wondered if I looked like one.

The band broke into their reggae version of Marvin Gaye's

"Heard It Through the Grapevine," and I felt lifted off the ground as I imagined myself in a world other than the Old Colony Project I'd go back to once I got kicked out of the Bradford Hotel. I ran into a bathroom when I heard official voices yelling about clearing the house and locking the doors before admission. I squatted on a toilet, thinking I could hide there until after the doors opened. Looking up at the dropped ceiling, I got the notion of pushing up one of the rectangular panels and seeing what was above. I pulled myself up through the bathroom ceiling, replaced the panel, then climbed onto a thick wooden beam. I waited there on the beam until I could hear that the doors had opened and people were pouring into the ballroom. I removed the ceiling panel closest to me and was about to climb down when I saw groups of girls coming in and out of the bathroom — I was in the ceiling of the *ladies'* room. I was afraid to go down and be accused of worse things than sneaking in to a show. Every time I thought the coast was clear, another girl would come into the bathroom below to fix her hair. I'd never realized how much effort punk girls put into their screwed-up hair.

Finally I spotted Remedios below me, powdering her face white. I knew she had a good fake ID, and was planning on going to the show. "Psssst! Reme," I whispered, making her grab her heart in fright. I told her to keep lookout for me as I climbed down. Reme told me the Bradford hadn't carded anyone, so my age didn't matter. On top of that now I had a whole new way of getting into shows for free.

Word got out, and soon the wooden beam was lined with people hiding out in the ceiling waiting to climb down and see bands like the Buzzcocks, the Gang of Four, the Ramones, and the Specials. I became friends with Springa, another underage kid, who was the competition for getting on guest lists at sound checks, and he revealed his ceiling system at another venue, the Channel Club. When the Cramps played there, we hid out in the bathroom ceiling, waiting to see yet another band I'd listened to through many sleepless nights in the project, and felt on top of my world.

Before long, though, as word got out again, the Channel's rafters became a place to party. People brought stashes of whiskey and vodka, and I had to sit on the far end because I didn't drink and was tired of handing the bottles to the next person. A few shows later, when Bauhaus played, our secret way in was finished at the Channel. As we heard the audience filing into the club, Reme tried to stand up on the beam to leave, and she slipped. Rita Ratt and I grabbed her, but her spike heel poked through a ceiling panel. A woman pissing below saw the foot above her head and let out a shriek — we all panicked and lost our balance, bringing down the entire ladies' room ceiling. We saw Bauhaus that night, but it was from the corners of the club, brushing off the flakes of asbestos that would have given us away.

As I swiped at the last bits of evidence on my pants, Rita Ratt shrieked "Are those Calvin Kleins?" as the crowd cheered for Bauhaus's song "Bela Lugosi's Dead." I'd taken a pair of dungarees from Kevin's stash, and washed and shredded them until they looked like jeans I'd found in a gutter. But there was still a dark spot where the Calvin Klein logo had once been. I'd been caught. I felt my face turn red as I tried to explain that they were my brother's. I knew she wouldn't believe me if I told her about Kevin's truck hijacking capers, and that I hadn't actually bought them.

"It's all right," she laughed, patting my shoulder, "we know you're a Southie boy."

I CUT BACK MY CALLS to patient information to once an hour on the hour, since the voice on the other end sounded fed up. "The same," she said, wearily. "Critical condition," like it was all same old, same old and unlikely to change. I had been planning for weeks to hook school that day to wait in line for the Elvis Costello tickets going on sale at the Orpheum. I hated big concerts now, and most of the bands big enough to play the Orpheum Theater were finished in my book, sellouts. But Elvis was an exception to a lot of us. And I hadn't hooked since that day Ma caught me in Copley, so I had looked forward to hanging out with friends in line, talking all day about this Elvis album versus that one.

Now, after the doctor came on the phone to tell me that they were trying to stop the hemorrhaging in Kathy's brain, that Kathy was hanging between life and death, and that if she did make it out of the coma, she would never be the same again, all music seemed stupid. After the doctor's words, my heart was racing, and I had to keep catching my breath. I'd been careening from thought to thought ever since the ambulance took Kathy away from Patterson Way the night before. There was no way I could sleep, not after what had happened with Davey when I went to sleep after he jumped. It seemed unreal to be back at the same place, on a deathwatch for someone who went off the roof.

We didn't know exactly what had happened to Kathy. She had been staying with her friend Joanie after a fight with Ma for staying out to all hours. I usually sneaked in and out the back door of our apartment, but Kathy was blatant about strolling in at five in the morning. She had dropped out of Cardinal Cushing High School, and Ma got her to enroll in GED night classes while taking carpentry. But Kathy would hook any class to hang out with her friends. Since she was nineteen, Ma didn't try to stop her from moving out. She figured Kathy would be right back anyway — and coming in at a decent hour — once she found out how expensive it was to feed yourself out in the world. Kathy packed her bags and moved into Joanie's project apartment down the street.

A neighbor of Joanie's said he'd heard Kathy fighting on the rooftop that icy cold night, demanding her pills and her keys to Joanie's place. Her new boyfriend, Richie, was the only one with her, but when he banged on our door to give us the news, he didn't tell us much more than that "she fell." And that was the last we heard from him. The doctors said Kathy's system was loaded with Valium, speed, and cocaine. A neighbor found Kathy's pocketbook and gave it to Ma. It had some coke in it, and some little yellow pills prescribed by one of the crooked doctors from "Pill Hill," in the nicer part of City Point. Ma told the story to everyone who called, so I'd heard it over and over. And when she told her cousin Nelly, who was close to Ma, she asked herself out loud why she ever let Kathy go to Joanie's. When Ma went to lie down, holding her head, I took over, answering the constant calls and telling the story over and again before breaking off to call patient information. At first it seemed like the only thing to do: tell the story and add the occasional news about contusions and hemorrhaging. But after a while the story made me feel trapped in my own helplessness, and I wished it were nothing more than a story, and that I could change the channel. I had to get away from the phone, get out of the house, away from the calls from relatives and Kathy's friends, away from the story going around and around in my brain.

As I left the house, Ma begged me not to worry, and as ridiculous as that sounded to me, I appreciated that she knew how devastated I was. I hadn't shown any closeness to Kathy in the past year or two, so I figured no one knew I cared at all. "And don't dare go to the hospital," Ma yelled after me. The streets were iced over. Halfway to the train station, I turned around, thinking I should be with my family in case something happened. Then, returning to the edge of Old Colony, I turned around again, needing to get out of the neighborhood. I did this three times, back and forth, until I heard a crow screaming at me from a telephone line. I thought it was a sign. I'd been looking for one all morning. I hadn't prayed much since Davey had died, but at that moment my beliefs felt as inescapable as my family. Not religious beliefs — Ma had always taught us to believe in things bigger than that. Ever since she was barred from taking Communion because she was divorced, Ma's church was down by the water, at Carson Beach. And even though she loved the saints and all they represented, she never taught us that the priests were holier than anyone else or that there was only one true church. Now I was desperate for a connection to something bigger than the life I was in, and when I heard that crow screaming, I took heed. I broke down and called patient information from a phone booth, resigned to Kathy's death. "The same. Critical." The crow kept screaming, then flew away to scream at someone or something else, or nothing at all. I was lost and didn't know anymore if there was anything to hold on to. I turned toward home again, into a lashing wind. Walking up Dorchester Street, I thought about Davey and how he had spent his days pacing the streets back and forth, always sick with worry.

After an hour of pacing, I finally sneaked onto a train. By the time I got downtown I was once again resigned to Kathy's death. I called patient information from a phone booth at Park Street Station, ready to hear she was gone. "The same," the patient information lady said wearily. And then "Critical," as abrupt as a door slamming in my face. But at least she was alive. I wondered if it would be better simply to have it over with, like Davey's death only hours after his jump. As I wandered through town that morning, all the talk at subway booths and newsstands was of it being one of the coldest Januarys on record, and of Ronald Reagan's inauguration. Eyes peeked out from between wool hats and scarves, and people jumped in place when they weren't walking fast. But I didn't feel a thing. Suddenly I needed, though, to tell the story about Kathy's brain bleeding again. I couldn't bear to go back home, where the story would get stuck in a closed circuit in my brain. So I wandered over to the Orpheum, where I knew Remedios was hooking school to line up for Elvis tickets.

Sculley was holding her tattered leopard coat together, hopping in place to get warm. She laughed when she saw me. "Look, there's Pineapple!"

"My sister went off the roof last night. She's in critical condition," I said.

"Oh, my God, your family's sooooo craaaaazy!" Sculley said. "Holy shit, I'm tripping my brains out right now and you look like a pineapple!"

"I thought your brother went off the roof last year," someone else blurted. I stared at the ground for a moment. I'd only recently started telling some friends that I was from Southie, but most of my stories were of characters from the neighborhood, for entertainment value. I didn't realize I'd told anyone about Davey. I hadn't yet figured out in my own head how to think about that day, never mind share it with anyone else.

"He did," I admitted, hesitant. Staring straight ahead, right through my friends, I realized that people might think I was making up this roof shit and that maybe I'd better keep quiet.

Maybe it's too much for people to handle. It all seemed so unreal, even to me.

I tried to focus again when I heard "What's up with your family and roofs?" I was so distracted, though, I didn't know who'd said it.

What is up with my family and roofs? I wondered. I had felt a nagging fear all morning that we might be cursed. And now, someone else pointing out the coincidence convinced me that my family was just bad, doomed, and there was nothing I could ever do about it.

The people in line behind us stopped talking about this Elvis Costello album versus that one to tell me that I couldn't just show up and cut in line. "What the hell are you thinking, man?" Beyond that, whatever they were saying didn't sink in. I was thinking about the curse and how I had to get away from everyone who couldn't possibly understand what I was feeling. Elvis Costello, obsessed music fans, crazy leopard coats, and making fun of everything. It all seemed alien. *And I'm not even the one tripping.*

"Tell us the one about your crazy mother beating up the neighbor, Chickie, for calling her a douchebag and a dickie-puller," Sculley said.

Remedios showed up, returning from a coffee run. But I had to escape. I told Reme quickly, "My sister went off the roof." I wanted to keep walking so I wouldn't have to answer any more questions about it. But I needed some reason for having come here, other than to talk about Kathy. "I only came by to see if you could get my ticket to Elvis," I said. Reme looked stunned. She was holding three cups of coffee, and looked down at them like they were pointless, the way I'd started to view getting Elvis tickets. I knew that I hadn't really come by for tickets at all, but I couldn't remember why I had traveled to the Orpheum in the first place, what the point was. I racked my brain, retraced *how* I'd gotten there — by subway — in hopes of remembering my point. I'd never felt so lost. It was like my brain had just fallen out of my head. Reme said of course she would get me a ticket. As I looked back at her, she looked almost as lost as I felt, which I appreciated.

"Goodbye, Pineapple!" Sculley waved, and I waved back. "Oh, my God, his family is sooooo crazy!" I heard the refrain become distant and shrugged it off, knowing Sculley was only tripping and probably meant "crazy" in a good way. Still, I was eager to disappear into the mob of passers-by going to work on just another Monday morning.

I sat for a couple of hours at the Frog Pond on the Boston Common, my favorite place that Ma would take me, Kathy, and Kevin when we were the "three little kids." I was the youngest in the family back then. Until Seamus and Stevie came along ten years after me with a whole new father, Coley, I had been the only one with a different father. That felt weird sometimes, if I thought about it. But Ma gave me the name Mac-Donald to be like the other kids, even though I'd heard that my father's last name was Fox. I had never met George Fox, and the other kids hadn't seen their father — "Mac" in family stories — in years. Being one of the "three little kids" used to make me feel connected to some grouping in the family, and to Kevin and Kathy more than anyone else.

It was a letdown to see the Frog Pond all these years later, as a fourteen-year-old. It looked like nothing more than a big puddle. And in the below-zero weather it was ugly, with sticks and beer cans trapped in the frozen brown muck. Being there made me feel like all the big things in my life — music and friends I'd thought superior to all the ordinary people in the world — were bullshit. I had to keep moving.

I had no idea what to do with the rest of the day other than call patient information every hour until there was no more information. Maybe no more Kathy. I decided to go to my aunt Theresa's in Jamaica Plain. Theresa looked after me when I was small and Ma was getting her degree at Suffolk. She had three kids at home, and they had once been like a second family to me. There was something calming about Theresa. She kept things simple, never talked behind anyone's back, always told the truth, and never asked insulting questions. If I showed up at her house these days after running the exciting gauntlet of people shouting obscenities about how I looked, Theresa would just shrug. "Oh, I don't care for the ripped-up old man's clothes too much, but whatever makes you happy."

She was family, but not as close as Ma to Kathy's situation. She was the person I needed right then. When I got to Theresa's house, no one was there, so I walked back up Carolina Avenue to find a phone booth to call the hospital. I couldn't help but notice the peace of Carolina Avenue during school hours, compared to Old Colony, where a lot of Kathy's and Kevin's friends who had dropped out kept the street corners busy even on the coldest school days. I saw Theresa walking down the hill carrying a bundle of groceries in her arms, looking excited to see me. I knew by her expression that she hadn't heard about Kathy. Ma's family was always the last to be told anything. I hadn't visited Theresa much since I'd become a teenager. But whenever I'd drop by her house out of the blue, she'd thank me fifty times over for visiting.

"Oh, Michael," she said when I approached her. "Isn't that nice you came over!" If her smile grew any wider I knew I wouldn't be able to break the news to her. And I had to let it all out again after an hour on the bus listening to commuters carry on like it was just another day. "Who gives a fuck about the weather?" I'd repeated in my head. "Who gives a fuck about Ronald Reagan?" I felt like I'd lose my mind if I waited any longer to talk about Kathy.

"Kathy fell off the roof last night," I said.

Theresa dropped her bundle, grabbed on to a nearby fence, and held her heart. Then she started bawling her eyes out, saying "Jesus, Mary, and Joseph" over and over again. As bad as it was to see her like that, I was almost relieved. I finally felt sure that it had really happened, that Kathy did go off the roof, and that it was horrible beyond all words.

MAD DONALD! YOU DON'T IMPRESS ME! Vat do you zink? You zink you impress me? No. You do not impress me. You vant to know vat impresses me?" Mrs. Savickas hovered over me, pacing and twisting a pencil. "Science impresses me!" she screamed, slamming her hand on my desk. "Vat's zis?" she asked, grabbing at the dog chain around my neck. "Now you vant to be a dog?" Her taunt startled me, because for a second I thought she knew the Iggy Pop song. I didn't know why Mrs. Savickas had picked me out of the crowd to blame. It wasn't me who had mimicked her high-pitched Eastern European accent while her back was turned. It was Matt Mc-Glaughlin, a football jock I let copy my answers during Earth Science exams, knowing I had half the answers wrong. He was probably just getting back at me, so I had to put up with Mrs. Savickas's critique of my outfit. "Vat's zese pants? You're vaiting for ze flood?" she asked, getting the laugh she'd hoped for. "Zese pants, zey don't impress me. Science impresses me!" she shouted, throwing her open hand toward the sky and then making a fist, to add power to the science she was talking about.

Mr. Savickas dressed like military personnel or a nun: plain skirt, crisp, collared man's shirt, and always an exactly fitted beige blazer. She walked stiffly and in a straight line, like someone who'd never experienced the sixties in America. I admired her. The uniform was intriguing, a radical rejection of lazy hippieness. But now she was turning on me.

"Look, I have seen it all. Ze Nazis. Zey took everything away from us. Ze Russians. They come into my home and take away my family." Suddenly everyone in Earth Science was gripped as never before by her story. I wanted to hear more about where Mrs. Savickas was from and less of her rant against me, but she cut her story short and breathed down my neck. "So you don't impress me. Science impresses me!" I hadn't wanted to show up for school that morning, since Kathy was back on the danger list and my stomach was sick with worry after hearing Ma talk about "being prepared for the worst." I stood up from my desk and walked calmly and resolutely out of class. When I unlatched the fire exit in the hall, I ignored Mr. Contompasis's incensed shouts of "Mr. Mac-Donald!" Once the heavy door slammed shut on his rage, I thought only of getting back to the hospital to see Kathy one last time.

I was hooking school most days, though I left the house every morning with a stack of Latin books under my arm so Ma wouldn't suspect. I couldn't go to City Hospital until ten in the morning, when they'd let me in to see Kathy. Before ten I needed a place to stay warm — the Mug-N-Muffin if I had a couple of dollars, or the library or a museum.

Sometimes I'd head for school, but right at the doors I'd turn around and decide to kill time at the Isabella Stewart Gardner Museum around the corner. I had discovered the museum one day when sneaking out the side door of Latin to have lunch at a nearby diner, Sparr's. It became my routine to leave a notebook jammed in the side door so I could get back into school for the period after lunch. I'd get a coffee to go and sneak it into the Gardner, where I'd sit and look at Rembrandt's *Storm on the Sea of Galilee*. I figured Kathy had about as much chance of waking up from the coma as the fishermen in the boat had of surviving the wave that was about to swallow them up, even though Jesus was on the boat with them. I was questioning my faith in anything, but the painting had pulled me back every day at lunchtime. Then I'd head back across the street to my rigged door at Latin.

One day at the Gardner I nearly fell off my bench when I heard Grandpa's voice behind me, explaining the Rembrandt painting to a tourist. I turned around and there was my grandfather in a museum guard's red blazer. "Grandpa!" I yelled in shock. He left the tourist, who looked like she hadn't understood much of what he'd said anyway. "Hello, Mike," he said casually, like it was nothing that we should bump into each other in the Isabella Stewart Gardner Museum at noon or that he was wearing a museum guard's red jacket. I didn't even know he had a job, since he'd retired from working as a longshoreman years before. He reached into his pocket, pulled out a dollar, and handed it to me. With Grandpa it was an automatic reaction to pull out a dollar whenever he saw one of his grandchildren. I took the dollar and, as he started to walk away, I said, "Wait, do you work here or something?" "Sure, it's only a part-time job," he whispered, adding that I needed to dispose of my coffee. *Dispose of?* I felt stuck in a strange dream.

Grandpa walked back to the tourist to tell her that Rembrandt was a very religious man altogether and that the painting she was looking at there had special powers. She looked at him doubtfully. I followed Grandpa around the room, and when the tourist ran away I told him he was making this stuff up. He agreed, squinting like he did when he held back a laugh, and said it was loads of fun. Grandpa had a habit of leaning up against a wall corner and sliding back and forth to scratch his back, and now that no visitors were around he was doing it in the Dutch Masters room. I wanted Grandpa to explain his secret life in one of the most proper Bostonian establishments, the last place I'd expect to see a relative of mine. But he hadn't yet asked me why I was out of school in the middle of the day, and I decided to cut it short. I had to get back to school. He said he was going to see Kathy that afternoon to bring her some holy water from Lourdes and asked if I'd like to go along.

Later that day, riding with Grandpa on the train, I found out that he visited Kathy as often as I did. I didn't tell him I'd already spent the morning at her bedside. From then on I felt like Grandpa was my new partner in crime. He'd meet me in the afternoon in front of the Rembrandt, and we'd take the train back to Boston City Hospital together.

After walking from Boston City to the Rat in Kenmore Square, I couldn't bear to go inside, even though my friends' band was playing that night. I didn't want to see anyone I knew. I felt I had more to talk about with Mac, my brothers' and sisters' father — "the worst bastard on two feet," as Ma said — than I did with any of my old Rat friends. Mac had recently been coming to see Kathy, along with his busybody second wife, Pauline. "Guilty as the day is long," Ma said about Mac's return after fifteen years in hiding.

When I saw two friends stumble out of the Rat, I sat on a nearby stoop with my aviator hat, a hand-me-down from Grandpa, pulled low, earflaps down. Pauline had asked Ma at the hospital if there was something wrong with me. "He looks like the homeless!" she said. When my friends disappeared I decided to look inside to see if Frank was working. I didn't want him to see me, though. It was always awkward to bump into him and have nothing to talk about. I tried to peek through the tiny window in the heavy steel door, but just then the door flew open, forced by a body that had been slammed into it. Frank had some skinny rock 'n' roll Ramones type by the collar and tossed him into the curb. "Mike!" he said, recognizing me in spite of the pulled-down hat. His backups stood behind him, ready to pounce if the rock 'n' roll guy tried to get back inside. I was shocked when Frankie called me to the doorway and explained to his friends that I was his brother. He yelled at the banished one to keep walking. I backed up a step, keeping a distance from both sides of the fight. Thrown off by Frankie's acknowledgment, I wasn't sure which side I was on. The guy walked fast up the street, yelling back with threats to sue the Rat. Frankie just laughed it off.

Everyone knew you couldn't sue the Rat. The owner had gangster connections and was immune to any recourse for all the beatings doled out there. Frankie stood next to me, leaning against the row of battered pay phones outside the Rat. We faced the approaching raucous crowds headed off to Narcissus, Kenmore Square's huge disco. He asked if I'd heard that Kathy was fighting pneumonia. I nodded. We were both silent for a painful minute, and I wondered how and when I'd get away. Frankie and I never had anything to talk about beyond the everyday reporting of Kathy's condition. He said he'd gone to the hospital before work and had brought a TV in for her. "A TV?" I asked, confused. My eyes caught his and we both looked away. "Yeah," he said, looking down at the pavement or at people passing by on their way to the nightclubs. "I figured it would be a good way to keep her head going, and maybe make her come to." I was amazed at the idea, and even more amazed that I never would have thought of it. Frankie said he thought Kathy would live, even though she was back on the danger list. "She has too much fight in her," he said. "Tougher than any guy I know." Frankie remembered the times Kathy had beaten Kevin in the family boxing matches Frankie set up for us when we were kids.

"Remember she stopped that girl from being raped?" I said. Frankie hadn't heard about that one. When Kathy first went into the coma, and I was sure she'd die, I went through the stuff in her room and tried to remember who she was, all the good things. Like the time she heard cries coming from the basement and ran downstairs to beat two neighbors off a suburban girl they had pinned to the ground. "She's as strong as an ox," Frankie said, shaking his head and reminding me of the time Kathy carried Ma, in labor with Seamus, down three flights into a waiting taxi to go to the hospital. Now, nearly four months into the deathwatch, I'd stopped thinking about these stories. Stories of Kathy now were only about neurological details and the fluctuations from danger list to "stable" and back again. I barely thought about Kathy herself. Even when I was around the people who knew her, like the friends who came and went during visiting hours, the uncomfortable silence always ended with casual talk of infections, catheters, and "the odds" of her living or dying. But this night Frankie had stories I'd never heard.

Just then my friend Bob came tumbling out of the Rat. Toohey, another Southie bouncer, came out behind him, fixed his collar to make it stand up stiff again, and folded his arms in the Rat bouncer pose. Frankie went to stand guard with Toohey, and the two of them laughed off Bob's calling them "meatheads" and "vulgarians," which was a new term for me. When Frankie and Toohey disappeared back inside to help with another fight, Bob came over to me to talk about "these fuckin' animals." I didn't tell him that one of the animals was my brother. I just said I had to go home.

I hadn't been to school in weeks — I couldn't remember how long. I walked toward the gigantic Corinthian columns of Boston Latin and joined the mass of kids herding in from the school buses. I thought the assistant headmaster, Mr. Vara, was probably standing in my path to congratulate me sarcastically on coming back — until he took the folded-arm stance of one of Frankie's crew of bouncers at the Rat, blocking my entry. Mr. Vara was short, which went comically with his Jimmy Cagney street-thug accent. I felt ready to laugh, anticipating a smartass greeting. Instead he told me I couldn't enter the building until school officials met with Ma about my absences, and even if they did let me return, I'd have to stay back a grade. After our phone was disconnected, I hadn't had to worry about phone calls from Latin. Even before that, Ma had stopped answering. She was worn out from the deathwatch calls coming in about Kathy and wanted nothing to do with the phone. But when the notices from Latin about my absences started arriving in the mail, I would wait for the postman in the hallway and rip them up before going to sit with Kathy. I didn't know what to say to Vara. Finally, frustrated with my silence, he ordered me to report to Mr. Flaherty in Guidance.

"Well, geez, where the heck have you been, Mister . . . um . . . um . . . ," Flaherty said. He opened my folder and scanned the papers inside, moving his head back and forth like he was crunching for a quiz on me. Mr. Vara knew me well — he was the one who always caught me sneaking in the side door late for homeroom. "Listen, kid," he had said once, looking up at me and poking at the air in front of my chest, "you're gonna set the record for being the latest person in the history of Boston Latin School." I was groggy, but I woke right up at the idea of making history. But I'd been ordered to see Mr. Flaherty only a few times, so he didn't know me as well. I fidgeted in my chair and tried to get up the guts to tell Flaherty that my sister was in a coma and that I needed to visit her instead of coming to school because she might die. But when I thought about saying all that, I choked up and couldn't force the words out. Finally I spilled it all out in a barrage of words I didn't hear myself saying. Whatever I said, it made him look up from my folder and peer at me from above the rims of his reading glasses. His forehead was crinkled and worried-looking. He sat up slowly, threw his eyeglasses on the desk, and leaned back in his chair with a look of sadness that made me choke a little more. "How'd it happen?" he asked quietly, making me feel less like a wanted criminal. I could only get through it by giving the bare bones, which was all we knew anyway. "She went off the roof. She was in an argument with someone up there." Then I immediately kicked in to the good news, that lately she'd had a few good days when the penicillin worked on her multiple infections and that she'd even beaten pneumonia in her sleep.

"Kathy's a real fighter," I said, repeating what had become Ma's mantra.

"Well . . . I . . . I just . . . ," he said, stuttering like he was frustrated and stopping to shake his head at the floor. Then he suddenly changed direction. Looking more like a judge and jury, he said, "What on earth do you think *you* can do for her?" I sat up in my chair and tried to respond, but the question was impossible to answer. Mr. Flaherty stood up, walked around his desk slowly, and looked out his window onto Avenue Louis Pasteur. He took the dramatic stance of someone looking reflective for an election campaign ad or a senior citizen commercial about life insurance. I was nervous anticipating whatever he was about to say but relieved that at least he wasn't looking at me. He began by saying how incredible it was that in this great country someone like me could be afforded the type of education that Boston Latin School offered, for free. "The rest is up to you," he said toward the end of his speech. "You simply need to pull yourself up by your bootstraps." It was the first time I'd heard that expression, and I looked down at my battered combat boots to imagine what he might mean. "In this country you can be anything you want to be, if you only apply yourself," he said. Then he carried on about hard work and struggle. I was confused, because the last few months had felt like nothing *but* hard work and struggle. When I left his office I agreed to bring Ma the next morning if I wanted to be let back in for the remainder of the school year.

But I wasn't going to 'fess up to Ma about not going to school all those days I'd left home looking studious, with a pile of books under my arm. I walked straight past Mr. Vara, who stood in the corridor underneath the school's insignia — the infants Romulus and Remus suckling from a she-wolf — and out the front door of Latin. The first smells of spring were in the air that morning, and I figured I'd walk with no destination until it was time to meet Grandpa and go to the hospital.

As I walked across town, it started to sink in that I wasn't going back to school again. It was official: I was a dropout. I would never go to some great college, as everyone had said I would do. I'd looked toward college with expectation ever since the day all eight of us kids piled into Joe's broken-down station wagon to see Ma graduate from Suffolk University. The Hynes Auditorium seemed palatial that morning, and the suspense grew with each letter of the alphabet, as black-robed graduates far younger than Ma accepted their diplomas. When they announced, "Helen MacDonald, cum laude!" we all stood on our seats to cheer for Ma as she walked onstage. I had no idea what "cum laude" meant until I went to Boston Latin years later, but I knew that to get the full scholarship to Suffolk Ma had to maintain all A's and B's. Her graduation robe was like everyone else's in the sea of black, except that Ma's was hiked up to show off her fishnets. When she walked offstage I was disappointed that it was over. But things got even more exciting when a *Boston Globe* reporter called us into a private room to take a picture of the whole family. We stood around Ma, who posed with sucked-in cheeks and a penciled-in beauty mark like Sophia Loren. Ma had clipped a red wiglet to the top of her head that day, and she wanted nothing to do with the flat graduation cap, which would mess up her look. "It adds height," Ma explained about the wiglet, which was the same shade of red as her hair. But the photographer wanted her to don the square hat. The reporter looked up from his notes and chimed in, saying that they wanted to do a story about the welfare mother of eight graduating cum laude and that they were going for a more scholarly look.

After that, while pregnant with Seamus and Stevie, Ma went for her master's in psychology. Davey was still alive then, and Ma said she wanted to understand better what was happening to him. Around that time Ma told me one of her professors was talking about how kids from one family can have all different types of skills, and she said mine were of the brain. "Analyzing things," she said. "Your father was like that." She said I'd always stand out in school and that wasn't a bad thing. But talk about what I was good at made me uncomfortable. I was glad when she changed the subject and asked me what I wanted to be when I grew up, so I could declare, "A psychiatrist, so I can help people!" Like Ma, I knew that the people I was talking about were the mentally ill, people like Davey.

It gave me a sick feeling now to think of the ambitions I'd once had and what I actually believed I *could* be. Like Johnny and Davey, I'd always gotten all A's. And like them I'd been accepted at Boston Latin. Now Davey was dead and Johnny was a lieutenant in the SEALs, on antiterrorist missions for Ronald Reagan's generals. *But what am I going to do?* I wondered. I'd imagined suicide after Davey jumped. I figured most people thought of it sometimes, and since I'd actually seen it, I couldn't help but wonder what it was like to do that — and what it was like to be dead. But I knew what Davey's jump had done to us, and I decided my family had been through enough. Killing myself was out of the question. And I certainly wasn't going to be like Johnny, an antiterrorist, whatever that meant.

That morning I came upon a sidewalk vigil for the Irish hunger striker Bobby Sands. Sands's face had been all over the news lately and Ma shushed everyone when updates came on TV. But all I knew from the news was that the Irishmen in prison refused to eat and that the British prime minister, Margaret Thatcher, called them terrorists. "We will not give in to demands by the men of violence," Thatcher said in broadcasts to the world. I knew nothing of the fight for a "united Ireland" other than the bits and pieces I'd heard from Ma's rebel songs on the accordion. I was focused on Kathy, and I didn't want to know about the hunger strikes anyway. On Southie's brick walls, IRA murals that said IRELAND UNFREE SHALL NEVER BE AT PEACE were painted alongside the graffiti scrawls of WHITE POWER, and REAGAN FOR PRESIDENT posters. The previous fall it seemed the whole neighborhood had voted for Reagan — ever since busing, any Republican would do. To most of the homeless people at the Boston Public Library, though, Reagan was the devil himself. The day he was shot,

Disco Train chugged by the library and shouted the news with a smile, and the homeless people all let out a big cheer. Most of the post-punk bands I liked hated both Reagan and Thatcher. I'd even heard that the Clash's recent album — the only music I listened to during Kathy's coma — was named *Sandinista!* because Thatcher had tried to ban the very word.

I stopped to look at the vigil for Bobby Sands from across the street. So many faces in that crowd looked uncomfortably familiar to me, reminding me too much of where I came from. I went back to walking and wondering where the hell I was going.

When Kathy woke up on Easter Sunday, I felt we'd experienced a real miracle, just like in Grandpa's stories about Lourdes. Through four months of Kathy swinging from bad to worse to just bad again, with constant infections, tracheotomies, and the danger list, I had tried to hope — against all probability -- that a miracle *could* happen. In reality I had little hope. Only the sight of Grandpa's welled-up eyes, and his witch doctor–like intensity when splashing Lourdes holy water over Kathy, kept me from giving in to the thought that we were on the threshold of another death in the family. It might have been a relief to let go of all hope, but fighting to the end had always been the family creed. I didn't know how to surrender, though at times I wished I did. Ma never let any one of us kids be sick with the flu. "Don't be so concerned with yourself," she'd say, even when I really was sick, not just lying to stay home from school. And if she saw us taking medicine or trying to sleep extra, she'd catch us. "Well, by God, you're awful good to yourself, aren't you?" she'd say. That's when I'd accuse Ma of being the twin of her father, which made her fume. I knew some attitudes were just passed down, and for better or worse, in my family surrender was a luxury, one to be ashamed of.

Even worse than the struggle to hope, though, I'd had to fight tooth and nail throughout Kathy's coma against my worst suspicion: that my family was cursed. Nausea snuck up on me when I least suspected it, overwhelming my head and my stomach with the certainty that expecting anything better than the worst possible outcome was useless fantasy. In my lowest moments, as I wandered all over the city or kept the deathwatch, I would nearly collapse from the recurring realization that the most any of my family could ever hope for was a fate like Davey's and Kathy's — crashing one way or another onto the twisted concrete of Old Colony. And these waves of doom threatened to drown all the fight I'd ever been trained for.

Before that Easter I'd never known what it felt like to experience a complete turnaround of luck. So I was taken off guard by Kathy's return from death's door. It almost made me uncomfortable, the idea that things could get better in the darkest hour. I wasn't sure how to deal with this whole new feeling. For a few days after Easter I had to spend my first ten waking minutes wondering if it wasn't all just a good dream. Like the ones I'd had about Davey being alive after all.

But Kathy *was* alive again, against all medical predictions, and against my conviction that my family was cursed. That day it didn't feel real walking into her unit and seeing her with eyes wide open. She turned her head to the doorway and looked at me in calm recognition, like she'd just woken from a nap on the couch. Her head was all there, the doctors assured us, and she knew all of us. But she remembered only bits and pieces of what had happened and had to be told that she'd been asleep for months. The doctors said she'd have to learn to walk and talk again. They said it would be like having to start all over, to learn everything anew. And as much as that was supposed to be the bad news, I liked the sound of it.

"Remember the old days, when punks were ugly?" Sculley asked. "Hideous," I replied. "That was the whole point!" We stared hopelessly at the New Wavers walking up Commonwealth Ave. to see Siouxsie and the Banshees at the Paradise, a concert venue in the middle of the "college land" of Boston

University. It was sad to see things changing so much. We were fifteen-year-old has-beens, jaded. We watched all the normal people in mass-produced punk and New Wave fashions get off the trains to line up for Siouxsie. There had been a time when, like Ma said, it was "one big ugly contest." But it was our own private club of uglies that no one could join without first earning their stripes by getting shoved down escalators or spat on while riding the trains. "Look, it's an alternative free-for-all: numbskulls thinking they get it," Bob said, appearing out of the blue to chime in on his favorite topic.

By now the smaller clubs, like Cantone's and the Underground, where we had easily snuck in to see the Cure and the Dead Kennedys, were closing. The bands we wanted to see were likely to play at bigger venues with long lines, professional security, and bolted doors. Siouxsie and the Banshees were from the old days; from that early group of teenagers who sought to destroy the world around them and start all over again. But Siouxsie's obsession with costume seemed to bring out all of the part-time punks. And it was now just two days before Halloween — no one would get any shit for what they wore anyway.

Springa caught up with us in front of the Paradise. He usually looked scruffy, with ragged dungarees and torn dress shirts scrawled on with a line from a Clash or Sham 69 song, or with the name of a song from his band, SS Decontrol, like "The Kids Will Have Their Say!" But tonight he looked like a priest, with an oversized black shirt formally buttoned to the top and hanging from his skinny neck. At the thrift shops where we all got clothes we never bothered with sizes — the more oversized, the better. Springa's hair was slicked back like Dracula's, or Dave Vanian's from the Damned. I was always glad to see Springa because we were usually in the same boat: no money, a bad fake ID that once belonged to a football jock from Boston College or a science whiz from MIT who looked nothing like us, and no way to get home on the Red Line — me to Southie and Springa to Quincy — after the trains closed down for the night. But Springa always had a will and a way, like Kevin. From the effort he'd put into his vampire look that night you could bet your life he would get in to the Siouxsie show. He even had dark circles smudged around his eyes, a risk for beatings on the Red Line even on Halloween.

I was pretty certain of getting in myself. Just an hour earlier, I had stolen from the Morgie's thrift shop what looked like undertaker's shoes. They were black patent leather, worn, and curled at the pointed toes. They looked like someone had died in them. Sculley told me I should have rinsed them in salt water to get rid of the last person's aura. She liked to think she was a real witch, not just posing like the passers-by in "Goth" clothing, as the look was starting to be labeled. As much as I enjoyed looking like death warmed over, Sculley's witch talk scared me.

Springa was always jumpy, and he was even jumpier now, on a mission, pacing the sidewalk and muttering fast about a plan to "slime in" for free. He said he knew a backstage door that would lead the three of us into the club. But first we'd have to make it past the bouncer taking IDs on the street. Ma was always saying I looked fifteen going on a hundred in Grandpa's big black wooly overcoat. Springa was sixteen but so scrawny he looked about thirteen or fourteen. The fact that he practically bounced off walls made him seem younger too. He was too goofy and slap-happy to pull off the ghoulish look he'd adopted that night. I couldn't imagine anyone believing he was twenty-one.

"Follow me," he said, without explaining the plan. We walked up to the door, and Springa said, in an attempted English accent that sounded more like someone doing mock Chinese, that we were roadies for the band. The jock doorman, obviously new to the job, cleared the way for us, even though we were just kids in oversized mourning clothes. We didn't even have to use our bad fake IDs. I believed it was my long black coat that did the trick. I felt like I was in a *Little Rascals* episode with Spanky and the gang on each other's shoulders and wearing a long black coat to get into a saloon, Sometimes, though, the college jock bouncers working the doors were so disoriented by the freak show that you could run circles around them — not like the Southie bouncers at the Rat, who were unimpressed and looked for any reason to pummel a weirdo punk rocker.

The doorman ushered us in like we were very important, directing us toward the booth where we would give our names for the guest list. Springa pulled Sculley and me into a huddle to whisper the rest of the plan, which was simply to continue acting very important. "Walk in there like you own the place," he said, pointing to the door that he said led backstage. I was to go first, which I learned only when Springa pushed me ahead. But I caught my composure and acted like I owned the place.

It worked! I was invisible! I couldn't believe what was happening. A guy who looked like a sound technician, a hippie with his hair cut short in front and a tail in the back, pardoned himself in the dark corridor as he walked past me. This was a revelation to me that could change the way I would sneak into shows for years to come. *Walk in there like you own the place,* I kept repeating to myself whenever fear of getting bagged crept in.

Then came the hard part, which Springa hadn't mentioned. After following the light at the end of the dark passageway, I was shocked to find myself suddenly onstage. Siouxsie and the Banshees had just broken into the song "Pull It to Bits." I was completely blinded by a spotlight and could only make out a silhouette of Siouxsie's spider-plant hairdo surrounded by white haze billowing from a smoke machine. She was coming after me, and her tambourine was raised for the kill. I jumped down a staircase into the audience and disappeared into a sea of people with black hair and black clothes. I stripped off the overcoat in case the bouncers had spotted me onstage. Then I saw that everyone was wearing black overcoats, so I put mine back on and hoped for the best.

Soon Springa appeared onstage. At first he looked surprised

by his rock star status, but he got used to it fast, bobbing his head in sync with the sea of ghouls jumping up and down before him. Siouxsie came at him from behind, looking like she was going for his throat with the tambourine. But just in time he dove from the stage, thrashing through the crowd, knocking people over, and causing what looked like a melee. Springa had been introducing the rowdy phenomenon of "slamming" to shows in Boston, even at shows like Siouxsie and the Banshees, though it seemed more appropriate for hardcore bands like Black Flag. Soon everyone, including some of the newcomer trendies, got into it, pushing and shoving until the whole club turned into one big friendly riot. Siouxsie looked appalled by the ruckus competing with her performance, and she sought revenge. She climbed over a few heads, supported by people's shoulders, and started hitting Springa over the head with her microphone before kicking him. Then the music came crashing to a halt and she stormed offstage, giving the audience the British two-fingered fuck-you. One of the more morose-looking fans near the front of the stage, a guy with black hair covering one eye, took Siouxsie's side, glaring at Springa with his one exposed eye. The crowd was stirring, and Springa was being blamed for the whole Siouxsie breakdown. But Siouxsie soon came back, and the bass player started into more foreboding bass lines. Springa disappeared into the crowd, slightly ashamed that he'd pissed off the icon. But he played it down, making the rounds with various cliques in the room and having a laugh. I was glad Springa had lightened up the show. I was getting tired of the gloomy vibe taking over a lot of music. I'd been hanging out at home more, watching Kathy take her first steps and string together her first sentences. And lately the darkness just didn't appeal to me as much.

Handwritten band flyers announcing ALL AGES! started to appear on lampposts all over Boston. More and more kids in combat boots and angry scowls were pouring into the city from the suburban outposts of the newly expanded Red Line. "Hardcore punk" was the new underground scene. While older punk bands like the Clash were getting huge crowds at expensive, sold-out shows in Times Square, bands like Springa's SSdecontrol and Gang Green were playing to mobs of kids in makeshift art galleries on Sunday afternoons. For once, at fifteen I wasn't the youngest person in the room, and my veteran status allowed me to casually join in when Springa brought up the old days, of seeing bands like the Buzzcocks or local groups like Unnatural Axe. I wasn't into most of the newer hardcore music, with songs even faster and shorter than the Ramones'. For a while there was a sort of competition among the groups to come up with the shortest and fastest litany of words to spit out over loud guitar. As soon as the song began, a sweaty horde of bald boys and girls would jump into the pit in front of the stage, thrashing and kicking and punching, and the song would end — sometimes only seconds after it began —just in time, before anyone got hurt. If the songs were about anything, they were usually complaints about boring, pointless suburban life, a world I'd never known.

As bad as Southie was, I was glad I was never allowed to feel sorry for myself the way these kids seemed to do in the pissed-off shouts and chants in unison that made you feel like you were at a football rally. Maybe, I thought, I was getting old, because I knew that when you get older you think that everything kids do is bizarre. Sometimes I thought this punching and kicking and chanting was just what rich suburban people did to rebel.

The hardcore shows gave me something to do, though, on Sunday afternoons, which I'd otherwise spend hanging out in my room listening to tapes. The only thing that scared me at the shows was that everyone was starting to look alike. In the "old days" you never saw two people who looked alike, other than the occasional Sid Vicious clone in black leather jacket and studs or the new morbid look, which at one time belonged only to Bob. But the hardcore crowd all had shaved heads and white T-shirts. One of the few hardcore bands I was into was the Dead Kennedys, which had been around from the early punk days anyway, and they sang about things that mattered, like poor people getting poorer under Reagan, which was becoming more important to me, even though most American punks didn't know what poor meant, and my neighbors in the projects pretended not to know.

Mostly I listened to bands that had come out of the earlier punk days — bands that the hardcore kids called "artsy" — like the Gang of Four, Pere Ubo, and the Fall. My preoccupation with roots reggae and dub got me to venture alone to see bands like Steel Pulse and Linton Kwesi Johnson. It was harder to slime in unnoticed, though, since I was always one of just a handful of whites in the room. And the mixtures of punk and funk coming out of New York, with bands like James White and the Blacks and the Bush Tetras, made me want to go there.

The first time I heard the Bad Brains, I became desperate to get to New York, where they often played. Newbury Comics' stoop had become a hangout where a lot of hardcore kids would pass the time sneering at the older artsy punks who worked there. One Saturday, whatever conversation was going on completely disappeared from my mind when the Bad Brains blared out of the store's windows, the sound hard and fast like hardcore, the drums and bass never getting lost in the power of loud guitar, though. Words spilled out of the singer H.R.'s mouth faster than any hardcore, but syncopated to flow like jazz. In all its apocalyptic fury, the Bad Brains' sound was more luminous and hopeful than any other music I'd ever heard. Besides the sound, though, was the ground-shaking disorientation of hearing hardcore punk music played by black Rasta guys.

I arranged to get a ride to New York with Springa's band to see the Bad Brains at the A7 Club on the Lower East Side. I told Ma I'd be staying over with some friends in Quincy and headed out to meet up with the crowds of hardcore kids gathering at Katie the Cleaning Lady's apartment in the Back Bay to get rides. Katie was a local personality who had worked cleaning houses and had started out doing scene reports on the punk radio shows. Now she took the role of mother-of-the-scene, organizing hardcore events. She always showed up with a clipboard of band flyers and looked very much in charge. As wide as she was tall, and wearing a man's topcoat that reached her ankles, she had a Mafia-like air of authority. The drivers of the different cars picked passengers one by one. The lineup felt like grade-school gym class, when you hoped to be picked among the first. I wasn't one of the bald hardcore types, so I assumed I'd be picked last, and by Katie, who would talk too much on the drive about this or that hardcore band.

But Springa pulled me out of line and into the SS Decontrol van with him. Lethal, the band's guitarist, drove. He had the shaved head and white T-shirt and also a big X on each hand, meaning he was a "straight-edger" — against drinking and drugs. So was I, but I'd never wanted to join a club over it. I was happy for the straight-edgers since I hated drugs even more after what had happened to Kathy. But most of the friends I was associated with from the old punk days were taking any pills, speed, or dope they could get their hands on. So I was surprised to find myself in Lethal's van, since he was known to be an exclusive and judgmental straight-edger.

During the drive I was amazed to recognize one of the bald guys, who chanted along to hardcore songs with a mean face and punched a clenched fist at the air. He even had a mean hardcore name, Choke. A year earlier some friends and I had snuck through a window at a Northeastern University hall to see a friend's band. We were embarrassed to find out that the band had been booked for a "New Wave Costume Party." Choke — with a sprayed green, curly poodle hairdo — won the "Most New Wave" contest and was awarded a B-52's album. "Sucks," he said to me and my friends, who'd watched the contest shocked at the state of the world. "I already have this album." Like everyone, I pretended I'd never liked the B-52's, but in the van, listening to a barrage of complaints from what sounded like chanting footballers, I would have killed to hear "Rock Lobster." Still, I just couldn't believe that New Wave Poodle Guy had become an angry bald straight-edger.

When we finally poured out of the van at the corner of Avenue A and Seventh Street on the Lower East Side, I was relieved to get away from the football-chant hardcore music. Getting my bearings on legs that had turned to rubber after the four-hour drive, I was stunned at my first sight of the beautiful, chaotic world we'd landed in.

The intersection was like something out of a dream, a crossroads I'd never imagined. All kinds of people walked in all directions, zigzagging across streets and somehow not bumping into each other. Some of the kids in front of the A7 Club I knew from punk fanzines: members of the band Reagan Youth; Harley, the thirteen-year-old veteran drummer from the older punk band the Stimulators; and some of the Beastie Boys and the Young and the Useless. There was a crowd of "Slits-y" girls, with tangled mops of spiky dreads and bag-lady clothes: layers of long skirts, slips, old-lady stockings, and orthopedic shoes. I was told these girls called themselves the Moppy Scuds, but I couldn't tell if that meant they were in a band. Some of the punks in front of the A7 were black and Puerto Rican, something I'd never seen at punk shows in Boston. Across the street from where I stood, transfixed, Tompkins Square Park was a shantytown filled with cardboard boxes housing whole families. Fires blazed from trash cans. When I wondered out loud, "What's going on over there?" a passing teenager with Clash slogans pinned all over his coat answered, "Reaganomics!" Cars sped by, never slowing for the constant jaywalkers at A and Seventh. Lights flashed and colors changed every minute on the street. The constant movement of this new place relaxed me more than anything I'd ever experienced. I could have stared at it like a fly on the wall and been happy forever. *I wish I could live here,* I found myself repeating in my head.

When two cars crashed, the Boston crowd gathered in awe to watch the bloody drivers get out to fight each other. None of the New York kids seemed startled by the crash. Ambulances showed up within minutes, and the gangs of kids in front of the A7 carried on smoking, hanging out on top of cars, playfighting, and talking about bands. They'd all grown up seeing plenty of action, like me in Old Colony Project — except on this corner of dirty brick buildings, no one in the chaotic swarms looked like anyone from Southie, or like anyone else.

Just then I saw H.R. of the Bad Brains walking down Saint Mark's Place toward the A7 in the state of Rasta transcendence I figured was ganja-induced. He carried a shepherd's staff and was followed by a legion of hardcore waifs. The Slitsy girls and Beastie Boys danced to a passing boom box playing Grandmaster Flash and the Furious Five. I was shocked that they could dance — the only whites I'd ever seen who could dance were from Southie projects. It seemed like all the lines people clung to in Boston were blurred here. The show was about to begin, so we followed H.R. into the A7. In no time the Bad Brains tore into their version of electrifying hardcore mixed with transcendent dub. In a space about the size of my bedroom, everything was shaken upside down and sideways as kids bounced off walls and dove from corners in a room that felt on fire.

When Ma discovered that I hadn't been going to school that year, she told me I'd have to be up every day at the crack of dawn to find a job. But instead of looking for work I went to a stoop on Queensberry Street that had become a gathering spot for young punks from all over Boston. The building had become known in our circle as a cheap place to rent, and many even ended up squatting there. I was usually the first to arrive at the stoop, since Ma kicked me out every morning. Before long, though, the front of the building was a circus of kids with nowhere to go. Jep, a girl who slept in layers of rags like a homeless person and who wore pointed librarian glasses held together with safety pins, would come and sit with her cat. She never had much to say except to show off where she'd been cutting herself. Soon after, Lolly Gag, an art student who broke into funeral parlors to take pictures, would appear. Sometimes she'd offer me her apartment keys so I could take her empty bed, but I usually refused because I was spooked by her roommate's bloody mannequin heads and upside-down crosses on the walls. Gluehead, named for the gallons of Elmer's Glue he used to turn his hair into a nest of spiky dreads, got up early to start his day as a bike messenger. His apartment had become a flophouse for skater punks, who'd soon come outside stretching and yawning after spending the night on a pile of blankets on Gluehead's floor. The only other person who looked busy was Dickie Barrett. He'd formed a band called Toxic Toast and was always drawing cartoons on the stoop for his band flyers. I usually avoided him, though, because he was obsessed with his Irish background, and after I told him a few stories about home, he wanted to actually discuss Southie as if it were a good place. He was from an Irish suburb but had relatives from around my way. "Hey, what about that Whitey Bulger?" he'd ask.

I waited on the Queensberry stoop every morning for my

new friend Clam and his girlfriend Debi to get up. Then we'd play my cassettes of Nick Cave's and the Birthday Party or Nico and the Velvet Underground before joining up with Rita Ratt to beg for change in Kenmore Square. After getting chased too many times by Red Sox fans coming from Fenway Park, we took our business to the center of tourism in Boston: Faneuil Hall. And before long we discovered we ould make a bundle of change letting tourists take pictures of us. Sometimes we'd return to Queensberry Street with as much as twenty-five dollars from tourists who got a kick out of waving to the camera surrounded by freaks. We shared the money, but everyone only wanted to spend it on booze. The stoop at Queensberry was starting to feel like the project to me, like everything I'd left behind: groups of kids sitting around telling stories of their drunken nights or of falling down the fire escape after stealing a keg of beer from a local barroom.

Looking for something to do, I began answering the phone for Sheena and Spenser, local radio personalities known as the Mystery Girls, who took me in like a little brother. The Mystery Girls weren't part of the drug scene. For them it was all about music, and they played everything from the Dead Kennedys to James Brown on their show. I had no interest in going back to school again. I'd lost my guilt about becoming a dropout. I made sure to go home after Ma was in bed so I didn't have to listen to her rants about getting my GED or finding a job.

Before long, though, the Queensberry Street flophouse scene — and much of the non-straight-edge punk scene in Boston — descended into the dark world of heroin. When friends were drunk or even on pills I could ignore it and still have fun. But now I didn't know how to ignore someone nodding out and then jolting awake over and over again or scratching an itch on his ankle until it bled. Before long I found myself surrounded by people helping each other find a vein to inject. I didn't want to judge anyone. But I felt like I might as well have never left Southie.

The streets of Southie, too, were getting worse. The neighborhood I'd once agreed was heaven on earth now felt like hell. More and more, the only talk at home was about who was serving time, or the previous night's gunshots, or who was seen at which kid's wake, and who didn't show up because they were related to the shooter. Kathy was slowly recovering from the coma, learning to walk with a cane and trailing far behind her old friends. As sad as it was to see her become aware that she might not ever be her old self again, everyone knew she was one of the lucky ones. Many in her old gang were getting run down or stabbed to death or shot in barroom fights on Broadway. I didn't hate Southie as much as I had, though. I was too excited about the world beyond it to spend any thoughts hating the world within.

I escaped to New York any chance I got; I would read the *Village Voice* to see what Boston bands had upcoming gigs there, then hitch a ride with one of them. And when Greyhound started offering ten-dollar fares to New York, I could leave home anytime I felt like it. I'd ask Ma for twenty bucks to spend the weekend with "some friends," and get a round-trip ticket. Once there I'd work out how to get food and sneak into shows. The worst scenario would be having to use my return bus ticket sooner than I wanted.

From Old Colony I'd walk over the Broadway Bridge and then about three miles to the Greyhound bus terminal. The bus drove through long stretches of Interstate purgatory — McDonald's, Friendly's, Bob's Big Boy — before finally coming in sight of the tall projects of the Bronx. Each time I'd be so ready for New York that I could hardly stay in my seat. After crossing the Triboro Bridge, with its first glimpses of the Manhattan skyline, and going down into the Queens Midtown Tunnel, I knew I was only minutes away from coming up for air. Feeling like I'd been underwater for too long, I'd pray for no traffic. I'd sink back from the edge of my seat to play a King Tubby cassette, the only music that eased my anxiety.

Finally the bus would roll onto the streets of Manhattan and into Port Authority Bus Terminal. Edging past the pushers and stepping over the sprawled-out homeless in the terminal, I'd walk down Second Avenue toward the corner of Avenue A and Saint Mark's Place. The landmarks were becoming more familiar with every visit, and I even loved the names people gave their businesses, like Disco Donut and Gasoteria. I'd eventually find myself on the radiant, dirty streets of the Lower East Side.

The street names were numbers and letters, like Southie's, but on these streets I felt alive and instantly happy. I could sit on a stoop for hours watching misfits from all over coming together to create a new life. Mohawked second-generation punk rockers, skinheads, Rastas, new romantics, drag queens, artists, and leftover hippies all walked past in droves. As in any outcast scene, there was dope, speed, overheard threats of suicide, all kinds of violence and drama. Plenty of battles played out before my eyes: junkies fighting over money, local stoop-ladies in housedresses calling someone out for a fight, disturbed-looking people with a train of shopping carts filled with found objects yelling at passing cars for no apparent reason, gangs of Puerto Rican kids looking for someone easy to jump, and Ukrainian immigrants watching the scene with a calmness that assured me it would all work out.

One night, sitting on an East Village stoop eating some Triscuits I'd taken from Ma's cabinets to get me through the weekend, I realized for the first time why I felt so different here. Even though it felt more randomly dangerous than Southie, it didn't feel like death, a feeling I knew too well from Old Colony. In fact, coming here — if only to sit on a stoop until it was time to go to CBGB, the A7, or to some basement reggae party — was the one thing in my life that felt like living. Here I could take it all in, every possible slice of life in all its chaos and glory.

And unlike Southie, the East Village chaos didn't have to drag me in, didn't have to kill me. I didn't feel trapped.

I woke up when my head bounced off the spare tire I was using as a pillow, and for a few moments I was stunned. I'd been in a sleep so deep that there were no dreams. I started to remember that I was on a ride to New York to see Mission of Burma.

I hadn't slept in two days because I'd had to help Kevin hide out from Ma and from the cops who'd come to the door to ask about him. I had to take whatever he needed to the back room, where he slept on a pile of clothes. I was the only one home when he came knocking on my window from the roof, asking me to open the top part and let him climb in. He was wearing a johnny over hospital pants. He said he'd walked through snow from City Hospital, and his foam hospital slippers were wet and worn out. I'd heard that a couple of nights earlier he'd been running from the cops and had jumped off a third-story fire escape to get away from them. He'd landed on his back, shattering the windshield of a car, and screamed in pain all the way to the emergency room. But Kevin told me it was all an act. His back only hurt a little bit, he said, limping around my room. Kevin was always running from the cops and claiming they were chasing him for nothing. They booked him from his hospital bed for attempting to steal a car — the one he'd landed on — but he knew he could escape easily from the hospital. If they'd taken him straight to jail after his fall, it wouldn't have been so easy. When I heard about the caravan going to New York for Mission of Burma's final gig, I left him at home to fend for himself. I figured I could catch up on sleep during the journey.

It was a good thing we'd gone over that last bump, though. Otherwise I would have slept through the feast in front of me. I'd caught the ride with Lou, Mission of Burma's soundman, and the van was filled with the band's equipment. The Mystery Girls and their friend Rona, who'd also gotten in on the ride, were in the center of the van with bottles of wine, fancy-looking cheese that Sheena called "brie," sliced vegetables, and pink cookies — a full-on picnic on an amplifier. Rona was excited to tell me that Benjamin Franklin had done the same thing as me, napping whenever and wherever he liked rather than sleeping eight hours at night like most people. I spent a groggy minute remembering my other similarity to Benjamin Franklin — we were both Boston Latin dropouts — and then I dug in. I was famished.

"Cunt cookie?" Rona asked, casually offering the tray of pink cookies, a maraschino in each center. I took two. There was no milk, I didn't like wine, and by the third cookie nothing else would go down and I couldn't talk. I mumbled with a full mouth about pulling over at the next gas station. The back of the van had no windows, but I thought I'd been sleeping for hours and we must be in Connecticut at least. When Sheena and Rona first stepped outside to shouts of "Whores!" and "Devo!" I guessed we were in some godforsaken nowhere off Interstate 95. After climbing out of the van, though, I realized we hadn't even left Boston. We were in Southie. I'd slept only ten or fifteen minutes. Lou said he'd driven this way to get to the highway quicker, and maybe we should get back into the van. But Sheena and Rona were already inside Rotary Liquor, the place Seamus and Stevie's friends called the "Irish Mafia store," Whitey Bulger's headquarters for controlling all of Southie's gambling, cocaine, and bank robberies. Sheena and Rona probably didn't even know that Whitey was the most feared and loved father figure in the neighborhood. And I figured they were better off that way.

I followed them inside, trying to keep a low profile so I could steal some milk. But we were being watched like hawks. No one would ever suspect a kid of being bold enough to steal something in Whitey's place, but my green plaid high-waters were causing a commotion, bringing me too much attention to get away easily with pocketing the milk. Someone opened the door to scream inside at me, "Hey, where's the fuckin' flood?" Rona walked along the aisle talking pretty loud about having to suck cookie bits out of a rear cavity. I finally put a small carton of milk inside my overcoat and was almost out the door when Donnie Hayden walked in and asked me how Kathy was doing. I stopped to talk to him, anxiously gripping the carton in my armpit and wondering if I looked as odd as I felt, with one arm sticking out farther than the other. I hunched over, pushing my other arm out to look more symmetrical. When I opened the door to leave, someone screamed, "Fuckin' weirdo!" from a passing car. I wouldn't have paid any attention except that Donnie called over to the driver, "Hey, watch your fuckin' mouth! He's a MacDonald!" *Whatever,* I thought, *just let me get the fuck out of here without getting bagged for the milk.* I was embarrassed that my friends might witness the ridiculous status I had as a MacDonald, honored by the people I wanted nothing to do with. Rona ran past us in the doorway, acting as if she'd stolen something. So we all had to jump into the van and be gone without goodbyes.

"God, what was up with that white-trash yahoo you were talking to?" Rona asked.

"Just a neighbor," I said, not thinking.

"You're from Southie?" she asked.

I was guzzling milk and almost choked. In those days I told only trusted friends where I was from, and I hardly knew Rona. I could tell, too, that she had a particular idea of what "Southie" meant.

"Well. Um. I used to be." I hesitated. "More like the border. Between Southie and Dorchester."

I skipped my ride home after Mission of Burma to spend the night at an after-hours club called Danceteria, where everyone went after shows. I had just enough to get home on the bus, and Danceteria was free if you crowded in with the VIP club kids who waited on one side of the velvet rope before being escorted past the admission booth. Sometimes I slept on the club's overstuffed couches before heading to Port Authority for the morning bus home. But that night I was kicked out while it was still dark, caught one too many times sleeping on a couch. So I walked downtown to people-watch.

I loved Tompkins Square Park just before the sun came up. At home, in my recent years of sleeplessness I avoided sunrise at all costs. One day when Ma thought I should wake up and look into getting my GED, she tore down the black cloth covering my window. "You can sleep when you're dead!" she shouted, storming out of the room. Still, I would bury my head under pillows or pull down the shades when the first light of morning invaded my room. But in New York I didn't mind morning so much, especially in Tompkins Square. The sky was beginning to turn blue-black now, and the trash barrels dotting the park were on fire. I watched another New York morning arrive before figuring the bus schedule to Boston.

At this hour I could make out only the silhouettes of the people warming themselves by the flames. Each one made a strange massive shape in the layers of coats cinched at the waist by a belt or rope. I caught a glimpse of a face lit up by the trash flames below. Across the street, a woman in a fur coat, who looked more Upper than Lower East Side, crouched in a gutter with a carefully folded napkin to pick up her dog's shit. Signs with stick figures scooping dog crap were one of the first things I'd ever noticed in this city, and here it was in action. Boston didn't have a poop-scooping law, and if we had, I didn't think the blunt depictions of shit-scooping would have been tolerated. And this woman's Boston counterpart would never have stooped so low. The bench I was on had become *my* bench, and I loved sitting on it watching all the contradictions of New York, the layers of class and grit peeled back and sometimes wrapped up again into one person.

The fluorescent-lit delis across Avenue A were as bright as noonday and busy as ever. Wilting drag queens worked the streets, pepping up for the occasional trick slow-circling the block. Shadowy clubgoers, wired and anxious to move on to the next haunt, flagged taxis, while others shivered and leaned into the wind, rushing home to hide from the coming day. Not even the Koreans at flower stands noticed when a man in high heels, red spandex pants, and a straitjacket walked down Avenue A. I thought at first that he had no arms and had somehow dressed to the nines for a night on the town. Groups of punks and skins with no place to go moved from corner to corner.

By six, just before the sun shined glory onto dingy Avenue A, most of the East Village seemed to be in hiding. In no time the sky turned pale blue, the fire escapes were dipped in gold light, and I could read the bed sheets hung from tenement windows proclaiming WE ARE ON RENT STRIKE or OUR LANDLORD SUCKS! A few of the homeless guys still huddled around a burning barrel, not yet sure of the sun's power to chase away last night's bitterness. Normally I would welcome the sun, but today I was holding on to every last minute before the journey home.

Soon it would officially be day; the night's denizens were dropping like flies. Even the nomadic groups of punks and skins were disappearing from the scene. I couldn't rouse myself to walk uptown toward Port Authority, and soon I was alone with the early risers going to work. The next hour seemed to last forever. I was reaching the level of tired that always made me feel crazy, first in a good way, wired and having a blast by myself, finding most things ironic and hilarious, but then in a way that made everything depressing. When a rooster crowed, I thought I must be losing my mind, hearing a rooster in the middle of the city. I needed a bed, or at least sleep. I didn't want to get on the bus back to Southie, but I didn't want to sleep on a bench and get robbed of the ten dollars I needed for the Greyhound. Worst of all, I had to call home to make sure everyone was okay, but I didn't have any money except the bus fare. So I called collect at seven in the morning, though I knew it would piss Ma off. She'd recently had the phone reconnected but was threatening to disconnect it because I'd made so many collect calls, checking in. Whenever I least suspected it, I would get a sneaking suspicion that something bad might have happened back home. We'd all noticed the increase in gunshots on Patterson Way, but no one was mentioning it. And I always worried about Seamus and Stevie.

"Mike! Where in God's name are you? I thought you were in your room." Ma said she'd accepted the charges only because she was shocked I wasn't home. I told her I was in Jamaica Plain staying with friends. "Is everyone okay?" I asked. "Oh my aching Jesus! Is that why you're calling at the crack of dawn?" I told her I was just making sure she left the breakthrough door unlocked so I could get in. "Where are the kids?" I asked. "They're right here! Sleeping! Mother of God!" She said I should get my head checked. Then she calmed down and told me the news about Frankie's latest bout, winning another Golden Glove championship in the light heavyweight class. In the past I'd gone to all of Frankie's matches, and I felt guilty that I was probably the only one in the family that wasn't at this one. Still, as much as I didn't want to be around Old Colony these days I couldn't help but feel lit up by the news of Frankie's winning streak.

Just then a middle-aged Puerto Rican woman in pigtails walked by with a boom box blasting Michael Jackson's "Thriller." I put a finger in one ear, thinking she'd pass by, like everything else on Avenue A. But she stopped, put her loud boom box on the ground, and started swinging on a child's swing in the playground next to me, soaring through the air with a fury, spike heels aimed at the sky, while Vincent Price's spooky voice talked about "grizzly ghouls" and "the hounds of hell" over a dance beat. I was distracted until Ma screamed, "What the Christ is going on there? Where are you?" She asked if I was listening to "that gloomy punk rock music," and I told her it was just Michael Jackson and Vincent Price, and that I wasn't "punk rock." I was about to describe what I was seeing on the street but realized she would know I wasn't in Boston. "I gotta go," I said suddenly, telling Ma I'd be home in a while.

Hanging up, I thought of how I'd like to be a moviemaker,

not to be famous but to be able to hire the people I was seeing all around. But thinking about that only reminded me I didn't know what I was going to do with my life. Recently Frankie had charged into my room, all excited to tell me what I should be: a tooth sculptor. He'd just come from getting his teeth cleaned. "You're an artist," he announced in my bedroom. "You'll make a bundle!" But I couldn't get excited about sculpting teeth. The one thing I'd inherited from the Irish was my hatred for dentists. Ma was the only one of the five sisters who still had all her teeth — the others had had all of them pulled as teenagers, by an Irish dentist. Ma, being the black sheep of the family, had missed out on her parents' trust in the Irish dentist. But Frankie's pronouncement that I was an artist gave me a shot in the arm. I'd never called myself that; I thought it was presumptuous and phony when people gave themselves that title, as if they were special. Since I'd been a kid, though, I was always drawing pictures of people's faces — faces that told a story but only to me. I didn't think much about it. But for Frankie — the family superstar — to acknowledge that I was good at something made me proud. I still had to hide from him, though, because he thought I should be a boxer as well and wanted me to spend hours hitting the heavy bag in his sweltering project apartment, when all I wanted to do in Old Colony was listen to the radio and make cassettes.

I felt awake again after calling Ma. As always, I was relieved to find that everyone was still alive. I was in a good mood now and decided to spend the day in New York and take the night bus home.

Later I bumped into Felix, my sidewalk artist friend from days at the Boston Public Library. She'd moved to Delancey Street on the Lower East Side, and told me I could stay with her for as long as I wanted in New York. I spent a month at Felix's, sleeping on a pile of old blankets in the corner of the huge open loft space. A homeless friend of Felix's, Albee, usually spent his drunken nights in the "guest room," a curtained closet filled with clothes and towels and blankets. At about sunrise each morning, after the three of us had spent the night listening to music and singing songs together, Albee would crash in the closet, his bare feet sticking out from under the curtain. When the rotten smell overcame us, Felix and I would wrestle his rock 'n' roll boots back on his feet, and the worn-down pointy boots would curl out underneath the curtain. We listened to everything from Jackie Wilson to Patti Smith to the Bad Brains. Felix's boyfriend, Greg, had been in the legendary band Wayne County and the Electric Chairs, and I loved listening to his stories about being in London in '77 around people like Sid Vicious, who'd once even broken a bottle over his head in a fight.

After Felix cooked us dinner, Greg would often stand playing air guitar while Albee walked in circles with a bottle of something, frantically rubbing his rock 'n' roll mop into new random formations. Felix knelt on the floor and rocked back and forth as she watched the record spin. Her feelings about the music showed in every move she made: closing her eyes, spinning around, pointing at the sky if the musician was dead, like Jackie Wilson, and sometimes even talking to them, dead or alive. "Imagine if there was no music?" I asked her one night while listening to Big Mama Thornton. "No!" she roared, jumping up and putting her fists to her hips like she was ready to take someone out. "I think I'd kill myself," I said.

It was the most amazing time to be on the Lower East Side. Felix's paintings, written up by the street-hustler art critic Rene Ricard in *Art in America,* had taken off. She was having fancy art openings in the same galleries where she'd once shown up to drink wine and tear off all her clothes and scream at the "art phonies." Many a night Greg had to carry her out, while Albee sneaked his last glass of free wine and I filled my pockets with brie. Most nights I would go on to Danceteria, which Felix wanted nothing to do with; she said it was too "hip" for her. But I liked the mix of people and music that came together on the club's dance floors.

Top left: Me and Nana, circa 1971.
Top right: Ma entertaining in
the project. Center: Kevin being
"Francis MacDonald" and
Frankie being "John Macdonald"
on summer jobs program IDs.
Left: Joe and Davey.

Clockwise from top left: Frankie on Patterson Way; Frankie at the gym; Johnny Rotten in Boston, 1980; Johnny Rotten: "Piss off."

Clockwise from top left: Clam, me, and Rita Ratt on Queensberry Street; Ari Up and Tessa of the Slits, Bradford Hotel, 1980; the kids of the Lower East Side; Joe Strummer posing for me on the Portobello Road; Dicky Barrett stage-diving at the Rat.

Top: Nana's childhood land, Glen Mackee, Donegal. Left: Ma with Castleisland friends, Easter 1998. Below: Me in the Gap of Mamore, Donegal, 1985.

In that first month away from Old Colony, I called Ma every night to tell her I was extending my stay in New York. I told her I was with Felix, who was almost thirty and rich. That quieted Ma down some.

"Well, tell me something about yourself," the admissions lady at the New School for Social Research said. I didn't know what to say — I'd never had an interview before. She did seem a lot more relaxed than Mr. Flaherty at Latin, the only other person I'd ever sat across a desk from.

"Well, how about this. Why are you interested in attending the New School?"

"Oh, I just want to live in New York," I said.

"Okay," she said, extending the word like she was wanting more.

"I just like it here," I added.

"Me too!" she said, leaning on her desk like she was getting casual. "What do you like about it?"

I couldn't explain what it was I loved about New York, because then I'd have to get into a whole whining story about how different it was from Southie.

"Everything just looks different here," I said, not sure what I was getting at but thinking about the streets of the Village and how I felt sitting on the stoops there.

I'd heard that the New School was "unconventional" and would admit someone who hadn't graduated from high school. I still had no idea what I wanted to do with my life. What I loved most was music, followed closely by books, paintings, and nightclubs. But it was music that connected me to most of the people I knew. I would gladly have spent my life listening to records, and I wished I could turn that into a real purpose, maybe even work. Most of the people I was around in New York were in art or music, usually. Felix was painting nonstop, getting ready for another opening. I would visit Jill, one of the Moppy Scuds from my first glimpse of New York. She and her Beastie Boy friends would be making demo tapes. Early on they played whatever they could get their hands on, like her two-string guitar; later they created serious hip-hop beats. The Beastie Boys, who hung out at Jill's house experimenting with rhymes, were becoming well known on the club scene with their hit "Cookie Puss." Spots like the Mudd Club and Danceteria were filled with artists like Jean-Michel Basquiat and Keith Haring. Scenesters like Madonna were disappearing and showing up on MTV, which was now in every home, even in Old Colony. It was strange to see familiar faces from the underground club scene, like Madonna — who chummed around with Debi Mazar, the elevator girl at Danceteria — on television. I had to wonder all the more what I was going to do with my own life. All I knew was that I didn't want to go back to Southie. So here I was at the New School for Social Research, wondering what the hell social research was about anyway.

"In what way does everything look different?" the admissions lady asked me.

I didn't want to tell her how it felt to come here from Southie and what it would be like to go back home. I just told her that things that made me worried in Boston seemed okay here and I didn't have to worry about any of it.

"Tell you what," she said. "Have you thought about going back for your GED and then maybe spending a couple of years at a community college?" That's what Ma had been saying whenever I was at home, trying to hide out from her and sleep in. "Get your GED!" she'd shout when, throwing laundry into my room, she discovered me sleeping on my mattress on the floor.

I shook the admission lady's hand and left. I was proud that I'd set up the appointment and actually showed up on time. Walking out into the streets I loved so much, I headed downtown to Felix's to rest up for another night at the clubs. My goal was to move to New York officially — no more sleeping on people's floors, finding someone to take me to breakfast, scamming my way into the clubs. But first, I knew, I had to go back to school. I pictured myself living on Avenue A, going to school at the New School, and working in some record store. It was an amazing picture. And I knew that once I wanted something, I'd make it happen.

I was too anxious to have a good time at Danceteria that night. I went up and down the elevator visiting the different floors, not liking the music at any one of them. On the first floor the gothic kids were swaying and spinning around to morose music like the Cocteau Twins and Dead Can Dance. Every time I went into that room I felt down in the dumps within minutes and had to jump back on the elevator up. On the second floor, B-Boys, people with Mohawks, and the Beastie Boys crowd all did the "smurf" to hip hop like Kurtis Blow and Newcleus, which was fun, but I found myself asking every other person what time it was, so I could catch the earliest bus to Boston. I was antsy, and no matter how much I smurfed I felt I wasn't going anywhere at all. I wanted to get home and figure out how I could go to school again. In most clubs I could gauge the time by the level of energy in the room as the night wore on. Finally, when the crowd thinned out and I was among a handful of beat-looking lingerers, I knew the sun was probably up. I pushed through the steel exit doors into a glaring sun that was even higher than I'd imagined. The breeze at my back felt warm, like it might be the first day of summer. Walking east on Twenty-third Street, I couldn't see a thing. But it didn't matter. I knew what this city looked like, and I was too busy imagining what it would be like to call it home.

"Forget about it now," Grandpa kept repeating, even though I wasn't the one bringing it up. "Forget it ever happened at all." That's what he'd been saying every time I visited with him in the City Point condo he'd been living in alone since Nana died. He said I should get on with my life, tell no one about Frankie getting killed in a bank heist. He said to forget that I was from the projects, even though I still lived there. "Nobody'll want nothing to do with you 'tall if you tell them anything about yourself. Sure they'll only be ashamed to know ye." I was trying to laugh, even though it was hard to do that now. But I was thinking too about the kind of world Grandpa must have come from to think like that.

I'd been trying to forget about it all, long before Grandpa's advice — but not for the reasons he was talking about. Some days I was doing a pretty good job of forgetting Frankie and how he was killed, until I went to Grandpa's and had to listen to him recount the bank robbery over and over again. "I told Frankie, 'Watch out who you shake hands with,'" he said, looking down at his toast like he wasn't sure he had the stomach for it. "Sure the bums he was chummin' with were a quare bunch altogether. I knew they was no good from the time I first seen them." Grandpa said Frankie just laughed whenever he warned him about gangsters.

I had spent years trying to find a life beyond Old Colony, and now, after Frankie died, I felt guilty for not having been close to my family. I was trying to stay closer to home, and to hang around the apartment more. If I needed to get away from the project, which seemed to me like a darkened catacomb, with so many street lights broken and hallways left dark, I'd go to Grandpa's on the nicer side of Southie. But I didn't know how much longer I could wake up to Grandpa walking around in his sagging long johns, deaf to the screaming kettle, muttering about Frankie and how I should "forget about it altogether."

"And don't tell no one where you come from!"

Grandpa didn't have to tell me about being ashamed of where I'd come from; I'd spent the previous few years doing a pretty good job of that already.

The last time I saw Frankie I was walking up Dorchester Street, returning home from a long stretch in New York. Only two minutes out of the subway station and staring at the sidewalk, I was in a good mood, imagining my future life in New York. I wore my usual bum gear: matted, spiky dreads, torn-up old man's coat, high-water pants, and old ski boots I had found on a bench at Port Authority. It had been another adrenaline-filled week of shows at the A7 and CBGB, followed by Danceteria until sunrise and crashing at Felix's loft on Delancey Street. Looking up from the ground to Boston's blanket of gray sky, I remembered where I was and immediately felt claustrophobic. I was dragging my feet toward Old Colony. Even though I now had a plan, a reason to be back home, setting foot in Southie always felt like going backward. My thoughts of the future were drowning in the reality around me.

Frankie was four blocks away, walking toward me on his way to Andrew Station. I knew his walk from any distance: the slightly slouched boxer stance, the left-right rhythm of his strut like he was in the ring. I never expected to bump into him walking, though; he was usually driving his Lincoln Continental, his pride and joy. It was strange to think of Frankie getting on the train to leave Southie. He loved the neighborhood and seemed to have no reason to venture beyond into foreign territories, except to drive to work at the Rat. Frankie was a big fish in Southie, a star, liked by everyone. Every time he saw me, even though he no longer complained about my looking "fucked up," he still stared at me like I was an alien. There had been a time when Frankie and I talked. When I was a kid going to underage discos in the seventies, he'd ask me about the latest disco and funk songs and the dances of the period: the freak, the rock, the drop, and the white boy. But years had passed since I'd traded my Kool and the Gang records for Slaughter and the Dogs. Now I was eighteen and liked to imagine myself independent of all things Southie and all things family. I did wish I had some connection with Frankie. But after discovering the world outside of Southie, I felt I had been deprogrammed in a way, and there was no going back. And I didn't feel I had much to offer Frankie, being a disappointment to him, the opposite of the world he'd embraced: boxing, being a bouncer, the cult of South Boston.

Those were the excuses I kept telling myself after he was dead. But when I saw him that day after the high of another week of late-night conversations with older jazz musicians, poets, and punks at the Holiday Lounge, and my wanderings at dawn through the East Village, I panicked at being reminded of who I really was. The shame of being from Southie was sometimes unbearable, and Frankie just didn't get that. I took a sharp right, certain he hadn't seen me as he strutted down Dorchester Street looking at the sidewalk and smiling to himself, maybe thinking about a funny conversation with Joe, or a date he had that night, or even just what a beautiful June day it was and how great it was to live in Southie.

I never saw Frankie again after that afternoon. It was my secret when he died, something I kept to myself when people recounted their stories of the last time they saw Frankie. For

Ma it was the day before he died, when he came up to the apartment, raided the fridge, and borrowed a twenty, which Ma said he'd never done before. She said he promised repeatedly to pay her back, even though she couldn't have cared less. "The funny thing is," she said, "today I found a brand-new twenty-dollar bill under my bed when I was cleaning." Ma's stories always had to end with the assertion that Frankie, like Davey and Patrick, was "in a better place." Seamus and Steven remembered Frankie's last words to them, a promise that he'd soon move them out of Old Colony and down to Florida, where they could go to Disneyland any time they wanted. "How would you like to be me?" Kevin asked somberly. "The last time I saw him we got in a fistfight." Kevin was originally meant to be in on the bank robbery, but he'd backed out. He'd just had a baby and was starting to settle down. He said he'd tried to talk Frank out of doing the job and they'd fought over it.

I just sat silently on the couch. I didn't think that story was as bad as my running away down a side street to avoid Frankie. At least Kevin had made contact with him.

"Hey, you probably saw Frankie at the Rat a lot, huh?" Joe asked, trying to bring me into the conversation.

"Not really," I said.

I'd taken my final GED test just before Frankie died. I'd been feeling on track with my goals, but now all I could do to get away from the constant questions in my family about the robbery was wander. I went back to the Rathskeller. The club had never felt so dark, and I'd never felt so sick, surrounded by people I had nothing in common with, no connection to. This was the place I'd gone for refuge so many nights, the place where no one had to belong to anything. But now it felt more like a dungeon whose four walls were closing in. And no one else seemed to notice.

The club was packed. Some of my friends were sliming drinks

from people at the bar. Others danced spastically in front of the band. The few who were shooting up in the bathroom made the most sense to me, from what I'd heard about how dope numbs. But I couldn't entertain the thought of abandoning control like that. I needed my wits about me more than ever, for I knew that the worst could and would happen at a horrifying moment's notice.

There was no one to talk to, beyond the passing nod. Before it hadn't mattered that no one here came from the place I did. The fact that you could be from anywhere and that you didn't have to be like anyone else was what had made me feel at home. But now, standing at the back of a room full of strangers jumping up and down in abandon, I wished I'd recognized my brother Frankie more when he was alive and in this very room.

Everywhere I looked in the dark basement I saw glimpses of Frankie: passing through the crowd and hoisting a keg over to the bartender, by the back door dragging an overenthusiastic punk by the neck, at the bar trying to talk to a Siouxsie clone who, I knew, wouldn't give a Southie jock the time of day. I was sure the bouncers knew more about the deadly bank heist than I would ever know.

I didn't mention the robbery to any of my friends; it was a Southie thing they'd never understand. Those who'd read about it in the papers, I imagined, either didn't connect it to me or didn't know what to say. What do you say to someone whose brother was just killed while robbing a bank?

"You know there's a hit out on that bastard," one of the bouncers whispered to me that night at the Rat. For once someone was speaking a language I understood, if only because it related to the earth-shattering catastrophe of the week before. "We don't know what went down or nothing," he added, "but we do know that prick left him to die." I didn't care about Frankie's cohort in the bank robbery. The pounding in my skull only had to do with my being in the small room where Frankie and I had lived parallel lives. I felt pummeled by the knowledge that I'd never see him out of the corner of my eye again. No revenge could cure that. But at least someone was trying to connect to me.

Before long two more bouncers gathered around me and offered their condolences. My friend Bob, walking by the huddled conversation, gave a curious glance at me talking to his enemies. The bouncers stood the way Frankie always had, like boxers, their massive shoulders hunched over, glancing furtively around the room like they were on a Southie street corner. They looked down and blocked their mouths with a hand when talking about how Frank had been used by his older partner, Toohey, the one Grandpa said "would steal the eye out of your head and come back for the other one."

When they went away I walked over to a dark corner where I couldn't be seen, just in case the choking feeling in my neck and the pain in my sinuses released something I couldn't control. The Outlets announced their new song, "Can't Cheat the Reaper." I thought I might feel like that if Grandpa had died. But none of my old friends in that room, for all their subversion, knew the real horror of a brother's violent, bloody death under a blazing summer sun. Only the clean-cut Southie bouncers, the so-called normal people in the room, knew what that was all about.

I wanted to get out of the Rat and never go back again. Katie the Cleaning Lady was leaving at the same time and offered a ride. Normally I would have accepted and asked her to drop me off on the outskirts of Southie. But I turned down her offer and instead wandered around Kenmore Square, waiting for the Southie bouncers, who I knew were going all the way back home.

After the funeral was over and all of Frank's loyal friends started to disappear from our lives, Ma had started keeping the apartment dark. The place felt too big and empty now that Frank was gone. Even though he'd lived across the street, his presence was a constant in the apartment. Now it seemed there were no constants. I had taken his presence for granted, and I felt he was right about my wasting my life with all that "punk rock bullshit." I badly wanted to get to know him better, to know the person everyone in my family — everyone in the neighborhood — had been so proud to be connected to.

Now I hardly ever left Southie and even worked to look like I belonged there. No longer wanting to forget about Old Colony, I wanted to *be* Old Colony, from the shell-toe Adidas to the buttoned-up Izod shirt that at one time felt like a straitjacket.

Whenever I ventured out to my old underground music world, where people were as obsessed with being individuals as I'd become with passing in Southie, I felt like an outsider. With vague rumors floating around about another person in my family dying, I was often floored by the dumb things people would say. One kid said Frankie's death was okay because I had a lot of other brothers and sisters. And someone else asked me, "Dude, were you even close to your brother?"

I decided it was safest just to stay home. Other than the occasional walk to Castle Island, I sat in the window of the apartment, worrying and keeping watch. I knew it was only a matter of time before something horrible would happen again. I just hoped it would happen to me this time, rather than to Seamus or Stevie or anyone else in my family. I'd decided to attend the University of Massachusetts, which was only a short walk over the Southie border into Dorchester. But I wasn't sure I'd be able to make myself leave home every day.

Sometimes I still felt like an alien in Southie. I felt I'd been to the other side, where people knew about things like Keith Haring and brie. It was like knowing another language that no one at home would understand. So I just kept my mouth shut about everything, even when Ronald Reagan won the election that fall with the help of so many of my neighbors on welfare. Even Ma voted for him, saying he was "tougher" than the Democrats. Southie people were stranger than ever to me now, but at least they weren't as clueless as people in the world beyond, who'd never experienced bank robberies and murder.

Sometimes, though, taking in what was happening from the window — the drug dealing, fistfights, and storytelling about who'd been locked up — and not feeling fazed by any of it, I thought I might be losing my mind. One day I suddenly became sure that I was dying. When I felt a lump on my neck, I jumped out of my seat at the window to get dressed for the emergency room. I ran past Ma coming up the front stairs in slow motion from all the Valium prescribed by a crooked doctor on Broadway. I didn't have the heart to tell her that my days were numbered. The lump turned out to be a bone that had always been in my neck but that I hadn't ever noticed before. Soon I developed a routine that became a pattern. I would notice a symptom and run to the emergency room at New England Medical Center, only to be sent home, told that it was all in my head. Each time, walking back over the Broadway Bridge and toward Old Colony, I wasn't sure I believed those doctors.

After Kevin died I wasn't afraid of death anymore. Eight months after Frankie's death, we were told that Kevin had hung himself in jail, though Ma didn't believe that, because she said a cop on Whitey's payroll had visited him the night he was found dead outside his cell.

I didn't expect to live much longer, and I felt guilty that I'd soon be putting my family through another funeral. I wished I knew what was killing me, so I could just get on with dying. But no matter what emergency room I went to, the doctors wouldn't pay attention to what was happening inside me: the shaking, the numbness, the forceful pounding sensation pushing through my bloodstream. The newest symptom was twisting and cramping in organs I'd never thought about before. I probably seemed ridiculous the time I went to New England Medical Center emergency room to be checked for Alzheimer's. But the special report on *60 Minutes* the night before had completely convinced me that I had all the symptoms, especially "memory loss," "confusion," and "sense of non-reality," as they said on the show. Dr. Metzger, who had seen me five or six times before getting cranky about my symptoms (and starting to send a nurse out to the waiting room to say he was busy), told me with a sigh that it would be extremely rare, maybe impossible, for an eighteen-year-old to have Alzheimer's. Hearing the word "rare" only made it seem worse, though. "Then how'd I get it?" I pleaded. Dr. Metzger told me there was nothing more he could do for me. He told me to start exercising and eating and sleeping more. He explained that many students who were new to college stress, as I was, complained of inexplicable ailments.

College stress? The deadlines at U Mass were always piling up. But my only real stress was from the knowledge that I was dying of an illness that couldn't be diagnosed. I hated to think of my family having to bury yet another — or, worse, having to take care of me for the time I had left. I gave up on Dr. Metzger and stopped going to New England Medical Center. *Mass General has a better reputation anyway,* I figured. *And there's no way, at this point, that Dr. Metzger will take my symptoms seriously.* On top of all the previous ones, I'd begun to experience sudden waves of tingling all over my body every day.

"I don't know, sometimes it's accompanied by this feeling that I'm soaking wet," I explained calmly to the doctor in the Mass General ER. "By the time I get home or to a public restroom to take off my clothes and see what's going on, I'm completely dry." I was relieved to have a new face listening intently, nodding and taking notes. Dr. Reynolds looked more concerned about what I was describing than Dr. Metzger ever had. I didn't mention any specific illnesses, like Alzheimer's, to him, since I knew the narrow focus would throw him off course. When he said I would need a full examination, I readied myself for the worst news, but I also knew that it was about time; I was tired of being in the dark. I'd lost all certainty about what would come after this life, but I couldn't take much more of the roller-coaster ride of being sick and being told that I wasn't. Along with feeling sick and twisted up in my stomach, I sometimes felt like a zombie, my brain completely hollowed out, like someone who has just stepped out of a car wreck. The real agony, though, was not knowing why I felt this way, what disease was killing me. At other times I just didn't care anymore. I couldn't feel anything, good or bad, couldn't think of a food I'd want to eat, a painting I'd want to see, a song I'd want to hear.

I got into a johnny and sat up on the freshly papered examination bed. I knew the routine and was ready and waiting for the nurse to place a thermometer under my tongue.

"How's it look?" I asked when she came back to read it.

"It's about 99.5," she said, inspecting it some more.

"Ninety-nine point five?" I panicked. "That's not normal, is it?" She told me that 98.6 was average. I felt vindicated by the confirmation that I was sick, remembering how Dr. Metzger had implied that it was all in my head.

I started getting the dry sweats and tingling and told the nurse, "It's starting up again."

"What's starting up again?" she asked in an impatient tone.

"Nothing," I said, seeing that she was one of the more skeptical types. But I knew Dr. Reynolds was taking me seriously, and I hoped he would give me some peace of mind by telling me — finally — what was wrong. Then I could research the details of my disease — no more mystery. Suddenly, though, the thought of breaking the news to my family made me want to jump out of my skin. I wished I could give them at least another year to prepare, since Kevin's funeral had been only two months ago. With a serious face and furrowed brow, the nurse started feeling my throat. Her expression seemed dire. She went back to one gland and wobbled it a couple times, stopping to take notes.

"How are the glands?" I asked. She seemed insulted at my intruding on her job but admitted that one nodule was raised. I felt my face go red with the pounding, which went right from my chest to my cheeks. I knew I would have to deal head-on with the bad news sooner rather than later. I felt sorry for people I'd come across who hadn't already learned that life was all about dying. But that knowledge didn't make the actual death sentence easier to take. When I asked her how raised the nodule was, she told me that a swollen lymph node could indicate something serious or it could just mean I'd cut myself shaving. I thought hard but couldn't remember the last time I'd shaved. Worn out, I began to let go and surrender to my fate. I was losing all the strength in every limb. Suddenly I got to the familiar place of feeling so drained that I was calm, and I couldn't imagine a better feeling in the world.

The nurse left me alone and I sat peacefully, thinking about how to tell everyone the news. I took deep breaths to relax my stomach, which had been aching only minutes before. I was at ease with the preparations for death that lay before me. Dr. Reynolds came in a few minutes later, apologizing for the delay. He was out of breath, either because the emergency room was busy or because he had just realized the severity of my illness. He stretched a latex glove over his right hand, and I realized that he was taking me more seriously than I'd expected. He told me to lie on my side. Now I wasn't sure that coming to Mass General had been the right thing to do — I might be better off not knowing what was wrong with me and just riding out my short life. *What does it matter how I die? Who cares?* I considered simply disappearing from my family rather than giving them a diagnosis and prognosis. I imagined jumping off a cliff in a remote place where I'd never be found. At one time I would have chosen to do it in a beautiful place, maybe in New Hampshire, which I'd heard was nice. But now that didn't matter. I had no energy left for a romantic suicide. It didn't have to be a cliff; I didn't think I had it in me to jump anyway. I could go to a remote spot and let the sickness eat away at me until I was free of it. That would be better than being alone in this hell. I was starting to feel like the guy in the myth who was left on a mountain to have his insides endlessly picked at by vultures while he was still alive. My death would have to take place so far away that I wouldn't be found, though. I'd just cease to exist, and no one would have to deal with another actual death, just a mysterious disappearance, which didn't seem as bad.

I jumped off the examination table, telling the doctor that I didn't feel so bad anymore and that I had a test the next day that I hadn't begun studying for.

"We just need to cover all the bases," he said, holding up his index finger. He told me he'd never heard of the symptoms I was describing — tingling and soaking-wet sensations — but he wanted me to have the peace of mind a full physical would bring. I told Dr. Reynolds that I was feeling nothing but exhaustion. "Suit yourself," he sighed, leaving the room while filling out some paperwork on a clipboard.

As I dressed, I figured I was done with doctors. But Dr. Reynolds came back into the examination room and handed me two jars, one for a urine sample, which I should try to give before leaving, and one for a stool sample "at your leisure." Unsure whether he was serious, I gave a hesitant laugh. I wasn't planning to come back, but wanting an easy exit, I set up an appointment with the receptionist anyway.

On the walk home from Mass General, I felt spent, done with trying to figure out what was killing me and what I should do about it. I had no strength left in my body or in my brain. I was glad the torment and worry were past, but my legs and arms felt like Jell-O and I just wanted to lie in bed. I walked to delay my return to Southie until everyone was asleep. I seemed to be the only soul out on the streets. Downtown Boston at night, emptied of all its daytime workers, was usually too still for me, like I was the only one to have survived an atomic bomb. But on this night I wasn't fazed. I'd learned by now that whenever I felt emptied of all feeling like this, completely over it, nothing could get to me.

The Combat Zone was more active than downtown, bustling with dolled-up hookers and dealers in spite of the cold winds that night. But it all seemed to be happening at a distance. I walked right through all the wheeling and dealing without putting on the discreet guardedness I'd learned from years of nighttime walks through the city. The night denizens, desperate for business, approached me from all corners with their goods, but their words had no meaning. I shrugged or shook my head, pretending to respond to the vague sounds coming from their mouths as I floated past them. Two miles farther on, I passed the homeless crowd around the Pine Street Inn. I didn't stop to say hi to those I knew, like Pippi and Scary Mary. I had no connection to them anymore — or to anyone else.

Just as I crossed the Broadway Bridge to Southie, I felt the dry sweats and tingling again. I thought about going back to Dr. Reynolds first thing in the morning. But morning wouldn't come soon enough; I wanted to turn right around and go back over the bridge. With Dr. Reynolds's sample jar in my overcoat pocket, I made a beeline for the Triple O's tavern, a bloodbath owned by Kevin O'Neil, one of Southie's protected drug dealers, a top lieutenant to Whitey Bulger. I hated the place, but the Cornerstone Pub next door was closed, and I had to find a toilet. Racing through Southie's favorite coke den, I passed the confused faces of many neighbors, no doubt wondering what the "quiet MacDonald" was doing at Triple O's. The more faces I recognized from Old Colony, the more cramped my stomach became.

By the time I got to the bathroom, I was bent over in pain. Someone I didn't know but who knew me as Frank the Tank's brother was in the bathroom doing lines. He looked surprised to see me, and we avoided the usual awkward silence over Frankie and Kevin — and everyone else who was dead — when I pointed to the stall, indicating my emergency situation. By the time I got out of the stall and back onto the disco floor, I couldn't believe I had actually stepped foot in the place. Almost at the exit, I was stopped by Kathy's old boyfriend Timmy, who was drunk. He shook my hand and told me, like he'd always done since I was a little kid, that if anyone ever messed with me I should come talk to him. People in Southie said stuff like that to give the impression that they had power. But I remembered when Timmy had chased down some older kids who had thrown a rock at my head, screaming that I was a MacDonald. I turned down a drink, but I appreciated his reaching out with the offer, and for a second felt a bit nostalgic for my childhood in Southie.

I returned to Mass General the next day with the sample in the jar, wrapped in a paper bag. My appointment wasn't for another ten days, but I went through to the emergency room and asked to see Dr. Reynolds. He looked frustrated at my early return but agreed to see me quickly. The cranky nurse took my temperature while the doctor took the sample out of the paper bag and waved it around while telling me about a friend of his who, going through the stresses of medical school, had all kinds of crazy physical symptoms. *He thinks my symptoms are psychosomatic,* I thought. I was sick of hearing about hypochondriac medical students whenever a doctor wanted to get rid of me. He wrote MACDONALD on a white sticker and stuck it onto the sample jar.

"Yeah, it must be weird to have all that pressure," I said, distancing myself from the doctor's stressed-out friend. I was relieved when he sent the sample out with the cranky nurse so I could focus on convincing him that I was in bad shape. I'd woken up with a whole new problem that day. "Heavy head," I told Dr. Reynolds. I must have invented the name, but I thought I remembered reading about it in one of the medical journals I'd been leafing through at the U Mass library. I explained that sometimes it took all the strength I had just to lift my head and keep it from flopping around on my shoulders.

Dr. Reynolds sat down at his desk, took a deep breath, and said, "There's no such thing as heavy head," pausing between each word like he was struggling for patience. And if there were such a thing, he assured me, I might be the first person in the world with both the symptom and the diagnosis.

He started asking all kinds of questions that sounded like they came from a "depression checklist" I'd seen in waiting rooms. I thought the questions were ridiculous because anyone could say yes to most of them.

"Are you no longer interested things that used to interest you?"

Check.

"Have you recently suffered a death?"

"Well, yeah," I said. "A few. But not recently."

"A few?" he asked, taking off his glasses.

I started counting with my fingers, never sure whether to add Kathy to my list of "Davey, Frankie, and Kevin," since she hadn't recovered to her old self.

Luckily he didn't want to know more than that. He started writing and explaining about the great medications that help people get through a period of grief. He handed me a prescription for Xanax, and I handed it back to him, saying I had tried some of Ma's Valium a few times and it just made me skip a lot of my homework, and Ma was walking around in slow motion from her prescription. *Besides,* I thought, *depression's not my problem. And that stuff will only zonk me out and make me less prepared for whatever is coming my way.*

When I refused the prescription, he changed direction and told me I might want to "talk to someone" about what I was going through. "A lot of people see therapists," he said. Now I thought he was really off-base, but I listened as he wrote down the address of A Family Service. "They charge on a sliding scale," he said, handing me the piece of paper. I looked at it and read the address, Joy Street, pretending to be interested so I could make a clean getaway. I left frustrated that I'd been diagnosed as crazy. I'd never be taken seriously, I thought, and the weight of my head was becoming unbearable.

Hands were laid on my shoulders, back, and head. I wanted so badly to be healed, but I wasn't sure that faith healing was the way to go. I couldn't believe I had actually wound up at the altar. I'd been wandering all over downtown with a heavy head when I came upon the sign at Saint Anthony's Shrine: FAITH HEALING TODAY. The word "healing" pulled me inside even though I wasn't sure I knew what faith was anymore. At one time I did have a sense of "faith," though I kept it to myself. Most of my friends were too smart to tolerate such ideas, but for a long time, through all the dying in my family, faith was all that kept me going. Nowadays I was alienated not only from most of my friends but from the person I had once been — someone who trusted a higher order and believed that everything was exactly as it should be. But since every emergency room doctor in town was hiding from me, I felt my options were running out. The Arch Street Church, as we called Saint Anthony's, had been a kind of mecca to Nana and Grandpa. When Nana was alive, they could be found there every morning, before their afternoon at the Woolworth's lunch counter.

When I walked into the chapel, I immediately regretted it, seeing the troubled faces turning toward me from the pews. There was way too much emotion going on. Faces were wet, some bodies shook, and scattered voices spilled out an inconsolable grief. The crying wasn't like any I'd heard before. There were cracks of sobs, followed by thunderous lamentations breaking through from depths I couldn't imagine. I wanted to hightail it out of there, but too many of the bereaved had spotted me. I let them see me slip into a pew. I was sure they were mentally ill, like Davey. I couldn't run from them now. I had to sit with their anguish.

Sitting among so many religiously obsessed people, I remembered the last night of Davey's life, before he jumped off the roof. In my memory of that night, Patterson Way was darker than it had ever been as Davey paced up and down the streets and across rooftops, shouting "Jesus, I love you!" like he'd been locked out and ignored. When he jumped the next day, he must have completely lost all faith in God.

As the sick people started moving to the altar for healing, I saw my chance to dart out of the church. I had come in at my wits' end about my illness, and I was curious about healing, and maybe even about faith. But these people had an altogether different kind of pain, one I knew nothing about, I thought thankfully. I had enough worries with the numbness and tingling, the sweats, the heavy head.

I slid out of the pew to genuflect and screw out of there, when I mistakenly made eye contact with one of the poor bastards — as Davey called the mentally ill — who had been crying a lot by the look of her.

"You're new," she whispered. She offered her hand. "I'm Sheila. Come on up!" *Fuck!* I thought as we approached the altar. I had no idea what they were doing up there, huddled like a football team. Every time I looked in Sheila's direction she smiled and nodded as if to assure me that I was doing the right thing. The huddled mass quaked, releasing occasional yelps and gasps. When Sheila disappeared into the huddle, I thought about making my getaway. But I had to see what was going on, so I circled the outside, standing on tiptoes to get a look over heads. Just then the crowd broke open to catch a body as it collapsed at my feet. A middle-aged black woman lay on the floor sleeping, with a look of contentment on her face. She woke up a little later and moved off to the side, holding her head and smiling like someone who'd just woken up from the most beautiful dream. The crowd huddled again, gathered around a priest who was touching people's heads to the sound of more gasps and yelps. I was stunned. The nuns at Saint Augustine had never mentioned anything like this. To me it seemed more like voodoo than a Catholic ceremony. I couldn't explain the people falling unconscious and decided it was a collective mental delusion, everyone agreeing to believe in the same nonsense. When the unconscious ones came to, they brushed themselves off and went out through the church's revolving doors, back into the crowded madness of downtown Boston. Some women fixed their earrings and hair in the glass of the exit doors, like they were going back to work.

My curiosity led me into the circle, but I didn't expect to end up at the center of a mob of crazy people or voodoo Catholics laying their hands all over me. First I felt one hand on my right shoulder. It was a woman's hand, and I could feel her weeping through my whole body. Maybe it was Sheila. I thought that her tears might be for me, that she knew something about the sickness and death coming my way. I wanted to ask her but I didn't dare turn around. I realized she probably had her own problems and knew nothing about mine. A large hand gripped my left shoulder, and I immediately pictured it as belonging to an older man. My hyperactive heartbeat — which I'd been paying a lot of attention to lately and wanted to have checked — competed with the pounding pulse coming from his hand. A third hand barely touched my back but was sending out even more warmth than the others. Soon I felt hands all over me. At first I was self-conscious, since I knew none of these people, and some of them looked like they had bigger problems than me. But then someone in the crowd gently lifted my heavy head. *How'd he know about that?* I thought. I stopped asking questions. I no longer felt hands. I only felt connected — to what, I didn't know. Maybe to people with bigger problems than I had. But they really believed in all the things I'd not been able to feel lately: faith and God. I could feel their hearts though, literally, in their racing pulses. It calmed me. For the first time in a long while I felt less nervous. And whether that came from their God or from their belief in God, I was too physically weak to turn it down.

Then the strong, warm hand of the healer came down gently on my brow, the heaviest part of my heavy head. He lifted my entire head with both hands and threw it back with such confidence, such belief in the Holy Spirit that he was invoking, that I lost all resistance. I hadn't even known my hands were clenched until I felt them open up. My knees buckled, and the last thing I remembered was falling amid a circle of faces and outstretched arms. As I was going under, I had the sudden fear that I was now part of a cult. But the supporting arms felt good, and I just let myself go.

When I woke up I couldn't move. Weak, plastered to the floor, I was far from the altar. If I turned my eyes to the left, I could see that people were still falling down and being caught. Other sleeping folks were being dragged off to the side, as I must have been. Their limp bodies and happily dreaming faces were so different from the desperate faces at the altar that wanted so much to be relieved of whatever weighed them down. I suddenly wanted to leave. I was done. I really had been knocked down, and I didn't know how it had happened, but I wanted to get out before they asked me to join or to give them money I didn't have. I couldn't move, couldn't even feel my limbs, and it felt kind of good. Within minutes, though, I started to feel my fingers and toes again. Then the arms and legs came back. But I lay on the floor until someone came over to lift me by the hands. Then they dragged Sheila over to my spot, like I was taking up floor space.

I left feeling I'd had the best sleep ever. I was in a good mood too. Seeing a phone booth reminded me to call home and make sure no one was dead, but I didn't. For the first time I thought that most likely everyone *wasn't* dead and that even if they were I could handle it. This was just life, nothing more or less. On the Red Line train home I saw Sheila but she didn't see me. She was with a man, probably her husband, and was playing with two kids. I wondered if anyone in her family could imagine her shaking like a leaf at the gates of hell. You'd never know that just thirty minutes ago she'd been out like a lamp in front of the sacristy. Her husband and kids were telling her about their day, and I wondered whether she'd tell of hers. I was amazed to think that she and the others in that service might *not* be mentally ill.

I thought about the whole faith thing on the train back to Southie. I still didn't know what faith was or how someone might get some. But I wondered if that was simply the way I was feeling now, calm in spite of being on the way back to Southie, where god-knows-what awaited me.

It was all I could do to carry my heavy head up Joy Street. Resting at a stoop on the way up Beacon Hill, I wondered if making the appointment had been the right thing to do. After all the symptoms I'd had came back along with some new ones, I gave in to the idea of seeing the therapist on Joy Street. Doctors were still avoiding me, and of course I couldn't talk to my family about my impending death. I thought maybe I could get the therapist to help convince the doctors that I wasn't crazy and should be taken seriously. From the foot of Joy Street the hill looked steep. I felt like one of the old people I saw stopping to hold on to every railing they came to.

The therapist watched me as I tried to answer her question, only her third in what seemed like small talk to get acquainted.

Shit, here we go again, I thought.

All my life I had struggled with the answer to the question "How many are in your family?" and it wasn't getting any easier. My mother had lost the baby, Patrick, a year before I was born, but we always included him in the count, since we thought of him as a kind of guardian sibling. As a child, sometimes I would say, "Eleven, but one died." People would ask, shocked, "*Eleven* brothers and sisters?" I was proud to be from such a big family. Only the Rooneys and the Noonans had more — eleven living kids, beating me by one. The Rooneys got the most shocked responses, all eleven being boys. So it was best not to be around any Rooneys when the question came up. Once I started spending time beyond Southie, though, my "eleven" would throw people for a loop, and they'd make the same old joke about Irish Catholics and rabbits.

After Davey died I started saying, "Eleven, but two died."
But then people exclaimed, "Oh my God!" and wanted to
know how the two had died. Once I saw how people recoiled
at the mention of someone jumping off a roof, I usually didn't
feel like talking about it. I learned to say, "Nine," relieved to
have to deal only with an "Irish Catholics" comment. But I felt
guilty about cutting Davey out of the count, even though I no
longer cared about childish birth-rate contests. I started including both Davey and Patrick again.

But now, with Frankie and Kevin dead and only seven of us
remaining alive, I had answered a few times, "Eleven, but four
died," only to see the person look horrified, not wanting to ask
how. Then, to comfort them, I'd explain that it wasn't that
bad, that I only knew three of them, that Patrick was a baby
who'd died before I was born. Which only made their faces
contort more. I had to do some quick math in my head before
answering at all, since Kathy was now permanently brain-
damaged and increasingly schizophrenic. She talked to herself
all day and wrote childhood rhymes on any paper she could
find, an existence that seemed somewhere between life and
death. I felt more like I was one of six, not seven, survivors,
and that brought me back to thinking, *Who's next?* Then I'd
want to call home to make sure everyone was okay or wonder
whether the strange feeling in my throat was cancer.

I'd only paused for a few seconds before giving my "eleven,
but four died" version, but the therapist looked confused. She
straightened up in her chair to pursue the question further.

"How did they die?" she asked straightforwardly. I was glad
she wasn't asking with the wide eyes that usually accompanied
the question. Anytime Ma had to answer the question, she said
they were in a car accident. I guessed she wanted to keep it simple, rather than getting into suicide, jumps and falls from rooftops, bank robberies, and prison deaths. And she would never
talk about the night she lost her baby Patrick. But a car accident? Tired of Grandpa's admonishing that I should "say nothing to nobody," I was saddened by Ma's shame about the

ways my brothers died. Ma was the one who had always gone against the hush-hush Irish ways of her parents.

Okay, here goes, I thought. *Remember Patrick even though you never met him. And keep Kathy off the list of dead.* I opened my left thumb to remember that Kathy was not dead and opened my right-hand fingers to keep the count limited to four. I started with the baby, Patrick Michael, who'd died of pneumonia, just to be done with that story. "I received his name in reverse," I said, glad to begin with a less tragic fact before telling about the baby being denied access to a hospital. *There, that's done with,* I thought, closing one finger and leaving three open. The therapist, her face somber, looked like she was really listening. "The hospitals didn't have to take welfare babies back then," I said, changing the subject from Ma's banging on neighbors' doors with the baby already dead in her arms, which was still lingering in the therapist's face. "Before Medicaid," I added, when she looked surprised at welfare babies being turned away. Then I tried to turn the conversation to how Reagan wanted to go back to those days. I was trying to feel out whether she was a Republican, in which case I'd have reason enough never to come back. But she didn't give away much about herself.

"What about the other ones?" she asked.

"Huh?"

"The others who died."

"Oh. Well, Davey jumped off the roof and killed himself. But he was mentally ill. He'd had a breakdown when he was fourteen. I knew he must have really wanted to go, though, because he put up a fight against the EMTs who tried to save him. So it's okay, I figure, what he did." She said nothing during my pause. "Suicide, I mean," I said, interrupting the silence. "You know, how they say they're going to hell. I know he must have been in a lot of pain every day to have done that." I added, "He died nine hours later," not sure what else to add in the face of her searching stare.

The therapist's eyes were glazed, and her expression became

sadder. "Oh no, really," I said, panicked, "it was rough at first, but I got over it. We all did. You have to." *Shit. I never should have come here. I should have lied when she asked how many were in the family. I could have said eleven, and we could have talked about other stuff, like how doctors pay no attention to how sick I feel every single day.* I couldn't wait to leave.

"What about the other two?" she asked.

I couldn't believe she wanted more. I knew I had to cut the rest short and get out, never to return. She looked like she was going to say, "Oh, you poor thing," which was always worse than when people said, "Holy shit!" Sympathy only made me feel embarrassed. And the sympathizer often looked unstable to me, not strong.

"How old were the others?" she asked, like she was regaining composure.

"Well, Frankie was twenty-four and Kevin had just turned twenty-two." *Fuck, should I pull the car accident thing, or just tell the truth and get it over with?* "Frankie died first. He got involved in a bank heist. You know . . . Southie." I hesitated, realizing that she, and most people, *didn't* know. "He was found in the first getaway car, covered in trash bags and pushed down under the seat. He'd been shot in the crossfire, but detectives say he could have lived if he was dropped off at a hospital or something. But, you know, I guess they thought he might have talked then. That's what the detectives told Ma, anyway." I almost added that Ma was now saying that one detective had told her Frankie was strangled to death in the back seat.

I looked at the one finger I still had raised. *Maybe after Kevin I can get to the fact that I am sick as a dog and need to find a good doctor who can diagnose my sickness.* "Then Kevin died after he did a jewelry store heist and went to prison. That stuff was much more Kevin's lifestyle than Frankie's. Frank was a Golden Gloves boxer and was much more into his body and lifting weights and stuff. Anyway, the detectives were working Kevin while he was in prison, trying to get information about the robbery Frankie had died in. The detectives said they had a video that showed Kevin trying to stop his partner from shooting the jeweler, and they were only going to show it if Kevin flipped. Word got out that Kevin was going to snitch for a lesser sentence." I felt it all spilling out of my mouth, but all I could think about was the weight of my head. "Long story short," I said, "he was found hanging in prison, outside his prison cell. Whether he did it himself because he couldn't deal with the prospect of snitching, or someone else did it because they couldn't deal with the prospect of snitching, he never did talk.

"Let me see," I said, still looking down, my head heavy. "Kevin died . . ." I had to stop to count months on my fingers. "Frankie died in July, and Kevin died the following March. What's that? They died eight months apart?" I raised my head to look at the therapist. She was buckled over in her chair, tears streaming down her face.

"Oh, my God! No, really. It's not that bad," I said. "This was all a long time ago."

She got out her tissues and wiped her cheeks and asked, "How long ago was it?"

"About . . ." Once again I had to stop and count. "Well, Kevin died about three months ago, and Frankie's been dead almost a whole year."

Walking through the Common to the subway, I couldn't get the therapist's tears out of my head. Even though so many Southie families had buried their kids in recent years, I thought, *most people don't live like this*. I saw that all the deaths in my family and in the neighborhood were not normal. All through my time with the therapist I'd planned to stop in at Mass General on my way home. If Dr. Reynolds could see that my head was lopsided and that I wasn't imagining the whole thing, he'd have to take me seriously. But by the time I got to Tremont Street, where I would turn left toward the hospital, I realized that my head wasn't so heavy anymore.

I went back to talk to the therapist a few times, each time

feeling a little lighter on the walk back home through Boston Common. But it didn't take long for the heaviness to return back in Southie. Ma had been going to a lot of wakes for Kevin's and Kathy's old friends. Each time I heard of another death from suicide or overdose, or a stabbing or shooting that no one present had seen, I wanted to start running again. So I would go to New York, where I could stay at Felix's loft. The geographic distance wasn't enough, though. On these visits I began to discover that whiskey was a great way to erase, to forget about everything. The only problem was that the hangovers brought more panic than I'd ever known.

I was spitting bits of mirror. I thought it was mostly my teeth pouring out of my mouth with strings of blood and drool, but when I closed my mouth I could tell by the crunch of small glass shards that I still had teeth. The pain shot through the front of my face up into my brain. It served me right for being so obsessed with my impending death. I had only held up the mirror to cast some sunlight into my throat to get a better look at it. I thought for a second about Narcissus and the damage caused by his self-obsession, but this was different. I didn't care what I looked like, I just wanted to know what that strange feeling in my throat was, and whether I was going to die sooner rather than later. I thought of what Ma always said if one of us mentioned feeling sick: "Don't be so concerned with yourself!" But I had bigger problems than throat cancer now that the initial shock of the mirror crash was wearing off. A sharp pain worse than I'd ever known was shooting through my skull, making me forget about my throat and everything else.

That morning, when I woke up in Felix's loft, everyone else had left. A candle was still lit, so I knew they hadn't been gone long. Last time I was awake, Albee was drunk and singing Screamin' Jay Hawkins songs to Felix. Greg was sitting in the corner sleeping, and Felix was doing a self-portrait. She'd had the flu for a week and said she wanted to exorcise it by painting herself and the flu, as a demonic beast sitting on her shoulder. When I woke up hung-over, I panicked about the pain in my throat. Grabbing the heavy antique mirror Felix had been using for the self-portrait, I held it up to the light to see down into my throat. I didn't see the mirror come out of its frame and smash onto my face. I only felt the crash.

I immediately thought of calling the dentist in Boston Frankie had recommended when he thought I should become a tooth sculptor. I remembered that the dentist's office was on High Street. That's all I had to go on, so I screamed at the operator, through blood and spit and a lax jaw, that it was an emergency. Sure enough the operator found the dentist on High Street. Looking into the bathroom mirror, I discovered that my front tooth was split up the middle and into the gum and that half of it was dangling. I tried to pull at the dangling bit gently while describing it to the dentist on the phone. But it wouldn't give. The tooth was split, but both halves were firmly rooted. The dentist took me very seriously and told me to get on the next bus to Boston.

As bad as the pain was, I felt flush with relief all the way back to Boston, for once having an ailment that was visible, with a gash no doctor could deny. All through the next month of dental work, I woke up every day feeling focused on my recovery from a wound that was obvious to all. The x-ray of my split tooth was even published in a dentistry journal because, the dentist said, "it was a highly unusual break."

I didn't know how long I'd been at the Allston apartment of my friend Katrina, whom I knew from the Queensberry Street days. There were five or six of us there, and we'd stopped paying attention to time after pulling the shades down on the first morning, when the sun tried to invade our smoke-filled den and stilted the conversation flow. I felt absolutely perfect while I was at the pinnacle of the speed high. By the second — or maybe third — night, Katrina, who always seemed to be the spokesperson for speed, summarized the feeling completely.

"You see, this is the most perfect drug in the universe," she said. "Everything is as it *should* be. There's complete clarity for once." And she was right. I'd never felt this on point before. I'd recently been seeking out my old friends from the club world and was willing to try anything to feel right. Booze only increased my panic when I wasn't drinking. I'd been trying trippy drugs with Katrina, like MDA, which kept us up all night talking and smoking and transcending everything. But nothing felt as enlightening as the speed I'd just taken.

For the next few days of speeding I could feel everything the others were saying, or trying to say, or not saying at all. We were beyond language, I thought to myself (or maybe out loud) at one point. We all understood each other completely. We talked, laughed, and chain-smoked. I experienced a wave of disgust only when I caught myself or someone else lighting a new cigarette with the fast-burning filter of the last one. That became my obsession. It felt degenerate, and I told everyone that from now on we could only light new cigarettes with a lighter. So we ventured out to the quiet, dark streets on a mission: to buy a collection of lighters. Toward the end of the journey for lighters, which also led to bags of useless snacks that no one would ever be hungry for, it was clearly time to take more speed. No one needed to say it, though. I knew I wasn't alone in suddenly feeling nauseated by the hideous sounds and smells of the predawn garbage trucks preparing for another day out there. The idea of going back to regular life, to the complete boredom of everyday chitchat alternating with panic and nausea, began to creep in right about when we noticed that the sky was turning from black to blue. The trucks were drowning out the perfection of conversation we'd come to live for in those few days and nights. Everyone was relieved to get back inside the apartment. Some shot up immediately, while others snorted. I could only handle drinking the speed in a lemonade concoction that Katrina had invented just for me.

For years I had heard about coming down, or "crashing," in stories told by drug-savvy friends. It had sounded scary. I had always been afraid of being high, afraid I might like it and then lose control. But now that I was high I wanted never to come down. Katrina had learned to manage her comedowns by drinking a tall glass full of vitamins with some swampy green liquid spirulina and always keeping peppermint oil in her purse for the nausea. She had been known to fall asleep in a dark closet for days after a couple of weeks on speed.

As my allies in speed began to drop that morning, finding dark corners and soft blankets to wrap themselves in, I was pissed off by their desertion and panicked at the comedown I had to face. There was no more speed, and the darkened blinds were outlined by creeping sunlight. I desperately wanted my perpetually dark room in the project back in Southie.

On the sluggish trolley ride home, all I could think was that I'd never before seen just how ugly the world was. After a few days and as many nights feeling alive on speed, every churn and squeal of the trolley car — sounds I'd never noticed in a lifetime of city living — made me sick, as the trolley twisted through the winding streets. It was a nightmarish morning and I was going home. I'd never known how depressing fluorescent lights were at sunrise, how sickly pale were the earliest commuters, or how nauseating my own faint reflection was in the window of a trolley descending underground. I was crashing hard.

I lay in bed all day listening to the noise outside, staring at the ceiling, and wanting to die. I didn't care that my shades were rolled up. There was no point in trying to keep out the hellishness of Patterson Way. It was all hell, no question about it, inside or out. I had no thoughts of my family having to bury another one. We were all buried. None of the ugliness or pain mattered. Nothing mattered.

Ma barged in before it got dark. I'd been in my room silently for the whole afternoon with no music playing. "What's wrong with you?" she asked. She was dressed to go out and play the accordion for some extra cash. Ma hadn't been out at all since

Frankie and Kevin had died. This was the first time I'd seen her dressed up in months. She was even walking faster since she'd thrown out her Valium, and seemed more resolute than I'd seen since Frankie and Kevin's deaths. How could she even think about going out, never mind playing the accordion for a bunch of hand-clapping foot-stomping Irish idiots?

"Don't you see?" I asked. "It's all shit." Ma was silent, looking out the window, and even though I hadn't said much, she looked like she knew what I was talking about. "Everything is fuckin' hideous," I said.

Ma kept looking out the window, not at me, and agreed. "Yeah, it is all shit," she said, her voice cracking as she looked out on Patterson Way. Then she threw open the window to yell at Seamus to "stay the fuck away from that no-good Sean Malone."

I admitted to Ma that I thought I was dying, and I started to cry but stopped myself fast, looking toward the wall next to the bed.

"Dying?" Ma said. "We're all fucking dying. Everybody's dying."

I pulled myself together and explained about the heavy head and all the other symptoms I'd been hiding from everyone. "Look," she said, "think of it this way. One of two things can happen every single day. You can live or you can die." That didn't sound like a good way to think about it. But she continued, "The worst possible thing that can happen is that you die," she said flat-out. "And that's not so bad. We're all going to die."

I was stunned that Ma would be so callous about the thought of dying. "Well, Jesus, you think I'm not sick to my stomach most days?" She admitted that if it weren't for Seamus and Stevie, she'd have done herself in by now.

Everything seemed to go quiet, all the noise on Patterson Way, all my focus on my own death. I was floored to think that Ma had been thinking of suicide. The only image she'd ever put out when we were growing up was one of strength and "holding your head high," as she liked to say.

Ma walked out of my room and got ready to go play the accordion. Soon Jeanie Gallagher came over to tell Ma all her problems, and I could hear in Ma's voice from the other room that she was all smiles as she told our neighbor to "dump the bum, throw on some friggin' makeup, and get the hell out of the house."

I was still crashing hard from speed, but I was too focused on the fact that my mother had wanted to die to be worried about myself anymore.

I was the only one home a few days later when I saw the knob turn and heard the door rattle like someone was in trouble. Before Frankie died we'd never locked our door in the daytime. We'd grown up with the idea that you just knocked once and walked in. Ma said everyone was getting crazy with all the cocaine in the streets, and no one knew who to trust anymore. I hadn't realized until recently what a rock Frankie had been in the family, the one who made us feel like no one would ever mess with us.

I crept to the door quietly and looked through the peephole, only to see Grandpa looking worried. Grandpa never came to the project. He said he was afraid of bringing the cockroaches back to his place. "For they'll climb in your pockets and go home with you," he'd explain. "And there's no getting rid of them cocksuckers at all." The few times he did come, he looked paranoid, like he trusted no one in our neighborhood. Through the fisheye lens of the peephole I could see Grandpa's Inspector Clouseau trench coat and his black pleather aviator hat nearly sideways. Looking like he believed there was a conspiracy to keep him out, he rattled the door and put one eye up to the peephole as if he might see through it in reverse.

"Michael, open up, for I know you're in there," he shouted. He backed up, and I saw him push his hand deep into the Inspector Clouseau coat, like he had a gun. These days I was always imagining the worst; nothing could surprise me. I opened the door, and he walked past me like he was on a mission, his hand still gripping whatever he was concealing in his pocket.

"Someone told me that you're in a cult," he blurted, his watery eyes examining me more closely than I was used to from anyone else in my family. I started laughing but wondered if I should be worried. Since Frankie's death, Grandpa had been coming up with every kind of conspiracy about the family, as if behind his back we all might have been dabbling in Southie's underworld all these years. We had been thrown off by Frankie's involvement in the heist. Kevin would have made more sense, since he'd been living that life for years. After reading in the newspapers that Frankie had burned off all of his fingerprints with acid before the armored car heist, Grandpa was worried that he'd been a professional bank robber for years. It made a big difference to Grandpa whether Frankie was a career criminal or had just been used for this bank job. I figured he thought it would determine whether Frankie made it into heaven or not. Now it was my turn for Grandpa's sneaking suspicion that he might not know any of us.

"Don't ask me who," he said, "for I swore by the life of me that I wouldn't tell." The conviction in his voice made me realize he was serious about my being in a cult.

"Cult?" I asked nervously. I was so confused lately that I had to rack my brain to remember whether I'd joined a cult or anything that might seem like one to Grandpa. I laughed. "You mean Saint Anthony's Shrine?"

"Don't laugh at me like I'm some kind of donkey from the old country, the way Frankie did," he spit out angrily. "I told Frankie to watch out for those bastards I seen him with. I gave him good advice, for I knew by the look of them bums that they was as criminal as the day is long. Sure, didn't I see the like of them all my years working on the docks in South Boston?" A tear streamed down Grandpa's face, and I held my breath hoping that his eyes were just watery from the cold outside. "And isn't Frankie dead now?" he said.

I got quiet. I didn't mean to hurt Grandpa's feelings by laughing. I was just nervous. I told him I'd never even known anyone in a cult. The closest thing I could think of was the way Southie felt ever since I started staying home all the time, with everyone being like everybody else.

"I'm here to tell you now that I know you're in trouble and I've come to help you," he said, going for the hidden thing in his coat pocket. He pulled out the jug of holy water from Lourdes. I knew that jug well. He'd kept it on top of his bureau all these years and only brought it out of the house for emergencies, like when Kathy was in a coma.

"Someone told me you were worshipping the devil with the punk rocks!" he said, opening the jug.

Ma walked into the apartment, and Grandpa repeated that I'd joined the devil-worshippers. "With the punk rocks," he added proudly, like he'd copped on to a new phenomenon.

Even years before, when my friends and I had "punk rock" shouted at us from passing cars — especially after MTV came on the air — we just laughed it off, never identifying with the term. Whatever we had been, no one I knew, even with underground music's slow dive into dope and depression, ever flirted with Satanism. Most people I'd known from the scene didn't believe in anything, never mind the devil. "That's heavy metal," I said, thinking I'd figured out the misunderstanding.

Grandpa said nothing and only looked confused by the term "heavy metal." Unyielding, he held out the jug and came at me like he was ready for an exorcism.

Ma told him to sit down "like a fucking rational man, for the love of Christ" and to explain what he was getting at. She looked worried about him.

Ma and I sat on the couch, but Grandpa refused. "I won't sit down at all," he said, adding that I was in great danger and would bring bad luck upon the whole house with my devil cult.

Ma told Grandpa to stop with all the foolishness and looked to me to explain what he was talking about. "I don't know." I shrugged. "Punk rock."

"The punk rocks all listen to devil music," Grandpa said. "They do a dance like this." He jumped up and down, and I figured he must have seen a TV special about London's punks of 1977 doing the pogo. Ma's jaw dropped — she looked horrified to see her father trying to bounce like he was on a pogo stick. "Then they give themselves a good wallop," he said, "like this," and he hit the side of his jaw with a closed fist.

"Daddy!" Ma yelled. "What in the Christ . . ."

Grandpa, continuing to pogo, opened his hands to slap each side of his face. Ma and I were more astounded with every phase of the dance. He had to stop to catch his breath, but in the next second he put his hand on his throat like he was choking himself. Finally, as a kind of grand finale, he collapsed on the floor.

There was a long silence, then Ma broke into her high-pitched cackle. "For Chrissake!" she said, laughing so hard she fell from the arm of the sofa onto the cushions. I was still stunned. Grandpa asked me to help him up off the floor, and when he was standing he continued with more facts about the punk rocks. He told Ma that they all wore symbols — "like a dyed piece of pink or purple hair, or a clothespin in the mouth" — to identify themselves to each other.

"You mean a safety pin," I said.

"Well he did get suspended once for painting his head some crazy friggin' color," Ma said. At first I thought she might be egging her father on. But then she looked at me and asked, "Mike, are you into Satan?"

I was speechless.

Grandpa told me to take just a little bit of holy water. I'd actually come to love the idea of holy water over the years, with my grandparents' and Ma's obsessions with Lourdes and Fatima.

"I'll take some holy water," I said, almost eagerly. "But not to get the devil out of me."

He came at me with the jug held out as an offering. It was beige plastic, molded to look like a woven basket. I noticed how dirty it had gotten over the years. Grandpa had told me many times the story of being in the waters at Lourdes along with hundreds of pilgrims "with every kind of a disease you ever heard of." He'd say grimly, "It's a wonder I'm standing before you this day, for I coulda been killed by the diseases was in that water. Only for the grace of God." Grandpa said a woman came to him in the water and handed him the jug she'd filled, telling him he'd need this for his family. We'd all come to know the jug, because Grandpa had brought it out during some of our lowest points, like at Kathy's bedside and at Frankie's casket. And now it was my turn for having once been with "the punk rocks."

I'd been feeling so unraveled and disconnected that I felt I needed the water — only not for the reasons that Grandpa thought. The holy water represented a connection to my family and to all the things — good and bad — that I'd experienced with Grandpa and his jug.

I took the jug from his hand, opened it, and took a swig.

"Christ, yer not supposed to fookin' drink it, you half fool!" he screamed. I told him I felt a little better, which kept him from lashing out any more. "Do you?" he asked calmly, scratching his head underneath the near-sideways aviator hat. He had a spark in his eye that I'd only seen the very few times he seemed proud of an accomplishment, like when he talked about his years of working longshore on the docks and putting food on the table for Nana and his five daughters.

He walked out the door then without a goodbye, as he often did, and Ma and I sat in silence.

I WAS LOOKING at my father for the first time. Ma said he'd come to see me when I was a baby, but I was nineteen now and he hadn't come to see me since. Until this night I could only imagine what he looked like, the way some people imagined ancestors from family stories. I knew I was looking at him for the last time, too. And no matter how hard I tried, I couldn't see the resemblance to myself. I had gone there looking for something. After burying Frankie and Kevin, and going back and forth between wanting to be closer to home and running as far away as I could, I was ready to look for any connection to my family on George Fox's side. He was, after all, my father, and I was his only kid.

I don't know what I expected to find. But as far back as I could remember, I'd heard aunts with folded arms whisper stories about George Fox being Ma's only decent boyfriend, then nod their heads in general agreement that I was the spitting image of the man Ma would have done good to marry. They'd said he was tall and smart and had a "big job" at the Navy Yard. Why Ma would marry a no-good blackguard the like of Dave MacDonald, the father of my eight older brothers and sisters, and not hold on to George Fox, Grandpa said he'd never know. This was said at tea, only among aunts and uncles who knew I wasn't really a MacDonald. "Your mother has no

shame, no shame at all" was the refrain I listened to throughout childhood as I sipped sweet, milky tea from their saucers
and wondered how great my father must be.

My brothers and sisters knew George because he'd stayed at
the apartment for a few months after I was born, and they
seemed to like him better than any of Ma's other boyfriends. I
always listened intently when they reminisced with Ma about
the time that Mac, their father, walked into the apartment for a
rare visit, only to come face to face with George at the threshold. Davey hated Mac, and whenever he told the story, he
made it sound like a Jackie Gleason episode, with the two men
stuck in the doorway, trying to pass in opposite directions. My
older brothers and sisters agreed when Davey used to say that
George was a head over Mac as they crossed paths, glaring and
never saying a word. My sister Mary said George Fox took all
the kids to Santa's Village a couple of years in a row, and to
hear Mary, an adult mother of three, talk with big eyes about
the elves and real reindeer and the rides through the North
Pole, you'd swear George Fox was just about the greatest man
that ever set foot in the project. Mary even liked him enough to
come along with me now, to see him one more time. To pay her
respects.

"Looks like he was a smoker," Mary whispered as we knelt
at his side. Mary hadn't seen George since she was maybe nine
or ten. She scrunched her forehead, nodding toward his stiff
hands folded into each other and wrapped in rosaries. Having buried three brothers and recently seen many neighbors
waked, every one of them looking like he had died saying a ro-
sary, I couldn't see what she was carrying on about. I looked at
George's hands and then back at Mary. "Tobacco stains," she
muttered out the side of her mouth, pointing quickly toward
his fingernails. She said it wasn't like him to be a smoker; he
had seemed more sensible than that. Then she stood up and
leaned slightly into the casket, looking for god-knows-what.
Mary had become a nurse in the OR at Boston City Hospital,
so casual observation of a corpse came naturally; "the detec-

tive" is what the other nurses at work called her. I'd often found myself tuning out her OR stories of car wrecks and body parts, made more horrific by her matter-of-fact tone. My stomach had been in knots the whole drive to the wake, and now, looking at my father's tobacco stains, I felt even sicker. Still, I was listening to Mary as we both blessed ourselves to pray. Instead of praying, though, I pictured the dead man before me smoking away and wondered whether I would make it to the toilet.

I shrugged off any sign of interest in how sensible George Fox was. *I wouldn't know.* I had decided in that moment that I had no connection to him at all, that it was too late. With that the churning in my stomach went away completely. Then Mary went silent to finish the praying so that George Fox's friends or relatives or whoever they were in the line behind us could have their turn. I turned to look behind me at a room full of strangers huddled in circles, shaking their heads and telling stories that all ended with exclamations of "I just saw him last Friday!" or "I just saw him three days ago!" Whenever it was that they'd last seen him, they were sure to let everyone know, opening their arms as if to include people beyond the circle of listeners, who couldn't believe someone they'd just seen was now dead. Some of the men — the ones with greaser hairstyles from their heyday, favorite dungarees and baseball jackets with BLARNEY STONE or MICKEY'S PUB stretched over broad backs — had seen him just minutes before his death. "There he was at the bar, big as life, healthy as a horse, and generous as the day is long, ordering a round for everyone." One of the ladies, with a man's Elvis hairdo, recounted George's last minutes. Had she known when he got up for the toilet that he'd not be coming back . . . she looked at the floor and shook her head in disbelief before straightening up to deliver the punch line: "I'd've made the bastard pay for the round before he went to the john!" A whole corner of the room, those who seemed to know George Fox better than anyone else, erupted into fits of laughter, holding their sides for fear of splitting. For some, laughter released tears that I knew might not have come out any other way. It was all looking very familiar to me. We were in Dorchester, and even though it was the next neighborhood over from Southie, I'd never realized until now just how close to home my father's wake was. Half the room emptied for a smoke on the front steps, and the laughter and uncontrollable coughing became distant, only to come pouring in every time someone opened the front door to go for a smoke. I turned back to George's face, and though I probably still looked like I couldn't have cared less, I was waiting for Mary to finish praying and tell me more about the stranger in a casket. We blessed ourselves again, even though I'd forgotten to say a single Our Father.

Mary said something about George's being "normal," and that's when I thought my whole stomach would pass through my throat. I looked at the corpse in front of me and felt my neck beginning to sweat, although I felt cold. From all the talk I'd heard over the years about George Fox — always referred to by his full name — and his "big job" inspecting ships at the Navy Yard, he had seemed like a different kind of man, one who wouldn't have nicotine stains on his fingers and wouldn't ignore his kid who lived in a housing project or die puking in the toilet at the Emerald Isle, only a couple of miles straight down Dorchester Avenue from Old Colony Project. My mother had mentioned seeing him on occasion when she played accordion at the Emerald Isle, and said he'd asked, "How's Michael?" as they passed each other in the crowd. She'd given him our number a couple of times. And each time one of my brothers died and it was splashed all over the papers about a fall from a rooftop, a bank robbery, or a mysterious prison death, I went to the wakes keeping a nervous eye out for George Fox, who surely had read about my family dying in Old Colony. None of them were his kids, but still, they were my brothers. I didn't know how I'd react if he had come to my brothers' wakes. I remembered thinking on the way to one of them that it was too late to get to know a "father" anyway and that at this point if the coward ever did show up I'd probably stab him as soon as look at him.

I suddenly felt my blood heating up through my entire body, spreading to head, hands, and feet. The rush felt good. For a moment I thought I might be truly evil, having such thoughts only seconds after making the sign of the cross at a casket, but at least my nausea had gone away.

Mary and I stood up from the kneeler, and when we turned around we bumped into Edie, who lived downstairs from us in Old Colony. Edie drank tall cans of beer at her kitchen window all by herself, facing no one on the other side of her table. She was always waiting, it seemed, for the chance to catch one of the neighborhood "little bastards" who came by like clockwork to bounce balls off the window where she sat. They threw all kinds of balls — superballs, tennis balls, Wiffle balls, basketballs — knowing that it would send Edie into a shitfit, roaring and hollering and calling them every kind of a sonofabitch in the book. As time went on and kids began to hate Edie more and more — not just wanting a rise out of her — they threw the balls harder, breaking screens and glass. Before long there was a collection of balls on Edie's kitchen table. And there she continued to sit, in the same window, facing directly across from no one, never budging and never once entertaining the thought of sipping her beer on the couch across the room. After Frankie's death, I'd sit in our third-floor window for hours, watching Edie in her second-floor window, wondering at her calling in life, and at my own. Now I was shocked to see Edie outside her apartment, never mind at George Fox's wake. She told me he was her buddy. "And what are you doing here?" she asked, looking me up and down as if I were on her turf, her after-hours world outside Old Colony. I told her I was his son, and she conceded, "Oh, yeah, I'd say there's a resemblance," leaning back and studying my face a bit. She said he was a good guy, "a gem." Then she walked up to the casket,

kissed her hand and laid it on her dead drinking buddy's forehead, and was out the door in a jiffy.

"I don't know. I guess he drank," Mary said, throwing up
her hands. Then she peered back at his corpse again from
across the room, looking as if she wanted to go back to check
for broken blood vessels or some other signature of alcohol.

We took seats next to strangers, who settled into an audible
hush when they saw me. I started to notice quite a few glances
at me from different parts of the parlor. One woman seemed to
be moving from one clique to another, telling people to take a
look at me. I figured she knew who I was, and it actually felt
good to be acknowledged, even in gossip. I thought I'd at least
wait for my aunt Eileen — George's sister — so that we could
thank her for her invitation and make a quick exit. I'd thought
it was pretty generous of her to go out of her way to find my
number and ask me to my father's wake. She'd said it was only
right that I should attend, and I had agreed that it was. As I
waited, the smell of carnations filled the air, just like at all those
other wakes.

I wanted to find something familiar at George's wake, something recognizable, something that might save me from the
doom I couldn't imagine escaping. I hated being from racist, backward Southie, living among people who talked about
niggers, buried their teenagers, and abided by the rules of their
neighborhood drug lord, Whitey Bulger. I hated the drugs that
surrounded me and the fact that for a while I'd fallen into that
trap of numbing drugs. I hated being poor. I felt like I wasn't
supposed to imagine anything more. Maybe I thought, going
to my father's wake, if I discovered that half of me was from
something else, then I'd be allowed to dream of living in New
York, to write stories, to draw, to eat strange food, and to
travel to places like London and Paris, where a lot of my
friends from my New York club days were going, and maybe
to not feel out of place in the world beyond Southie. I knew
there had to be something else that I had come from. My father

did, after all, have a "big job" at the Navy Yard, whatever that was.

Mary stood up to look at the corpse again, and I just sat, somewhat anxious about Eileen Fox. I had met her only once, when she showed up at Frankie's wake. She introduced herself to me as my aunt, expressed her sympathies, and left. Frankie's wake was still a blurry memory, and I couldn't recall what Eileen looked like. She'd brought her daughter Julie, my cousin, who I remembered because she looked like me, except in a dress. But the fact that they had shown up, unlike my father, meant a lot to me. Eileen had sounded smart on the phone the day before, too, pronouncing her *r*'s and referring to our ancestors from Ireland: Foxes, Plunketts, and Cavanaughs, who she claimed were some very dignified people. She didn't know much about them except that they were some very dignified people. But it was the first I'd heard of dignified Irish ancestors, and I wanted to know more.

Mary sat down, looking distraught at her investigation into the life and death of George Fox. When I asked her what Eileen looked like, so I'd know her when she arrived, she told me that Eileen would have been pretty except that she had a rotten angry face, like someone who'd spent a lifetime sucking a lemon. Mary said Eileen used to come screaming and hollering into the projects to fight with her mother, Gertie, next door to us. She said everyone was afraid of her. I knew my mother was no fan of Eileen, but I figured she must have changed. After all, she had called the night before to tell me that my father had died, that it was only right that I should attend his wake, and that we came from some very dignified blood in counties Meath and Cavan. She had even invited me to come visit her house in the suburbs and meet her daughters, my cousins, who she bragged looked like Christie Brinkley.

A flutter of activity erupted at the door to the funeral parlor, and Mary nudged me, looking scared. Eileen Fox looked distressed as she waved away all the gathering well-wishers. She was well dressed and seemed well mannered. Julie stood next to her and lit up with recognition when she saw me approach. But then she seemed to stop herself. I put my hand out to greet Eileen. My aunt put her hand out, and I noticed how well kept it was, all manicured and decorated in gold jewelry. Someone took the fur coat off her shoulders, and Eileen's hand held mine. Her hand was warm.

"I wanted to thank you for inviting me," I said.

"Who are you?" she asked, doing a double take.

"Michael," I answered. "Your nephew, George's son."

"My brother never had a son," she said, pulling her hand away and turning her back quickly.

She approached the casket and made the sign of the cross.

On the drive back to Old Colony Project I thought I must be insane. It had been a strange few years of deaths and burials, worry and confusion, followed by more deaths and burials. If Mary hadn't witnessed the interaction with Eileen, I might not believe it had really happened. I kept replaying it in my head: being denied by the bitch who looked like she'd spent a lifetime sucking a lemon and her daughter, who looked like me, football-player build and all. I began to get that drained-of-all-life feeling I'd come to know. *Why would your aunt invite you to your father's wake and then pretend she'd never called you and tell you that your father is not your father?* Nothing seemed real anymore, not even the drive home.

I remembered that on my tenth birthday, home alone and minding Seamus, I looked up George Fox's mother in the telephone book after learning from Ma that her name was Gertie. I knew from Ma that he was living with her in Dorchester. I spent the whole morning getting up the guts to call, and when I did, Gertie answered with a cranky voice. I asked to speak to George. I told her that I was his son, Michael, and that she was my grandmother, as if we'd all be in for some kind of happy family reunion. "He doesn't have a son!" She yelled so loud I had to pull the telephone away from my ear. "Who put you up to this?" she asked. "Your mother?" I told her my mother wasn't home and that I'd just called because it was my birthday — hoping now that I might get some kindness, which the mention of a birthday usually brought. Then a man's voice came on the phone. "Michael?" It was the first time I'd heard my father's voice. I told him it was my birthday. "Who put you up to this, your mother?" I hung up the phone and went back to minding Seamus.

That was the only time I heard George Fox's voice, and every detail of his tone had stuck with me to this day, nine years later. I wished I had never made that call. I wished I had never gone to his wake. Mary dropped me off in the project, and I went to my room and threw open the windows, letting out the day's pent-up heat and cockroach fumigation. My room was bare these days, no cutouts, no posters, no found objects nailed to the wall. I no longer barricaded myself in the world I'd created there; I didn't have the energy for that these days. I let the nighttime's whistles and hollers fill my room, preferring them to the stifling project heat.

The next morning Ma came into my room and asked how the wake was. I told her how Eileen had acted. I told her I could have sworn she'd called me the day before, inviting me to my father's wake. "Oh," Ma said, like she knew something. "She always was a cute bitch." *Huh?* I thought. I didn't know what Ma was getting at. All I knew was that I was late to my father's funeral, and it was too late anyway to make up for never getting to know him. "That cocksucker," Ma said. Ma's swears only reminded me how wretched our lives were. No wonder Eileen would deny the likes of me.

"Don't you see?" Ma said. "He must have left money! Eileen must have found out after she'd called you, and then had to deny you, since you would be the next of kin." Ma reminded me that George was not named on my birth certificate, since she hadn't been married to him. She'd given Dave MacDonald's name as father, like all the other kids.

I was proud of Ma's detective work, and I was determined to show my face to Eileen Fox one more time. I felt I should be proud for once of where I came from and who I might become, and for a moment I was ashamed for ever having felt otherwise. I got Mary to drive me to the funeral. We went to the funeral parlor first, to see the body one last time, as families are invited to do. The funeral director closed the casket, though, as soon as I came into the room. We went to the funeral Mass and afterward walked down the steps of the church behind Eileen and Julie, who by now was well trained not to acknowledge me. When I walked by the black limousine reserved for family, I stopped to look in. Eileen called out to a gang of George's drinking buddies who had no cars, and they all piled in, telling more stories of days and nights at the Emerald Isle. Eileen caught my eye by accident, looked away, then slammed the door shut.

Mary had to get to work at Boston City Hospital. I was going to take the train home, but after Eileen's limo took off, I found myself surrounded by George Fox's cousins and aunts, telling me they knew who I was and offering me a lift to the cemetery. I called Ma to tell her I was going to the cemetery, and she told me she had done some investigating and found that George had left about $75,000 between his savings and his life insurance policy. It pissed me off to think he had even a dime. I took a lift from the woman who, the evening before, had been alerting different cliques at the funeral parlor to my identity. She was George's cousin Louise, who said that George hadn't talked to Eileen in years and that he hated her. Louise said she'd always known about me, because George had taken me to her house when I was an infant, wanting her to help him shop for baby clothes. She had wondered if I'd be at the wake, and when she first laid eyes on me it was like seeing George Fox back from the dead. She said I looked even more like his brother Jimmy, who I'd heard was a heroin addict who'd died just a few years earlier.

When we got to the cemetery I was greeted by a woman who had been George Fox's fiancée for ten years. She said that all of her family was staring at me in the church and that her own son from a previous marriage said, "Who is he? He even walks like him!"

It felt good to be acknowledged. But I'd never had to think about my walk before now. And trudging over the spongy cemetery grass and mud toward a stranger's burial, I wondered at how someone could walk like a man he never knew.

AFTER SOME JOLTS and bumps during takeoff, the plane began to fly smoothly. We soared upward, then tilted left and circled back over the city. I was already nervous about flying for the first time, and the older woman sitting next to me and moving her lips in whispered prayer made me even more worried. "I've never been on one of these things before," she interrupted her Hail Marys to say. I looked out the window, trying to make out the streets and buildings floating next to me. It was Southie, and it looked almost upside down, which of course meant that *I* was practically upside down. The plane adjusted and Southie sank below my window. I peered out, my face against the glass, trying not to lose sight of it. Old Colony was easy to find — its maze of bricks and concrete looked like something unnatural kerplunked on the edge of Boston Harbor.

Watching it become smaller and smaller with our ascent, I could imagine the people below having the time of their lives on the brightly colored lawn chairs I saw scattered across rooftops or in front of circular blue wading pools in the concrete courtyards. "Like they're on the fuckin' Riviera," as Ma always said. I counted streets and buildings by the green copper stairwell exits on the roofs. When I located our building, I wondered what Seamus and Stevie would be doing right then. I looked for the ladies on our front stoop, figuring Kathy was probably sitting outside with them, agreeing with whatever they said, then drifting off and talking to herself. But now Old Colony was getting tiny, and any people I had been able to see were disappearing. One side of the labyrinth of buildings was turning golden in the sunset.

I wondered about all the times I'd heard planes above me as a kid in Old Colony and had paid no mind. I'd grown used to the airplane noise that every so often drowned out *Wheel of Fortune* or *Family Feud* on television and the fistfights of the Duggans next door. I knew it wouldn't occur to anyone down there that I was up here, on my way to London and Paris, and looking down at the maze of bricks fading from view.

Within three weeks I'd gone through almost all of the four hundred dollars I'd saved from my dishwashing job back home, but I didn't care. I hadn't expected to get as far across Europe as I had. Sometimes, especially at landmarks I'd read about in books or had seen in movies, like Trafalgar Square, I had to wonder if I was dreaming and would wake up still in Southie. During my first days in London I stayed with an American woman who was a friend of a friend of a friend. She was working for a hotel and was happy to let people crash there. I walked from one end of the city to the other, each day seeing landmarks like Big Ben before spending my nights in pubs I'd read about years before, like the legendary punk hangout the Hope and Anchor, or at nightclubs like the Wag in Soho and the Fridge in Brixton.

In Paris I spent my days at the Louvre or taking pictures at the Arc de Triomphe and nights staring at the illuminated Notre Dame, imagining medieval Paris and remembering scenes from *The Hunchback of Notre Dame*. Some days I wandered in Père-Lachaise, finding the graves of Edith Piaf and Oscar Wilde, or in Montparnasse, where Rimbaud was buried.

Once I learned to sneak onto trains, I went even farther. I'd simply hide underneath a bed in a sleeper cabin, my face pressed up against the springs under someone's mattress, breathing through a vent to the train corridor. I'd hold my breath whenever I saw a conductor coming my way. I made it to the Berlin Wall, rode a gondola in Venice, and sat with the stray cats in the Colosseum in Rome. After Spain, where my friends and I were kicked off a train in Madrid for trying to use some expired tickets we'd found, I went back to London for one more visit. I felt as if I'd seen more on this trip than I'd ever imagined seeing in my lifetime.

Even upon my return to London, it seemed as if everything had been laid out for me like magic. Everywhere I went I met people I'd only imagined seeing when I was younger. Just two nights before, I'd sneaked in to see the Damned and Johnny Thunders and the Heartbreakers try to revive their old selves. Bored, I noticed Poly Styrene from X-Ray Spex standing next to me, looking equally unimpressed by Johnny Thunders's flailing around onstage. I almost didn't recognize her. She looked like a grownup now, albeit a hippie one. I'd read somewhere that she'd become a Hindu, which explained the calming scent of sandalwood. Before long we were talking, but when I asked if I could take her picture she looked at me as if she didn't know why. When she realized that I knew her from her old self, she happily complied.

Walking through Hyde Park the next day I ran across Tessa, the bass player from the Slits, looking like a regular mom wheeling her two-year-old daughter in a stroller. She was with Neneh Cherry of the post-punk band Rip Rig & Panic. I told them how I'd learned to sneak into shows at a Slits gig and had once followed the band all the way to New York. "That's so sweet," Tessa said, sounding more like a genteel British mum than a raging teenage Slit. I hardly ever listened to music from my punk days anymore, other than the Bad Brains, which I guessed I'd listen to for the rest of my life. Most of my home-made cassettes were mixtures of music from Jamaica, old funk and soul from the seventies, or pre-punk classics like the Velvet Underground, Patti Smith, Brian Eno, and T Rex. I owed my appreciation for that range of music in part to groups like the Slits, which had broadened the definition of punk beyond a particular sound to include all those who'd ever challenged the way things were. I thought about how these regular adults walking around London had had an impact on the way I now saw the world.

But now, after a night out at the Wag, I knew I had to call home to see about borrowing money from Ma to go back to Paris before returning home. It would be another six hours, though, before I could place the call. To kill time, I walked all the way to the Portobello Road to browse in my favorite Jamaican record store. As I began to flip through the LPs, in walked Joe Strummer. I gripped my camera, then thought, *How can I treat this guy like a rock star? The point of punk was to destroy the very concept of rock star.* Joe Strummer had by then actually crossed over into the realm of rock star with the huge hit "Rock the Casbah." But I didn't want him to think I was one of *those* Americans, the ones who liked "Rock the Casbah." He bought some red, gold, and green wristbands and walked out the door. I followed him in what I hoped was a nonchalant way. "Joe! Um, Mr. Strummer!" I called after him. He turned with a smile, and I jumped right in, explaining that I wasn't a new fan, that I actually hated "Rock the Casbah," but that I'd like to take a picture of him, since "Black Market Clash" and "Sandinista" had changed my life. I realized I might have insulted him when he twitched and squinted at what I was saying. He looked like he was wondering if maybe he hadn't heard me right — he even cupped one ear forward to hear me over the dub music blasting from sidewalk speakers and the patois shouts on the Portobello Road. I repeated the part about taking his picture, and he was more than pleased to oblige. He struck a mean pose, one leg jacked up against a wall that was as orange as the screwed-up brassy hair he was sporting. We shook hands and off he went. I didn't want anything else. Just being able to tell my friends I'd met Joe Strummer was enough.

After that meeting I decided not to go back to Paris right away. I wanted to spend a few more days in London. I'd ask Ma to wire the money by ten in the morning Boston time so I could pick it up by five London time. And I knew a hostel that cost ten pounds a night, where I could hole up until I had to go back to Paris for my flight home.

"Jesus Christ, what the hell did you go over there for with no money?" Ma wasn't yelling at me, she was just screaming *to* me, since I was all the way across the Atlantic. Ma always yelled through phone lines, but whenever I called her long distance I had to pull the phone away from my ear.

"I have no money!" Ma shouted, enunciating each word. It sounded like she was cupping the mouthpiece to direct her voice. *Jesus, how bad were the phones when you were growing up?* I wanted to ask. "Mike, are you there? You're going to have to call my father and ask him for money!" Then she hung up on me. I realized she must not have been able to hear me during the last half of my call. A recording came on asking for more money. I hung up, then picked up the receiver again to call Grandpa, only to hear a British voice telling me I owed fifty pence. I had only a few pounds to my name, so I hung up again. No matter how long I waited, every time I picked up the receiver, there she was, accusing me of dodging my debt. So I fled that booth and walked a few blocks until I found another. I hated these phones. I had exactly enough change to call Grandpa and talk for five minutes. And this call had to work, since afterward I wouldn't even have money for another day's worth of coffee to keep me going.

"Ireland?" I felt sick at just the thought of it. Ireland was the last place on earth I wanted to see. And now, when I was only calling to borrow some money, Grandpa was making me promise I'd use his loan to go there. After a lifetime of plastic shamrocks and leprechauns, wisecracking, bigoted politicians named Bulger and Kelly, and a neighborhood filled with enough fear, superstition, and hatred to make medieval Paris look enlightened, I had no desire to see the corny "auld sod." I preferred to think that I'd severed myself completely from the ancestors I was sure must have been a wretched ignorant lot, in spite of Eileen Fox's airs about our lineage. But Grandpa was offering two hundred dollars, more than I'd hoped to get for the rest of my trip. I ended up promising him that I would see the land of his birth. At the same time, I couldn't figure out why he was insisting that I go, since he was always cursing the country he'd left at age nineteen as a "depressing auld fookin' place you never seen the like of."

"I never said that, you fookin' half fool!" Grandpa loved the opportunity to call anyone a half fool, which I always reminded him was better than being a whole fool.

I told Grandpa he *had* said that — and much worse — about the place. "You always said it was a lonesome old place with nothing but TB and dying cows."

Grandpa used the word "lonesome" where his American grandkids would say "depressing" or just "fucked up." But Grandpa also told me some happier stories, and after the telling, he'd look down and scratch his head underneath his cap, as if doing so would change the subject. I didn't know whether he missed Ireland, or his family, or maybe just childhood. He liked to tell the one about the first time he got lost in the mountains near his home and ate blueberries until he puked from the excitement of it. "For ever since I could walk I wanted to go up and look around from the top of them mountains," he told me. Some of his favorite stories were about the nights when his cousin Dan would sit all the younger kids around him on the floor to hear tell of ghosts, banshees, and deaths foretold, stories that would make the surrounding room disappear until they all had to snap out of their trance for the lonesome walk home along pitch-black country boreens. Grandpa said that on the walk home the slightest rustle in a ditch "would send ye running home for the life of ye."

As a child I looked forward to Grandpa's stories at tea around Nana's kitchen table. I couldn't believe that the old man in front of me with a crooked cap and slow-motion slurps of tea was once a child running up a dark boreen in wide-eyed terror. "See, there was no street lights back in those times, no lights at all," Grandpa would explain when he caught himself revealing too much weakness. "Sure, anyone would run, for there's no telling what kinds of animals was in the ditch." Stories like those had made me curious as a kid about Ireland, but by now I'd lost all interest in boreens and banshees, no matter how much I had once loved the sounds of those words. Eventually I accepted Grandpa's insistence, in his more negative moments — whenever he saw too much celebration of all things Irish — that it was a "lonesome old place with the durtiest weather you ever seen." Those moments had no stories to go with them, I noticed.

"The best thing I ever did was leave," he'd often say. And when I got older and hated all the celebrations of Irish ignorance in Southie, I'd agree with him that it must have been an awful place. Then Grandpa would turn on me, defending Ireland and threatening to kick me out of his house. One time when I woke up at his house on Saint Patrick's Day, I put on my favorite orange mohair sweater — one I had been wearing for a week — thinking I might fit in for once at the parade, since orange was part of the Irish flag. That's when he did kick me out of his house, no explanation. I knew practically nothing of William of Orange, who'd slaughtered thousands of Irish Catholics, but Grandpa had assumed I was a fan.

Grandpa never looked sure of himself when he expressed his dislike for Ireland. Eventually I would try to change the subject no matter how it came up. Now, hoping he'd wire me money so I could get by in London for a little longer, I thought Grandpa was going to come through the phone at me, shouting that I'd never step foot in his house again if I didn't go "home" to Ireland. "Home?" I asked, thrown off by his choice of words. "Ireland?"

I shook it off and explained that I was only going to stay in London for a few days before heading to Paris. He said I had no business going to England in the first place, that it was a "cruel country that never brought nothing only slavery to the Irish." I only had a few coins left for the call, so I got back to the point of me borrowing money, promising to repay him as soon as I got another job dishwashing back in Boston. Grandpa screamed that there'd be no lending of no money if I didn't go to Ireland and that I wouldn't be coming over to his house again.

My time in the big red telephone box was running out, and the voice telling me so sounded like the queen herself. "Your call will be terminated in thirty seconds," said the proper, judgmental voice, drowning Grandpa's culchie brogue. And even though he was calling me a "son of a bitch of a bastard," I was distracted long enough to notice how much I liked Grandpa's brogue over the queen's English. Grandpa waited for the recording to go away before confirming that it was a horrible accent she had. "Jesus, Mary, and Joseph, isn't that a horrible way to fookin' talk," Grandpa said under his breath, as if the recorded lady might be listening. He carried on, saying again that he didn't know what I was doing in England anyway. He said the British were "awful, long-faced fools" who had built their empire on the backs of the Irish. Hoping to make him less agitated, I told him I'd met some good English people and that many of them hated the queen as much as he did. "Sure, aren't they all the same," he said. "Anytime an Irish man trusted an English, wasn't it the death of him?" He said he'd never met a good Englishman, and I came close to reminding him that he'd probably never met *any* Englishmen, having lived only in counties Kerry and Boston.

Grandpa's occasional bouts of Irish nationalism were always a surprise to me, and I was struck by just how much it meant to him that I go to Ireland. I deposited more of the odd-shaped, heavy British coins into the telephone when Grandpa added that I should meet Nana's people in Donegal, since his own in Kerry were dead or had emigrated. "Wasn't Nana good to you?" he reminded me. His voice was cracking and sounded tired from all the excitement. Then, out of the blue, he said he had to go and hung up, an odd habit he had of cutting off a conversation before it was done. No goodbyes. Sometimes he'd say he had to run to the toilet before abruptly hanging up, but this time there wasn't even that excuse. And I still needed to borrow money. So I called him back, collect. After saying yes to the charges in a subdued and polite manner, put on for the British operator's live voice of authority, Grandpa started right in again. "Isn't it an awful fookin' shame you don't want to see Glen Mackee where Nana was reared?"

I knew then I would be taking a train and a boat to Ireland. I'd go for a few days, get it over with, and still have money left for a few nights out in London and Paris. Later, on the trek across town to a Western Union for Grandpa's loan and then to Euston Station to buy my ticket west, I thought about Nana for the first time in years, and how much I'd like to see her again. I felt, in a way, that that was exactly what I would be doing in Ireland. I decided to make the most of my bargain with Grandpa by trying to bring to life those vibrant images of Ireland's boreens and banshees from stories passed down.

"Aren't the Americans mad for finding their roots?" *Roots?* I thought. I knew the expression only from the Alex Haley movie. My mother's cousin Dennis, in London, meant well by the question, but it pissed me off to think that he would mistake me for someone at all interested in my "Irish roots." I couldn't tell him I was only going to his mother's in Donegal because I had been bribed by Grandpa. I had looked him up because I had a day to kill before leaving for Ireland. Also, though he and his wife were from Ireland, I knew they had kids my age who were English and raised in London, which was much cooler to me than Ireland. Dennis said he remembered Ma coming over to Donegal with her accordion at the age of seventeen. "Your w'an was wild," he remembered fondly. Ma loved to tell everyone how she got the Donegal side of her family all up in arms because she had hit on her cousin Dennis by the fireside during an evening of song and story. On that same trip she'd gone off entertaining with the "tinkers," causing more stir among her mother's relatives. "I fit in more with the Kerry crowd," Ma liked to say, which meant nothing to me.

Dennis's wife, May, came into the kitchen, tying on an apron before rummaging through pots and pans to make a feed. "I suppose you'll be looking for your roots," she piped in by way of introduction. When they first invited me over for "tea," I thought they meant a cup of tea, maybe two cups. But "tea" meant three kinds of meat, five boiled potatoes, and about five cups of tea. May told me they'd be seeing me in Donegal, as they always went home for a month's vacation in August. Their daughter, Jackie, rolled her eyes at the thought of having to spend another August in Donegal.

"Wot's all this about roots, then?" Jackie asked, examining me from across the kitchen table. I couldn't believe I had a cousin with the London accent I'd admired for so many years. I shrugged my shoulders, explaining I'd never heard of the roots thing.

"Yanks are mad for their roots," May explained to her. "Isn't that the truth?" she asked, slapping me on the shoulder and looking for backup. She said they were known to be all over Ireland with maps and family trees trying to find out where their ancestors came from. "Sure, you could tell them anything and they'd believe you." Everyone laughed at the Yanks.

"So, wot's this?" Jackie asked incredulously. "They actually *like* Ireland?"

"You keep your filthy English trap shut, you," May said, laughing and waving a big wooden spoon at her daughter. "You should have seen this one," May said to me, pointing at Jackie and pulling up a chair for a break from the boiling on the stove. "Go ahead and tell him, Dennis!" she said, knowing that he'd shrug his shoulders and defer to her to tell the story. "This one," she said, pointing at Jackie with the wooden spoon again. "Here we are in Donegal, about twenty of us." She stopped to count on her fingers. "Let's see, me, Dennis, the three children, Patrick and Sheila, their two boys, Rose and Oweney and their two boys, Packie Noel, his wife, his mother, Susan — that would be your granny's sister now — Dennis's mother, Elizabeth — she's your granny's sister too."

Dennis interrupted, "Christ Almighty, wouldja tell the story, you're doing his head in!"

"Anyway," she continued, "here's us, singing songs, some of us full with the drink, and the craic was mighty. And here were these young fellas from Derry singing the old rebel songs. And we're all taking turns singing a song. Oh, the craic! Wasn't that some craic, Dennis?" Dennis just shrugged again, then nodded in agreement when he got a wave of the big wooden spoon. "So this here republican fella from Derry looks to Jackie and tells her, 'Give us a song.' And what does this one say?" She went back to the boiling pots and told Jackie to tell the rest of the story, which Jackie didn't seem to know. May came back to the table, wiping her hands with her apron. She sat on the edge of a chair. "This one here opens her mouth with the bloody English accent and a sour puss and says, 'Oy don't know any Oyrish songs.' Well, the whole room went silent," May said, "and that was the end of the craic. I thought we'd be found dead in a field, so help me God."

Everyone got a kick out of that story except me. I didn't really get it. I just looked around and smiled at these cousins I'd never met and hoped for some information from the younger ones about good clubs for non-Irish music in Ireland. I knew there had been a good music scene, with bands like Stiff Little Fingers and the Undertones, and I figured there might be at least a tolerable club for new bands or DJs. Dennis asked if I was looking forward to seeing Ireland, and I said I was, unable to say much more.

May stirred the pot and nodded in my direction. "Well, what do you think?" she asked Dennis, as if he'd asked a stupid question. "Sure, the Yanks are mad for their roots," she said, repeating the refrain to keep the conversation going when it seemed like things might go quiet — just like Ma and most of my relatives had always done.

On the bus ride from Dublin to Donegal town, I almost forgot how much I resented having to go to Ireland. I'd never bothered much with scenery before, though on most drives Ma always had to comment about any place with water or grass that it looked just like Ireland. The bus window's framed view bounced and shook constantly with every pothole or mound. But I couldn't take my eyes off the passing scene. Waterfalls spilled, twisted, and leapt from the greenest hills imaginable. I'd thought the bit about Ireland being really green was a lie, like every other fantasy I'd heard about the place. The people with the biggest imaginations about Ireland were the ones who'd never been there, it seemed. I thought I was hallucinating myself now, especially whenever we passed another bearded mountain goat standing nearly sideways on a craggy slope. The rickety bus must have been built in the sixties. It was like our school buses in America, hard plastic seats and all. But it barreled along narrow roads that hadn't been paved in years. I held on to the seat in front of me. When I saw that a few teenagers were getting a kick out of the Yank who couldn't take his eye off the goats, I became self-conscious. "The fookin' head's gonna spin right off of him," one said. I guessed they were used to all this.

I couldn't imagine growing up in a place like this instead of Old Colony Project. To me it was like being in a cartoon or a dream: that shade of green I'd never imagined, the bearded goats, the clouds that seemed to move faster than the speeding bus, breaking open to funnel columns of sun, like searchlights that raced across faraway fields. One minute the sky threatened rain, and in no time the sun broke through just for our bus, while clouds across the glen got blacker still and moved away. Then, right after an ancient woman behind me laughed about "the Yank bringing the fine weather with him," a sudden downpour hit without any warning drops. "Durty, durty auld fookin' day," muttered the bent-over farmer passing me in the aisle with a smile and a sideways jerk of the head, like he was proud to be telling me the surest thing he knew.

In Cavan a woman climbed onto the bus and handed me her baby before heading back down the steps with the bus driver to load bundles and a pram. The bus took off again over bumps and holes, and I held the tiny infant while its mother brushed her wet hair and redid her kerchief on the seat behind me. I kept looking back toward her but didn't want to seem bothered; I kind of liked being welcomed into the family, realizing how differently I had felt as a tourist in London and Paris, more like an outsider looking in. I guessed the mother might have thought I was Irish. She asked me what part was I from. "I'm from the States," I told her, and she got a great kick out of that one with everyone else on the bus. "Fook sake, sure I know that," she said. "What part?"

The bus stopped bumping, and we were on a good road when suddenly we were pulled over by soldiers. "Jesus Christ, gimme that there child. They'll probably think you've planted something in her. Jesus, why'd you have to wear that American hooded thing. And it's fookin' green! They'll think you're Noraid, for fook sake." I looked down at my green hooded sweatshirt. The old lady who said I'd brought the five minutes of fine weather shook her head and laughed with the others until the soldiers stepped on board. Everyone came to a complete silence, looking straight ahead like they didn't notice the soldiers in camouflage carrying machine guns. I'd never seen anything like it. My heart pounded and I felt guilty — for what, I didn't know, but I sure as hell didn't want to get caught. I knew nothing about the Troubles in the North other than that Catholics and Protestants couldn't get along and that the Northern Aid guys from Southie were in on some of the bank robberies and gun smuggling to the IRA. I'd never wanted any part of it. As far as I was concerned, the Catholics were probably the bad guys. They had to be, since so many racists from Southie supported them. At the end of my street in Old Colony was a mural portraying an IRA sharpshooter on bended knee, taking aim. So many times, passing that mural after another death in the neighborhood, I fantasized about scrawling over it DON'T WE HAVE OUR OWN TROUBLES? But I wouldn't dare. The Noraid guys were no joke.

"American?" the soldier asked, and I nodded, my heart racing, blood pumping like I'd suddenly been found out. A big knot took hold in my gut. He asked me to step off the bus and to bring any luggage from the rack above. I thought I was finished, never to be seen again. I had to remind myself that I wasn't a criminal or a terrorist. *I know nothing about this Catholic and Protestant shit,* I wanted to tell him, but he might be a Protestant, so I better keep the Protestants out of it. *But it might be too obvious if I curse the Catholics, like I'm trying too hard to distance myself from the IRA. And then, if it works, I'll probably be dumped by the Catholics on board in a mass grave.* So I said nothing. I grabbed my bag from above and thought how much I hated Grandpa for sending me to his backward, screwed-up country. The others on the bus barely looked at me. They seemed only slightly bothered, like this was an everyday occurrence and they were going to be late getting home, once again.

Three soldiers with machine guns led me to the side of the road. I handed over my passport, and one of them took it to a Land Rover to call in the information. "South Boston, eh?" he yelled back at me.

"Yeah," I said, scowling, like I wanted them to know I was ashamed of it.

"So, wot, you on 'olidays, mate?" I nodded. " 'Ow long?" The one asking the questions acted all friendly-like while another soldier searched through my bag. "Donegal? Wot you going to do there?"

I honestly didn't know. I'd never been there before. *Look for rainbows and leprechauns? Drink tea? What the fuck am I do-*

ing here anyway? I said I was going to meet my grandmother's sister, who was about ninety.

"Sounds lovely, mate," said the soldier as he handed me my bag. "I suppose you're looking for your roots, then." The soldiers all laughed and motioned for me to get back on the bus.

The driver looked at me like the delay was all my fault and shut the door, mumbling something about "black bastards." None of the soldiers was even black. I figured the Irish were so racist they called everyone they didn't like "black bastards" whether they were black or not.

"Ach, ye don't mind, do ye," said the woman, putting the sleeping baby back in my lap so she could apply her makeup. At this point I didn't want to be part of the family — I was done with Ireland. *I should have stayed in London or gone back to Paris.* I thought how James Joyce was right to leave this place and never want to return; the same for Samuel Beckett. The way I felt about Southie and Old Colony.

I asked the woman how she knew I was American in the first place. "Th' fook," she said, looking me up and down, "look at the size of ye! Tell ye one thing, the food must be very good over there. Plus youse are always coming over here with the big bright green jumpers. I bet ye have a big Aran jumper too in that there bag, and maybe some tartan pants to go with it." I forced a laugh with everyone else, picturing the types they were talking about — the retired Irish Americans in Hyannis with their plaids and Irish knit sweaters wrapped around their shoulders, all fresh and clean as a whistle, like the ads for Irish Spring. Little did my fellow travelers know that my bright green hoodie was pure accident. That it was all I had with me for the rain. And that I hated the Irish.

"Ach, I'm only slaggin'," she assured me, reaching over my head to take her baby back.

We arrived at Donegal town after passing back through the border into what some passengers called the "free state." There were no more British soldiers or Land Rovers and tanks out the window, and the roads were bumpy again. I'd always assumed that Donegal was in Northern Ireland, since it was the most northern county on the map. But the people getting off in Fermanagh, who told me they'd only crossed the border to the "free state" for some cheap shopping, referred to Donegal as the "free state" too, when I told them I was going there. They assured me I'd have a good time and there'd be no black bastards to ruin my holidays. I didn't even fake a laugh at that one. I hadn't seen one black person — or even a tan person — in all of Ireland and still, here were the Irish, carrying on all racist.

"Last stop! Donegal town!" the driver barked, coming to a screeching halt. When I got off the bus I was spooked by the sight of Nana everywhere. All different versions of her, though: fat ones, tall and lanky ones, even male Nanas. They all had the same face, high cheekbones like American Indians and wide-set, sharp eyes, squinting like they were bothered by the slightest bit of sunlight, even in cloudy Ireland. There was Nana buying vegetables in an open-air market. Nana was selling the vegetables too. There she was driving a tractor. Even the kids running in circles around another Nana's hips and grabbing on to her housecoat had the face of my grandmother. I was in a country that I wanted no part of. I was around people I liked to think I had nothing in common with. Only most of them had this face I knew like I knew my own.

I had to wonder if they knew I was one of them. As a kid sitting at Grandpa's table with all the aunts and listening to them banter over whether I was the spitting image of George Fox or if I was more like Nana's people, I always wanted to vote for the Nana team. After going to my father's funeral and being told by so many that I was like him back from the grave, I couldn't ignore the facts. But I liked to think Grandpa was right when he told me I had the same "ways" as Nana, something in my expression. And that's partly what I was seeing all over Donegal town, something familiar but not necessarily on the surface, like a nose or a walk. It was deeper than that. Besides Nana's features, which I saw on every corner, everyone seemed to have her "ways."

I wondered about my disposition, which everyone said was quiet, and about Nana's calm, easygoing nature. When Nana was alive we'd often catch sight of each other in the midst of a ruckus between Grandpa and Ma, and we'd sneak a laugh, especially when Grandpa was telling Ma she was never any good from the day she was born or when Ma would tell Grandpa he was a dirty rotten piece of shit that never cared about anyone but himself. Nana had this calm habit of rocking from side to side and twiddling her thumbs, which drove Ma to the brink but reassured me that everything was all right.

My aunt Rita said that, like Nana, I was always able to see humor in the midst of chaos. But they didn't see me in later years, when I was always nervous, running to doctors, or walking the streets of Boston all hours of the night just so I could think. Like Nana, the people in Donegal town, on the border and just down the road from the "armored cars and tanks and guns" of one of Ma's songs, looked like nothing bothered them either. And in spite of the soldier episode, I wasn't feeling a bit nervous anymore, what with the sight of Nana everywhere.

After walking to the bus station, which looked more like a shed, I found out there'd be no more buses that day to Inishowen, where all the addresses I had in my bag were located. None of the addresses included a street or a house number, only a name, townland, and county. Ma had told me that hitchhiking was an everyday thing in Ireland, so I walked to the road that headed north and put out my thumb. I'd gotten rid of the bright green hoodie and was now wearing a T-shirt — even though it was pouring rain — so as not to be tagged as a Yank so easily. I figured an Irish person would get picked up sooner than a stranger. The driver of the first car to come my way pulled over and threw open the door. A man who looked too fat for his tiny Mini leaned toward the flung-open door and shouted at me to get in. I jumped in out of the cold rain, breathing a sigh of relief. "Ach, some holidays for ye! I wasn't going to stop for anyone today, but seeing as you were a Yank I figured I'd give you a lift."

"How'd you know I was American?" I asked. I knew it wasn't the "big guy with the bright green jumper" thing. My T-shirt was a drab gray, and he was fatter than any American I'd ever seen. "Don't know," he said. "Yer a big fella," he added, looking at me like he didn't really want to break it to me. *The fat fucker,* I thought. *Seems all the Irish ever do is welcome you in so they can insult you.*

The driver's name was Martin. I told him I was going to Carndonagh and I was looking for some O'Donnells up there. "Half the county is O'Donnell!" he said, shaking with laughter. He said he'd only be going as far as Letterkenny. "But I know a man that do be going to Carndonagh every day," he assured me. "We'll call in to him on the off chance he's going up there today." *But why would he do that?* I thought. *Escort me from one lift to another when we'd just met?* Now I was nervous again, reminded that I was near a contentious border. I spent the rest of the hour's journey figuring out how to escape going into the house of some stranger who was supposedly going to Carndonagh.

The sky went black, and the tiny car rocked with the rising winds. We pulled up to a farmhouse and Martin walked in after two taps on the door, just like anyone could do at our apartment in Old Colony before Frankie was killed. I rolled down the car window to hear if the yelling inside was friendly, like they were family or had known each other forever. Martin had a booming voice, but I couldn't make out much of what was being said. The people inside weren't speaking Gaelic, but the words ran into each other so fast that they might as well have been. I was more used to the *dun-derrun-derrun!* downward-thumping cadence of Grandpa's Kerry accent; a few times I'd even had to translate to shopkeepers who thought he wasn't speaking English. But the Donegal accent was harder. It was more of a *dee-duru-duru?!*, each utterance sounding like both a question and exclamation. I could only make out "Yank" every once in a while, and every time I heard it Martin stared out the kitchen window, looking at me and scratching his head. Before long an older couple stood in the doorway to get a look at me, motioning to each other in all directions and saying something about O'Donnells, as if they were trying to figure out whether I was related to someone in one of these hills. But there was no other house in sight. Martin came running out through the rain to tell me they'd like me in for tea, and he rubbed his hands together like it was one of those "teas" that meant a feed. I felt a little standoffish, but I hadn't much choice. And none of these people seemed to be in a rush to do anything besides figure out who my cousins might be.

I assumed they'd serve a few biscuits or maybe sandwiches for the "tea." But by the time I got my bag out of the back seat and made my way into the kitchen, the table was spread for a full dinner, with three kinds of meat cooking on the stove and a boiling pot of spuds. Martin was already seated and digging into the first course of sandwiches. Throughout the feast with strangers, the actual tea for which the ritual was named flowed endlessly.

I hadn't eaten during the whole day's journey north from Dublin, and I was trying to be polite, eat slowly, and make conversation by asking questions once in a while. But the older couple — who sat away from the table, watching Martin and me eat — didn't say much except to urge me to "eat up now, God only knows when you'll eat again. Sure, it's a long road ahead." Whenever they spoke to me, they spoke at a normal speed. But mostly they talked to each other, and their words came so fast that I couldn't make out what they were saying. But I enjoyed listening, because every sentence had that rhythm and ended with the uplifted note of a question and an exclamation of certainty. They sounded like they were sure of whatever they were saying, like no one could tell them any different. Their sentences twisted and turned like the roads I'd traveled from Dublin to Donegal. I listened mesmerized, no longer trying to make sense of it all.

They asked me what were the first names of the O'Donnells I was related to. "Well, some might be Doughertys," I said. "Sure, most of Donegal is O'Donnell or Dougherty," asserted the old woman, whose name I still didn't know, even though I was eating her food. I told them the cousins' names I'd always heard, like Rose and Patrick, which didn't help much. I asked if I could use their phone to call my grandfather collect. But they had no phone and didn't know anyone nearby who did. The old man said he'd take me to some O'Donnells he knew of in Clonmany who were probably my relations. "That's it," I said, "Clonmany," suddenly sure of the name I'd often heard. Taking a final chug of tea, Martin said he'd better be off, and he left me in the care of the old couple.

On the drive to Carndonagh I learned from the old man that he barely knew Martin. They had only known each other "to say hello" a few times over the years, even though Martin seemed to know all about the man's daily drive to Carndonagh.

The old man drove me up a long driveway, explaining, "Patrick O'Donnell lives here and he'll look after ye well.

"Packie, this here Yank belongs to you," he called out to the old man running toward us. Patrick O'Donnell shook my hand and took me inside. "Well," his wife said, greeting me. In minutes another feed was being laid out on the table, and seeing the old couple run around the kitchen for me, I didn't have the heart to tell them I'd already eaten. They sat away from the table watching me eat and questioning me about this relation and that relation. None of the people they mentioned were familiar to me. And each time I said a name they looked at each other perplexed. Halfway through the meal we realized they weren't the O'Donnells I was looking for at all. I stood up as if I'd made a terrible mistake, but they looked offended that I might be getting ready to leave. "Work away," they said, motioning at the plate in front of me. As filled up as I was, by the way they stared at me eating I knew it would be an insult not to eat everything they'd offered. Patrick O'Donnell figured out who my cousins were, but he was in no rush to get rid of me. We sat talking and drinking cup of tea after cup of tea, each one bringing me back to the extra-sweet cups Nana had always made me as a kid.

When I finally got to the house of my mother's cousin Patrick in Anaugh, the next townland over from Clonmany, his wife, Sheila, looked hurt when I turned down another meal. But I simply let out the truth that I'd already been fed twice by complete strangers. I agreed only to some more cups of tea. Then Dennis and May walked into the house, having arrived from London for their August holiday, and everyone sat around asking me questions about America.

"Is it true they drink green beer on Saint Patrick's Day?" the teenage son, Patrick, asked.

"Is it true the craic is something ye smoke over there?" another teenage cousin from down the road asked, just walking through the door and throwing herself into the conversation.

"And what's all this, what do you call it . . . corned beef and cabbage?" Rose's husband Oweney piped in before changing his question: "What is it ye call trainers? Sneakers?"

I found out that the Irish didn't really celebrate Saint Paddy's the way they did in Southie but that they were starting to bring in the green beer as an American thing, along with over-the-top parades. But corned beef, Oweney told me, was basically meat you might feed to the dog.

Then came the question that made me almost fall out of my chair. "Is it true youse Irish Americans hate the blacks?" asked Big Patrick, as he was referred to, puffing on his pipe. I was shocked at being questioned as a racist by an Irish man. I listened frozen as my cousin said he'd heard all kinds of terrible things about American Irish being racists.

"You *don't* hate black people?" I asked. They all looked at each other confused.

"Sure, there's no blacks here, but still it's a terrible thing to imagine how they be treated in America," Nana's oldest sister, Elizabeth, offered, speaking slowly from a table in the middle of the room. I knew Elizabeth had lived in America, having moved to Cambridge when she was eighteen, and had worked to bring Nana and her sister over before deciding to go back to Ireland.

"So if a black person walked by, across that field," I said, pointing at the glen and realizing how unlikely that would be, "what would you do?" They looked at each other and laughed, not because it was so unlikely but because they didn't understand why there'd be anything to do over it. "There would be in Southie," I told them. "He might not make it out alive." I told them I'd thought racism was an Irish thing, "like green beer and plastic green shamrocks." They agreed it was an awful thing, racism. Young Patrick added that it was no different than how the Catholics were being treated over the border, "not far from here," he added.

But I pushed them further, asking, "Would you talk to a black person walking across that glen?"

"Well, I suppose it'd be strange to see an African out there in that there glen," Big Patrick said. "I did meet a man once, a tourist in Dublin, and he was as black as that there stove — from Africa he was — and he was the nicest man you'd ever want to meet."

Sheila added that anyone who walks by her house is invited in for tea. "And that would go for a black fella just as well. Aye, surely! If he were black as soot."

"What about all the talk I've heard of 'black bastards' in this country, even though you never see black people here?" I asked, which made everyone laugh.

Patrick explained that the term referred to the Royal Black

Preceptory. "Protestant loyalists to the Crown of England," he said, adding that they were a bigoted brotherhood like the Orange Order. "Them and anyone else who want to run the Irish out of Ireland," he added.

I was speechless. I had come here expecting to meet the original Irish racist, in the motherland of all ignorance I'd ever known, and was instead hearing of the shame felt over the stories of Irish American racism.

"So you'd invite him in for tea?" I asked hours later, after another meal, about ten cups of tea, and five whiskeys. No one knew who I was referring to.

"The black guy!" I said.

On my second day in Donegal, I walked out of Rose and Oweney's, where I was staying, and stopped to taunt the geese. They chased me halfway down the hill as I set out on the main road to Carndonagh. It was "just down the road," my cousins said, but down the road meant a good five miles away. As soon as I set out, though, a stranger in a car offered a lift. And so did a second and a third, and finally I gave in and accepted. Before long the driver was asking me who I belonged to. "Let me see," she said, "that would mean you're my . . . ," and then she started calculating in her head until she came up with "fourth cousin." But she said it casually, and she dropped me off with nothing more than a "good luck," as if it weren't the most amazing thing to have just met a complete stranger you shared an ancestor with.

By the third day I knew you couldn't set out on a walk without being offered a lift wherever you were going. But I was determined to walk to Carndonagh this time because I was thinking a lot about Nana and picturing her walking this very road and seeing these very hills. A farmer delayed me for fifteen minutes with nothing more than the directions to Carndonagh. I knew the directions to Carndonagh: straight ahead. But I'd learned by now that it was true — Irish people loved to talk, and they'd turn the simplest directions into a beautiful story.

After three days in Ireland I never wanted to leave. It was a strange thing to traipse through muddy fields where I knew family had walked for hundreds, thousands, maybe millions of years. I said yes immediately when Big Patrick put on his Wellingtons and offered to take me to Glen Mackee, where Nana and her sister Elizabeth and five other brothers and sisters were reared. It was on a hill so far removed, and the bumpy road took so many twists and turns this way and that, that I had no idea where we were in relation to the landscape that had already become so familiar to me.

When we got to Glen Mackee, Patrick called out to the old man who'd bought the land years before. I saw what remained of the old, whitewashed stone house Nana had grown up in, which now served as sheds for a big modern house that was attached. Suddenly I felt like I couldn't talk to anyone because my face hurt from holding in my crying, even though I wasn't sad about anything. The glens of Nana's childhood play were lined with trees that led down toward a stream I could hear gurgling below. When Patrick handed me a nut from one of the trees, I stood stunned, remembering Nana's stories of these hazelnut trees — stories I'd forgotten until this very moment — and her promise that someday she'd take me home to eat from them. I'd never tasted a hazelnut before; it wasn't sweet yet and tasted only the way the air smelled, like fresh water from a stream, and dirt.

"Them nuts is meant to give you great wisdom and healing when you eat them," laughed the old man who now lived on Glen Mackee. "Go ahead," he said. "Work away."

"Which one do you fancy?" my cousin Michael was asking me, pointing to a table full of girls our age. *Fancy?* It sounded so old-fashioned to me, even more old-fashioned than everyone in Donegal's calling the dance club the "disco." I fancied none of them, because they looked too much like the girls in Southie — pretty, but too tough, like they might belt you if you said the wrong thing. I ended up talking to a girl who looked a little different from everyone else, as if she'd grown up on punk music. Maybe it was because she leaned on the bar looking bored by the Duran Duran song being played.

"Do you have to show ID here to drink?" I asked. She laughed at that one. It seemed like all the kids in the room were drinking openly, so I ordered a pint of beer. Mary said she was from Derry, so I decided to ask why every sign I'd seen called the Northern Ireland city "Londonderry" while everyone here referred to it as Derry. Her answer was so volatile that I didn't understand a word she said. Her northern Irish lilt rose to crescendos of rage and exclamation, and her face looked like she wanted to rip my head off for asking the question. I wanted to walk away then, but instead I asked her to speak more slowly. What I got that night was the entire history of the town of Derry, which included language about "British occupation," "uprisings," "civil rights," and even "racism." *Racism?* I thought. *But both sides are white.* I decided to keep that puzzle to myself, lest she loose another fit.

"So why do people fight over religion, anyway?" I asked casually, thinking it an innocent enough question, until I got a finger poking my chest along with accusations I couldn't understand about "youse Yanks" not understanding anything.

"I don't want to understand anything," I protested, explaining that I was only making casual conversation. She shouted that it wasn't about religion at all, that the Catholics were the colonized Irish who got the shit jobs and shit housing and that the Protestant ascendancy were the Scottish and English planted by the Crown and that they considered themselves English and wanted the North to remain part of Britain. Then she said something about us Yanks treating the blacks just as bad. Before I could argue that I wasn't like that, or change the subject to the Thompson Twins song playing and how bad music had gotten lately, she recited her family's litany of tragedies, including an uncle who was in jail, interned by the Brits, and a brother who was shot dead by loyalists.

By the end of the night, my head felt split open by Mary's

accounts of trauma after trauma suffered by family and neighbors. I didn't have to understand half of what she was saying in her Derry accent. By now I recognized the way she looked and probably felt. Her hectic fits of anger and sadness and laughter were the same combination of feelings I'd known for the past six years of my life, through all the deaths in my own family and neighborhood. Feelings I mostly kept to myself, since no one I knew from the world beyond Southie had experienced anything remotely close. I wasn't a smoker, but that night I smoked cigarette after cigarette, since Mary followed the Irish custom of handing you a cigarette every time they lit one for themselves. And after a few coughing fits, it felt good to connect through cigarettes. When I finally told Mary my own family's litany of tragedies, she didn't flinch the way girls had in the past or make light of it by talking about "white trash," like my family was kitschy and fun.

By closing time I told my cousin Mickey which one I fancied, and he said he'd never seen her around these parts before. She had no phone, so we agreed to meet the next day in Carndonagh. For the rest of my stay in Donegal I hitched regularly to Carndonagh for more of Mary's history lessons. As I learned about the troubles in Derry and got closer to someone who'd experienced them but also was aware of the history, geography, and politics of it all, I thought I might want to move to Derry to settle down. But I knew that wasn't possible. People were fleeing Ireland by the droves to find work in the States. So as the days wore on I got more and more distant from Mary until I disappeared. I'd lost enough people in my life and didn't want to lose any more.

It was a two-mile walk to the nearest phone, Rose said, but I needed to call home. It was the sixth anniversary of Davey's death. Being in Ireland had made me think of him often, since he'd spent a few months here before he got sick. After Davey ran away from home and started to get into trouble, Ma thought Ireland would be good for him. She had sent him to stay with her cousin Dan Murphy down in Kerry. After being in this country for just a few days, I couldn't imagine that it hadn't been good for him. I couldn't see anything bad happening here. Then I remembered Ma once saying that Davey had run away from Dan Murphy's, gone to Northern Ireland, and been arrested by the police. I had felt the tension in the air in the North, and after hearing Mary's stories, I wanted to find out more about Davey's experience. I couldn't wait to call home, and now I had an excuse other than my usual anxiety. All day I'd resisted the urge to call, though, and it was a good thing, because I'd felt it first at about noon — six in the morning at home. Ma would have been pissed off if I'd called that early to ask if everyone was still alive. It had been a few months since my last worried call home. Now it was almost eleven at night in Ireland, and I couldn't sleep. I knew I'd be up all night unless I called.

The two-mile walk down a winding country road with tall hedges and no sidewalk was blacker than any that Grandpa had ever described in story. I wasn't sure I'd see a phone booth unless I tripped over it. On the edge of a field I finally saw the silhouette of a rectangular shape blacker than the night around it. No one at home would ever believe me when I told them the phone had no rotary dial. I didn't know what to do with it at first, but then I remembered, from a *Beverly Hillbillies* episode I'd seen as a kid, that each number was given by the number of clicks of the lever. But I didn't know how to indicate zero to get the operator, so I just kept clicking continuously. Sure enough, a woman's voice came through, sounding groggy, like I'd woken her. She sounded like just any woman in her kitchen, and when I apologized for waking her she explained she was the operator and asked would I like to make a call. I gave her Ma's number so she could do the dialing and ask Ma if she'd accept the charges.

"Oh, sure, operator, is he there?" Ma yelled. "Mike!"

When I said hello, Ma and the operator kept talking like they couldn't hear me.

"Well he was here a minute ago, so he was," the operator said.

"Hello!" I yelled, but they carried on without me.

"Where are you from?" Ma asked the operator.

"Carndonagh," she said.

"Hello!" I screamed again, hoping they might hear even a trace of my voice. I looked around at the blackness beyond the now lighted booth, thinking about the walk home after a useless attempt at calling Ma.

"For God's sake, that's where my mother's from!" Ma shouted, excited, like she and the operator were long-lost cousins. Even in Boston Ma always acted like it was an amazing coincidence to meet someone from Ireland. And now she was talking to someone from a small town filled with her mother's people.

"Hello!" I shouted, not wanting to give up so soon. I started clicking the lever over and over, since I had no idea what it had done in the first place to get the operator.

The operator asked Ma what was her mother's name and her mother's mother's name and whether her mother's mother married this O'Donnell or that O'Donnell, and Ma kept up with her, and before long the two of them figured out that they were third or fourth or fifth cousins, depending on how you count generations. (The Irish operator introduced the whole new concept of "once removed," which threw Ma off, but before long Ma was referring to her and the operator as just "cousins.")

"Can you hear me?" I screamed into the mouth of the phone, cupping it with both hands. "Hello!"

The conversation went on for forty minutes, with Ma getting into whether this or that person she'd met when she was eighteen had ended up in a good marriage or a bad marriage or had stayed a bachelor or run off with another woman to Australia or America — "an Irish divorce," as she called it. Ma and the operator got on like a house on fire, and the conversation could have carried on all night, until Ma turned the questions to the operator's love life and whether she was in a good marriage or a bad marriage or no marriage at all. That's when the operator quickly started wondering, "Where's the boy gone to?"

"Well, did he sound all right?" Ma said.

"Ach, he sounded grand!" said the operator. "So he did," she added.

"Well, that's all that matters, isn't it?" Ma said.

"Aye, surely," the operator agreed.

"How's he looking?" Ma asked. I thought that one was ridiculous but was floored when the operator actually had a report to give, saying she hadn't seen me herself but that she'd heard from her sister's husband, who'd crossed paths with me on the Carndonagh road two days earlier, that I was "in good form." Ma always said you can't take a shit in Ireland without everyone knowing, and now I knew what she meant. It was like the grapevine in Southie, only worse.

The two cousins said their farewells, and Ma told her to say hello to this cousin and that cousin. "Mother of God, wasn't it strange to meet this way, to get a call like this out of the blue." As if I had nothing to do with it. "Hello!" I attempted one last time before they hung up.

"Operator!" Ma screamed, and I thought she'd heard my shouts.

"What is it?" the operator said, a bit startled by Ma's urgent tone.

"You're not going to charge me for this, are you?"

"Och, no!" she laughed, and the two of them hung up.

On the walk back through the blackness I couldn't get over that my family had come from this strange but familiar place. There wasn't even a passing car to light the road occasionally.

There was complete silence and the peaceful echoes of crickets in fields that were too black even to look at, for fear of what else was in there besides crickets, what ghosts.

"Now don't be talking to anyone strange on the train to Belfast," my cousin May warned me, laughing, as if she wanted to scare me about Catholics and Protestants at war. "You never know who you'll be talking to on the other side of that border," she said more seriously. I was crowded into the back seat with Sheila, Big Patrick, Little Patrick, and another cousin I'd just met, on the way to Derry to be dropped off for the train to Belfast, where I'd board the boat to England. I looked out the window at the landscape and weather constantly playing with each other in ways that could almost make you forget everything else. But if it was one thing I had learned on this trip it was that the Irish forget nothing, even across generations. Even in Southie, where most of us Irish Americans knew nothing about this place, we still somehow remembered that you never surrender the fight.

As we drove through Derry, I was getting a tour of the town's history. The streets looked so much like Southie's that I couldn't help but make comparisons between the two places. Listening to my cousins, I thought how shocked my neighbors would be to find out that the Irish Catholics they claimed allegiance with identified as much with American blacks. May pointed out a gable wall that had been painted with the words YOU ARE NOW ENTERING FREE DERRY during the Battle of the Bogside in 1969. At the height of the civil rights movement to gain access to fair housing and the right to vote, residents had barricaded the Bogside — a neighborhood of housing projects — against violent incursions by loyalists and the police. The Battle of the Bogside sounded like Southie's busing riots of the seventies. But in Derry the people organized marches modeled on the black civil rights movement in America and ended up having to barricade their neighborhood, while in Southie my neighbors, under siege from a forced busing policy that pitted poor whites against poor blacks, lined our streets to shout at passing buses, "Niggers go home!"

At one point May cursed Prime Minister Margaret Thatcher out loud. When I asked, "So you don't vote for Thatcher back in London?" she answered with no hesitation, "I'd choke the bitch as soon as look at her." I wondered why people in Ireland, and in England too, knew their place and where they stood in relation to their politicians, while at home my neighbors on welfare had voted for Reagan.

The medieval walls of the old city towered above the streets where fourteen unarmed civilians were shot and killed in 1972 by British soldiers on the day known as Bloody Sunday. Now, on the sidewalks below those fortress walls walked people who looked exactly like my Southie neighbors: tough Irish faces, uptight hairstyles, and jogging suits. It amazed me to see such familiarity alongside murals depicting uprisings and a history that spoke of solidarity with American blacks.

From the train window I waved to a group of relatives I'd never cared to meet. May followed alongside the moving train, laughing and shouting something that sounded like another slag, which I now recognized as a high art form of affectionate insult reserved for people you felt safe with. Later, passing cattle that watched unmoved as the train raced by, soaring above the rocky cliffs and crashing waves of the Antrim coast, I wished I could delay my arrival in Belfast and with it my departure from a country that had begun to feel better than home.

I was strip-searched for explosives before getting on the boat to England, which was carrying hundreds of British soldiers home for their August holiday. From Liverpool the next morning, I crossed the gray, smoggy British countryside by train back to Piccadilly and Soho, where I wandered, killing time and missing Ireland. I looked forward to getting back to Boston just so I could get another restaurant job and repay Grandpa. I was grateful to him and hated the thought that he might spend even a week wondering if I'd pay up.

On the boat to France I saw Tessa from the Slits again, as she walked aboard with her baby and her boyfriend. I flagged them down to sit with me. I was glad to have someone to tell about Donegal, about how you couldn't pass a house without being invited in, how no one ever lit a cigarette without offering one to each person at the table. Most important, I told about the living history and about leaders like Bernadette Devlin, who, when the mayor of New York gave her the key to the city, handed it over to the Black Panthers.

After a night of rambling on to a member of the first gang of British punk kids who'd helped me break with everything I'd come from, I arrived in Paris at sunrise. Looking at the gleaming white city that had once seemed beyond reach from Old Colony Project, I realized that my world had changed completely. When Tessa and I parted ways, I felt lucky to have stumbled, as a kid, on a small underground movement of destruction and reinvention. But I knew that it was Ireland that would make everything look different from now on. Exhausted and completely broke, I looked at the plane ticket in my hand and wondered how I would get to the airport that day. But I wasn't worried.

MOTHER OF GOD, aren't they a strange-looking bunch!"
Ma said.

"Who, stewardesses?" I whispered, trying to lower the volume of the conversation. Ma was staring at one of the British Airways flight attendants at the front of the plane who, like all the others, was a platinum blonde and was decked out in tartan.

"No, the fuckin' English," she yelled. "The long faces on them!"

Just then one of the English offered me a hot towel from the right aisle, and I nudged Ma with my left elbow to stifle her. Ma was one step ahead of me, though. She was already politely unrolling the steamy towel handed to her by one of the English on the left aisle, attempting a halfhearted smile while examining the woman for more strangeness. We both used our hot towels to wash our faces, behind ears and all. When I noticed that fellow passengers were washing only their hands, presumably in preparation for breakfast, I elbowed Ma again in judgment. Just in time, because she was reaching into her sweater to give her armpits a once-over. Ma opened her mouth in wonder every time a British accent passed us down the aisles. "It's a terrible accent, isn't it?" She had no idea, with the noise of the airplane, just how loud she was or where her voice might travel on the plane. So I nudged her again. I guessed she hadn't seen many English — or even people of English descent — after a lifetime in Boston's Irish circles. Ma had gone to Ireland a few times since her first trip at seventeen, but never by way of London. We were headed to Heathrow, to make the connection to Dublin by bus and ferry. No relatives in Ireland were expecting us, so we could play it all by ear.

Trying to mask her curiosity, Ma feigned a smile and gave a nod of the head whenever she was caught staring by a Brit. When we were served tiny versions of the big British breakfast, Ma shouted over the volume of her headphones about how the English were cheap sons of bitches too, on top of everything else. "God, they're an odd breed altogether," she yelled, staring at her beans on mini-toast. That's when I started to pretend I didn't know her, the way I did when I was a kid.

I leaned back in my seat and reminded myself that we were just two adults taking a trip. I was thirty-two years old now, and I ought to be able to travel to Ireland with my mother without reverting to my teenage persona. A lot had happened since I was a teenager. My brother Joe had spent time in the air force in Colorado and had liked it there enough to get a house and move Ma, Seamus, Stephen, and Kathy out with him. Though Kathy had recovered enough to walk around Southie, she had deteriorated mentally. For a while she was missing, until Ma found her living in a crack house in New Hampshire, pregnant. In Colorado Ma spent all of her time taking care of Kathy, who had descended into schizophrenia. But her daughter, Maria, now ten years old, was beautiful and healthy, and Ma was raising her as her own.

I'd gotten closer to my family after my first trip to Ireland. At U Mass I concentrated on the history of Ireland and of other colonized countries. In and out of college I was trying to understand all the things I'd hated as a teenager, whether the over-the-top shamrocks and leprechauns or the race riots of Southie's busing days. And the more I traveled to Ireland, the more I appreciated the best things passed down to the Irish American world of my Southie childhood. I'd even allowed friends from my teenage years to meet my family in the project. And some even came to Southie to hear Ma play the accordion on St. Paddy's Day. When I started doing community organizing in Boston's neighborhoods, working on all the issues that had affected my family — violence, poverty, guns — I realized that the sooner the Irish of Southie came to better understand their history as an "inferior race" by English standards and learned what it meant to be Irish beyond the happy-go-lucky tunes and bloody fistfights of Saint Patrick's Day, the sooner they would acknowledge Southie's poverty and its manipulation by gangsters and politicians. And maybe even work with black people in neighboring Roxbury on common issues, like the fact that both neighborhoods had been declared "death zones" by sociologists. I also became obsessed with the connection between the work I was doing and personal recovery from trauma, as I got close to a number of mothers whose kids had been murdered in the city.

I'd come away from my first trip to Ireland wanting to understand more about Southie, and Irish America in general, but also more about my own family. After Grandpa refused to accept my two-hundred-dollar debt to him, I decided to repay him in stories from the Ireland I'd experienced, since he wasn't able to go back himself. I spent a lot of time at Grandpa's until he passed away, seven years before my trip now with Ma. The more questions I asked Grandpa, the more I heard stories that helped me see my family in new ways. Grandpa helped me through my anxiety and sense of doom after Frankie's and Kevin's deaths by admitting to me his own "nervousness" in his teenage years before he fled to America. Seeing that I was often afraid to go home, he told me he had been the same way when a TB epidemic was taking the lives of his family's cows. At first I was insulted that he'd even think of comparing the deaths in my family and in Southie to an epidemic among farm animals, but he explained that the cows were considered important members of the family back then, because they were a family's livelihood. To lose even one cast a dark shadow of gloom on any house. Grandpa said he'd started staying away from home then, fearing he was from an unlucky house, that his family was cursed. He said that whenever he started to have fun with people his own age, his thoughts would turn in an instant to which one might be dead back at home, until he left home for good at the age of fourteen and traveled around Ireland to work on other people's farms.

Grandpa's voice, weakened by age in his last year, quivered when he finally talked about the "awful fookin' shame" he had when he was eighteen and his mother died from blood poisoning caused by a pulled tooth and bad medical care. He did make it back to see her one last time while she lay in Tralee Hospital with her face all blown up from the poison, but he said that when he got word of her death later that night back at home, right then he made up his mind to leave Ireland forever. He told me that the guilt for ever having left home in the first place was something he'd lived with all these years.

The more I got to know Grandpa and the parts of his story he'd never shared before, the more I began to understand Ma too. And I knew that on this trip with Ma I'd be getting even closer to home.

"Ladies and gentlemen, for your safety, all unattended packages will be confiscated and destroyed," threatened the polite computer voice at Heathrow Airport. It was six in the morning, and barely anyone was in the terminal other than Ma and me. I watched Ma across the way at a coffee counter, talking away to teenage employees who were barely awake, while I called my friend Buddy in London to see if he wanted to meet up before Ma and I headed off to Ireland. Suddenly I saw Ma racing across the floor toward her battered accordion, which was sitting all by itself, abandoned-looking, in the center of the stark modern terminal, as soldiers approached it from all directions. Ma had owned that accordion from the age of ten, and by now it definitely could be mistaken for a suspect device, patched up through the decades with electrical tape and wire. The soldiers stopped at a distance. "Bloody 'ell, wot is it?" one asked, while another started circling and studying it. Ma called out to the soldiers that everything was okay, that it was just her Irish accordion.

They asked Ma to bring her Irish accordion into a back room for a little test swab. Waiting for the soldiers to inspect the accordion, I thought it mightn't have been a good idea for her to call it "Irish," since we were in London. But that was how Ma always referred to it. After passing terrorist inspection, Ma and her accordion were free to go. She threw the strap — an electrical cord she'd cut from an old radio — over her shoulder and swore not to let go of the accordion again. Then she said we should get the fuck out of England. "Jesus Christ, did you see the morbid faces on them? They're a dreary race altogether."

In the meantime, though, I had arranged to meet up with Buddy Riordan, and thought we could all spend the morning seeing London. Buddy was my good friend Danny's brother. I'd met Danny when he'd moved to Boston from Castleisland, Kerry, five years earlier. I'd never met anyone from Grandpa's town in Ireland, and from the first day Danny and I were like long-lost cousins. Being from a family of eleven kids in a housing estate, Danny had stories like my own from Southie, minus the guns and gangsters. But if Grandpa, who passed away before I met Danny, had heard his stories of the drugged-out kids, fistfights, and pregnant teenagers in Castleisland — and not just among the tinkers he liked to blame — he'd never believe them. The country of Grandpa's youth had been engaged in revolution and civil war. But his stories of growing up in Castleisland, at least the ones that weren't about sad farewells and dying cows, had made it sound like a fantasy land of lush glens, wildflowers, and endless summer days.

Ma knew Danny from talking with him on the phone. She'd check up on old friends of hers from Castleisland, like the Widow Leary, and ask about some of the tinkers she'd gotten on with, like Black Hannah and Foxy Mary — nicknamed, Ma explained, for their hair colors. It seemed like nearly everyone in Castleisland had a nickname, just like in Southie. When she spent hours on the phone reliving what sounded like the time of her life in Castleisland, I had to wonder how bored she was now with her less colorful life in Colorado. One time Danny, joking that his ear was sore, passed the phone to his brother-in-law Mikey, visiting Boston from Castleisland. Being the local bread man and making deliveries at sunrise every day, Mikey was more up-to-date on the town's old-timers. He and Ma carried on about this one and that one until Mikey got so wound up that he fell down my hallway stairs. I looked down at the landing below to see Mikey, one hand still clutching the phone and the other one cupping his free ear to drown out noise. After a few calls like that, Ma said the Riordans were like long-lost relations, even though she'd never met one in person.

Buddy had said he'd meet us at a Wimpy's in Leicester Square, and Ma was thrilled we'd be spending the day getting updates on all the characters of Castleisland. We had a couple hours yet to kill, so we took the Tube to Piccadilly and walked the rest of the way toward Trafalgar and then Leicester Square. Ma was amazed at first by the ornate majesty of the older buildings and by the neon light shows of Piccadilly Circus, even in the early morning. As the multitudes of commuters started to pour out of the Tube stations, Ma couldn't get over the armies of men and women in uniform slick dark outfits, marching off to work. At first I thought Ma had been too long in Colorado, where life was slower. But before long we were both feeling we might be mowed down and left to die on a London sidewalk. "For Chrissakes, they're doing a goose step!" Ma shouted, trying to catch up to me and bumping into yuppies with her battered accordion. I didn't remember London being like this in the eighties, but of course back then I'd have been going to bed at this hour after a night of clubbing and wandering the streets.

I told Ma she should put on her sneakers instead of the

strap-on spike heels she was now jogging in. Ma was turning sixty-five, and in Colorado she had become open-minded to sweatpants and sensible footwear, even in public, after a lifetime of spike heels and clothes to show off her figure in spite of having had eleven kids. "Oh yeah, good idea," she said. She threaded her way through the horde and leaned on a sidewalk railing to change her shoes. By the reaction from passers-by, you'd think someone was breaking rank to get naked. But Ma was oblivious to all stares as she stuffed her spike heels into her pocketbook. When we got back onto the treadmill of London's sidewalks, Ma shook her head in wonder at how much the world was changing. "Imagine, Davey and Frankie and Kevin never lived to see the world come to this," she said out of the blue. She was out of breath, and I couldn't tell from her tone whether she thought that was a good thing or a bad thing.

Struggling to keep up with the crowd of bankers and traders on their daily mission, I was thrown off to realize how well Ma usually pretended that she wasn't thinking of the kids all the time. That she was somehow over it. It was hard for me ever to look at Ma and *not* think about their deaths. Almost fifteen years later, it was still frustrating whenever she'd insist that she never thought about them at all and that they were in a better place. "We're the ones you gotta feel sorry for." When she'd say that, it was a relief to think she might be referring to her own sense of loss and grief. A relief — until she followed it with her more dire sense of reality: "After all, we're living in hell!"

Buddy showed up at Wimpy's, his eyes puffy from interrupted sleep. I felt bad we'd woken him with no prior notice that we'd be in London. He looked a lot like Danny except that he had a shaved head and the build of a bouncer. Before he could introduce himself to Ma, she was already looking up at him, making conversation like they'd known each other all their lives. "Buddy, what do you think of all these crazy English people?" she said. "It's like they're doing a friggin' power walk!"

Ma probably figured she could talk to him about the "crazy English," since he was from Ireland. I let out a panicked "Shhhhhh!" Buddy looked alarmed too, scanning the Wimpy's to see if anyone had heard Ma's Irish whisper. But then he lowered his head to bring down the voice levels. "Sure they're right cunts," he muttered. "So they are."

"See, he knows all about them!" Ma yelled at me. "Never mind with the goddamn *shhhhh!*" Ma knew instantly she'd be the best of friends with Buddy, and she told him, "For Chrissakes, you remind me of my father, with the Kerry brogue and all!"

We followed Buddy into the Tube station. We'd decided to stay with him overnight and take our bags to his place before spending the day seeing the sights in London. Waiting on a bench for the train, Buddy finally got up the guts to ask Ma about her accordion. Ma pulled it onto her lap and popped the fastened snaps. She stretched the bellows as wide as she could, and the accordion let out a long wheeze and rattle. Then Ma broke into an Irish rebel song just for Buddy.

> So they buried him out on the mountain
> 'Neath a cross that stood facing the sun
> And they wrote, "Here lies a true Irish soldier
> Who was shot by a Black-and-Tan gun."

Buddy looked at me and begged, "Tell her to stop. We're liable to get the heads knocked off of us, or locked up, for a song like that. This is London, for fuck's sake." He was half laughing but looking around nervously. I just shrugged. At this point in my life I might still try in vain to hush Ma when she talked too loud, but I'd certainly given up on attempts to restrict her singing and playing. Once she started a song I knew there was no stopping her.

Ma interrupted her song, and Buddy looked relieved until she asked, "Hey, Buddy, you ever hear about the Black and Tans? They were the English criminals — real bad sonsabitches — sent to Ireland in the fight for independence and given

208

shoot-to-kill orders. They'd shoot you as soon as look at you, if you were Irish." Buddy said under his breath that he knew all about the pricks but explained to Ma that we were surrounded by English and that you couldn't talk about this stuff, lest people think you were a terrorist. And then Ma broke into another song, and we figured it was a harmless one, until she got to the line about being off to join the IRA. Buddy looked thankful to hear the powerful ruckus of an oncoming train drowning out Ma's tune.

Buddy's neighborhood of Willesden Green, along with the adjacent neighborhood, Cricklewood, was said to be an Irish section of London. We saw a few Irish pubs and Irish butchers, but the area had recently been settled by waves of Pakistanis, Jamaicans, and Arabs, along with the Irish immigrants. When we came out of the Tube, Buddy said Ma could sing any song about British colonialism and slavery wherever she wanted around there. So she did just that, after leading us into an Irish pub called the Snug and playing for a handful of Irish workers on break. Emerging from the pub two hours later we walked across the street to Buddy's apartment building, which said HIGHBURY MANSIONS in fancy raised letters over a graffiti-covered entryway.

"Jesus Christ, Buddy, if I'd ever known I was going to a mansion," Ma said, out of breath from our four-story climb. Buddy told her they'd called a lot of buildings mansions at one time, but that it was actually a council flat, "like Section Eight in the States," he explained while we stopped to catch our breath. Buddy knew a lot about America because he and the first five Riordans — including Danny — had been born in Chicago. They returned to Castleisland, where their mother and father were from, when Buddy was just five and Danny three. Danny had once told me the story of how, when they were planning their return to Ireland after hard times in the States, he was often warned they might not have a toilet and would have to go outside. So Danny thought he'd get some practice in Chicago and took a shit on the front stoop of their apartment house, then proudly called his mother over to ask, "Is this how they do it in Ireland?" Back in Kerry the Riordans really didn't have a toilet at first, which wasn't unusual in some poorer parts of rural Ireland in the seventies.

"Yeah, but Buddy," Ma said, ignoring his explanation that he merely lived in a glorified project, "did you ever think you'd be living in a mansion?" Buddy would have been happy with any council flat, but just then he looked around at the gritty stairwell we had climbed as if he really did live in a mansion. "Christ, I never did," he said, puffed up with pride now. Ma liked to make the best of everything, whether telling people they looked like movie stars or asking them if they'd ever thought of going to law school. The exaggerations often drove me crazy, but I kept it to myself, since Ma's optimism always seemed contagious.

Buddy's flat actually was the most impressive subsidized housing I'd ever seen, with high ceilings and huge windows. Much better than any in the States. And Buddy told us the government allowed people to rent-to-own. In the living room, a whole welcoming committee waited for us. "Sit down now, we got the kettle going," Buddy's sister Noreen ordered. To look at Buddy's sisters, you'd never know they were from any place referred to as "the old country," even though the affectionate sit-your-asses-down-and-drink-some-tea greeting was a dead giveaway. Mary wore black elevator shoes and an electric blue fake fur coat and had a diamond stud in her cheek. Noreen wore a leather jacket, micro-miniskirt, and heels, and had a pretty but pissed-off face. A speedy-talking Irish traveler named House looked more "old country" in his curled-up tight shoes and high-water pants. He stood and bowed repeatedly, offering Ma his seat on the couch next to Trampus, a long-haired, disheveled man who slept seated with his head tilted sideways and mouth wide open. Trampus looked like he was in a blissful state until Ma began playing songs next to him. Two minutes into "It's a Long Way to Tipperary," he woke up holding his ear like it was sore from the playing. But he instantly got focused, rolling a gigantic spliff of hash without asking so much as who we were. Between songs Ma did more damage to Trampus's head, asking him all kinds of questions about his life and his hometown of Listowel, Kerry. Looking askance at her, his scrunched face got more and more pained. I wasn't sure whether he was trying to understand her Boston accent or just trying to keep up with questions about things he didn't like to think about, like who he was and where he came from. When Ma went off to the toilet, he finally asked Buddy, "Who's your w'an? Christ, she's stone mad."

Ma called me into the kitchen to look out the window at the people passing in the street. "Are those Irish people out there?" she asked. I shrugged, not knowing what she was looking at. "Look at the big feet on them!" she said. Ma didn't realize platforms were back that year, and she whispered that the Irish were just now catching up to our disco days, "with the goddamn Frankenstein shoes." I told her they were wearing the same thing in Boston, that the seventies were back. "Well, by God, if they step on your foot tonight you won't be defending them. You'll be in the emergency room."

That night we went back across the street to the Snug. Michael, a younger brother of Buddy and Danny, had shown up. He too looked more London than Kerry, and Ma optimistically told him that she loved his "great big shoes," that the Irish were right on top of all the styles. I knew the Riordans were all eager to meet us, as friends of Danny's. I had the sense that Danny was the family's magnetic center, the life of the party, that all the Riordans felt connected to him. We didn't talk about him, but it was clear that it was for him that they were entertaining Ma and me. When his absence became obvious, though, we all felt uncomfortable. With each round of drinks we got quieter and looked across the room for diversion. Watching Ma mingle with the crowd of Irish old-timers, we laughed whenever we could at the sight of a joke we couldn't really hear. Then Ma took the guitar away from a band member and hijacked the stage. I knew we were in trou-

ble with the first notes of her country version of "Danny Boy."
The Riordans looked panicked. Ma stopped after the first line
to announce, "This one is for Danny Riordan from Castleisland, Kerry. He died only a year ago. And he was a beautiful,
beautiful kid."

Mary Riordan looked at me, trying to hold herself together
as tears streamed down a face with no expression. I couldn't
tell if she was pissed off, if she felt trapped and was blaming
me. Noreen looked away, smoking harder and looking defiant.
Michael disappeared through the crowd, and Buddy lit up a
cigarette, taking a slow haul and holding it in for an extra long
time. When it was over, we all seemed to breathe freer. The
heaviness lifted, and everyone looked relieved to have made it
through. The pub band tried to reclaim the stage, but Ma
rolled right into some wilder hillbilly tunes with the guitar.
That's when the whole pub broke into fits of exaggerated "yee-
haw"s and handclapping. Ma knew the Irish loved American
country, and she got the whole place going. Our own table
went back to normal too. We kept the conversation light, still
talking about anything other than Danny, but feeling his presence now as much as his absence, since Ma had turned the
room into a place he would have loved to be.

We decided to extend our stay in London. After that first night
at the Snug I thought I'd never get Ma away from Willesden
Green. The crowd in the pub loved her, and she was stalked by
an Irish laborer who insisted that her American accent was a
put-on. "I never seen a Yank the like of you," he said, following her from one end of the bar to the other. He was about
Ma's age, but she referred to him as "that old fucker," wanting
nothing to do with him. Ma hadn't been much for dating since
her days in Southie. In Colorado she mostly kept to herself,
staying tuned to CNN and being my only link to every big
story, from Jeffrey Dahmer to Monica Lewinsky. Now Ma
seemed to have no idea that her peers were the guys with canes
who sometimes fell asleep at the bar. She was ready to party,

even though to her that never required a drink. Most of us couldn't keep up with her as she kept us out until the bars closed.

Buddy's place was like a home for wanderers, like Ma's place had always been in Old Colony Project. Trampus was a regular fixture. He came over every afternoon to smoke hash and fall asleep seated on the couch, always with his head tilted sideways and mouth wide open. He and Ma became the best of friends. Ma was like a therapist to him, a psychic one, holding his hand to tell his fortune and saying all good things about what kind of person he was. She even took a hit off the spliff, which Trampus habitually offered to the person next to him after every toke. No matter how many times I refused, he'd pass it to me while holding it all down in his lungs. Each time I'd wave my hand and let the next person take it. "You're like a fuckin' Jehovah's Witness," Noreen growled, like she'd heard about me. In recent years I had stayed away from drugs, but I refused Trampus's offerings mostly because it seemed too weird to smoke hash with my mother. We were both adults, but she was still my mother. That didn't stop Ma. She said she wanted to try it out, and hours later in the dead of night she yelled to Buddy from her bunk bed, "Hey, Buddy, that's some good shit!" Everyone else seemed used to Ma's wanting to keep the conversation going. But even after all these years, I wasn't used to it. So I let out a big "shhhhh," waking Trampus on the couch opposite mine and sending him into a tailspin about "dese fookin' mad Yanks."

By the third day we were pretty well settled into Buddy's place. We'd seen some more late nights with Ma playing the accordion and everyone telling stories. Even Trampus had started to come to life. Ma figured it must have been the ma huang herb she'd given him — her last batch, since it had been banned from the natural food stores in the States. Since taking ma huang, Trampus had been full of stories, stopping only to ask Ma once again for the spelling of those Chinese herbs. And since we were all telling stories, Ma asked me in front of everyone, "Mike, wouldja tell us a story about Danny in Boston?"

Then she turned to explain to Buddy, "Well, my God, I'd love to have known him." She said she'd have gotten on great with Danny if he was anything like the rest of the Riordans. Buddy nodded quickly, as if to shake off the reminder, then looked down at the floor and took a drag of his cigarette.

I started with the one about how Danny had brought life into my first apartment. It was my first Christmas in Southie after four years away. Since all the deaths, no one in my family had been into the holidays much. It felt like we were always holding our breath through them, and for years December 26 couldn't come soon enough. Then, after Ma shipped off for Colorado in 1990, I moved around Boston like a gypsy, from neighborhood to neighborhood, as friends' couches became available. I sometimes went through the holiday motions with friends just to avoid talking about how awful Christmas is once anyone in your family dies, especially people so young.

"Jesus, he's awful fuckin' morbid, isn't he?" Ma interrupted my story. "Never mind the depressing old parts," she said. Trampus, snapping out of a watery-eyed daze, agreed. "Christ, that's sad. Give us one of them fightin' rebel songs with yer accordion," he said to Ma, his new best friend. "What did yer man — that old fecker — say? 'I never seen a Yank the like of ye!'" But Buddy hushed them both, wanting to hear more about Danny's recent years in America. So I continued.

When I first moved back to Southie in 1994, finally drawn back to all that I loved and hated about the place, Danny helped me move in. He knew how much it meant for me to be going home. A few months later, during the first blizzard of the year, Danny showed up on my doorstep with a Christmas tree twice the size of him. I hated the sight of Christmas trees, but of course I couldn't tell him that, since he'd gone to the trouble of kidnapping it from the plant nursery where he worked. His girlfriend was in the car and I invited them in. Up the stairs they went, singing songs, squeezing this big fat tree through a narrow stairwell and leaving a trail of fresh snow behind. Loose pine needles bounced off the stairs, ceiling, and walls, releasing memories of all those Christmases when everyone was alive. I followed them, plotting how I'd get rid of the tree as soon as they left.

Danny put the tree into a paint bucket filled with wet sand he'd gathered at Carson Beach. He conjured up a bag of decorations and went to work on the tree, stepping back once in a while to take a good look at what he'd created. No one could interrupt his flow. He took fast puffs of his cigarette and looked focused and intense. In the end it was colorful, lopsided, and kind of crazy looking. Danny said that never before did a pack of tinkers put together a finer tree.

After all that work I couldn't throw the tree into the trash, but I tried to avoid it as much as I could in an apartment you couldn't swing a cat in.

"And what would you be doing swinging cats in your apartment?" joked Trampus, full of life from the ma huang. "I never heard of that."

"It's an Irish expression, isn't it?" I asked everyone. I'd decided to throw it in rather than something American, like comparing my apartment to a shoebox. But everyone shrugged and looked puzzled by the cat-swinging.

"Must be some fookin' Northern Ireland thing," said Trampus, elbowing Ma for a laugh.

I couldn't get rid of the tree because every day Danny would come to look at it with satisfaction. Over the weeks, I got used to it and actually felt like I was celebrating Christmas for once. I even had people over for a Christmas party one night. And as people talked about their Christmases past, I slowly became less afraid to remember my own. I started to like Christmas so much that I kept the tree up well after New Year's. By late February, though, it was leaning diagonally against my parlor window and the branches were downturned, making it almost like an upside-down tree. My floors were covered in pine needles, anchoring the dust clouds in my apartment. The pine scent was still there; I'd become so used to the memories it brought that I didn't want to sweep any of it away. But the Christmas lights were leaving burn marks on the branches. I knew I had to face the sad task of taking the tree down.

The tree had widened so much that it wouldn't fit down the stairwell. I had to break it apart, branch by branch, making a pile on the floor and breathing in the scent on my hands, sticky with pine sap. After getting through half of the tree I was shocked to come across a perfect bird's nest perched on a branch. At first the nest spooked me, like I might find a living bird in the half-destroyed tree. Or even a dead one. When I lifted the nest I couldn't believe how sturdy and tightly woven it was. I put it on my mantel while I took apart the rest of the tree. I wasn't keen on anything to do with birds in the house, which in the lore of my relatives portended bad things. I wondered where the nest came from and what it might mean, overlooking that I was taking apart a tree, that birds nested in trees, and that it probably meant nothing.

I became obsessed with the nest and wanted it to have meaning. It was my first Christmas in ten years, I was living in my first apartment on my own, and I was finally feeling at home in Southie. When Danny barged in to put up the tree on that miserable snowy night in December, I sensed that he knew how I felt about the holidays, that he was on a mission that night. I keep that nest on my mantel not only as a nudge to celebrate Christmas but also as a reminder that life can change, that painful things can transform, that you don't have to stay stuck. One year you might hate Christmas and the next year love it again. I look at the nest today with gratitude. In a way it brings Danny back to life for me. And it represents home to me, something I can have no matter where I go and no matter who's missing from the picture.

"Do you know that American song about 'give me a home where the buffalo roam'?" Trampus asked Ma. "Christ, that's a cracker of a song!" But Ma ignored the request and looked to Buddy, who was staring out the window. She asked him some questions about Danny and what he was like, until he left to get some beers from the fridge. When he came back he was wearing his sister Mary's blue Muppet-fur coat, dancing around, carrying a six-pack and a boom box blaring techno music. "Buddy, what in God's name is that music?" Ma asked. "It's techno, Helen, you gotta get with the times, never mind that old squeeze box." He pulled Ma up from the couch and they do-si-doed to the electronic blips and beeps of techno. Before long Trampus had locked arms with them and nearly swung himself into a wall. The party lasted until four in the morning, and when it wound down, everyone gave Ma permission to go back to playing her accordion. "But none of them sad fookin' Irish songs," said Trampus.

We were running late for the bus that would take us through Wales to get the boat from Holyhead to Dublin, so we squeezed into Buddy's Mini, and he sped all the way to the station. Buddy lit up his morning spliff and passed it to Trampus, who passed it to Ma, who said she'd try it one more time. I frowned at her in judgment. Ma took the spliff with both hands and leaned between her knees to take a big hit. We were stopped at a red light, and when her head came back up, with her sucking in like she was drawing oxygen, a car full of Rastas blasting heavy roots music lit up in shock at the sight of Ma smoking up Buddy's Mini. Buddy opened the window to let the smoke out. "Irish?" one asked, and Buddy just nodded. "Yeah, sistren!" another Rasta called to Ma with recognition. "Jesus, Buddy, look at the blacks with the crazy hair," Ma said, waving back to them and laughing.

At the bus station Ma hugged Trampus, telling him she'd miss him like one of her own and holding his hand one more time to tell his fortune: all good things, including that he'd soon be meeting the woman of his dreams, which made his eyes light up. He asked her to send some of those Chinese herbs back from America. I told Buddy we'd definitely make it to Castleisland and would visit with his family. He made Ma promise she'd play the accordion at Danny's grave and she was thrilled to.

Minutes after we got on the bus, Ma let out a big sigh. "My God, they're really not over it, huh?" In my community work with mothers whose kids had died, I'd learned that talk of getting "over it" was just about the worst thing they could ever hear from friends who didn't have a clue. And here was Ma, even after losing four kids, suggesting the possibility. But I figured, whatever works for her. I didn't need to be splitting her open.

Ma talked constantly on the bus through Wales. At one point she said she worried about Trampus "with what he's going through." She told me all about Trampus's brother getting killed only months before. She said that was probably why he was at Buddy's all the time, even if he didn't know it himself, for the company of someone he could relate to.

"How the hell did you get all that out of him?" I asked. My thoughts returned to Southie and the recent spate of suicides by hanging and the epidemic of painkiller use, especially heroin. I'd been run ragged by months of young deaths, bringing back everything that had originally made me flee from Southie. I'd been frustrated by the city's solution: send in teams of psychiatrists to medicate the neighborhood rather than deal with the causes. And I thought how that wasn't much different from Trampus and his hash.

During the passage across the Irish Sea, I drifted off to sleep, only to wake up to the ruckus of a full Irish seisun — fiddles, uilleann pipes, guitar, and, of course, accordion. There was Ma on the other side of the boat surrounded by a group of musicians. Small kids had gathered around and were doing Irish step dancing. "Come on over, Mike," Ma called to me, giving away that I was with her. I went over and she whispered, as if no one else could hear her, "I think these are tinkers." "Travelers," the fiddler corrected Ma, taking no real offense. "Travelers, that's right, travelers," Ma said. "That's what they call them now," she assured me. The entire boat turned into a party, and I stared at the first sight of land, still about an hour away, wondering where we'd end up.

"Let's get the Christ out of Dublin!" Ma said, amid hordes of marching pedestrians as relentless as downtown London's. I studied a map from different angles, trying to figure out the way to the car rental.

"Look, it's James Connolly!" Ma shouted like she'd just spotted an old friend. The bronze statue of Connolly was instantly recognizable. Anyone who'd grown up Irish in Boston knew the songs about the Irish martyr who faced the firing squad for his part in the Easter Rising of 1916. After being lost in Dublin's side streets and then nearly trampled in shoppers' gangways, it was a relief to happen upon something we knew. The statue stood in front of Liberty Hall, the headquarters of Connolly's Irish Citizen Army, made up of workers. It was from here that the militia had marched off to the General Post Office to base its operations that Easter. Behind Connolly was the Plough and Stars, the Citizen Army's symbol of the workers' present and the workers' future. The songs always referred to the workers but never mentioned Connolly's being a socialist. And it's a good thing, since for a lot of Irish Americans, and especially in Southie, being a socialist was akin to being a Satanist.

The monument made us want to see the General Post Office, which had been seized by the armed rebels all those Easters ago in an uprising that, as I understood from the Irish reading I'd been doing over the years, some call suicide and others call a blood sacrifice for Ireland's freedom, like the Crucifixion and Resurrection. The Rising failed, and commanders like Connolly were put before the firing squad. Still, their brave fight and gruesome deaths at the hands of Britain showed the way for even more fierce fighters for Ireland's independence.

But the Irish of 1998, with Easter just days away, had more

shopping bags than arms. Ma tried to corner one shopper to ask where the famed General Post Office was where the rebels had stationed themselves. Ma even went into detail about James Connolly and Parnell and this one and that one in the Easter Rising, walking faster while the woman — cupping her hand over her mouth and cell phone — started running from us. I told Ma the woman was probably on an important business call, and anyway I knew where the General Post Office was, on nearby O'Connell Street. As usual Ma just wanted a good conversation with a stranger. She tried to flag down two more Dubliners, who pointed apologetically to the cell phones at their ears. Cell phones weren't that popular in the States yet, but it seemed everyone in Ireland had one, including the kids coming home from elementary school. And they were using them nonstop. I was as baffled by it as Ma. But I *shhhhh*'d her again when she yelled out in disbelief, "What the fuck happened to the Irish?"

We got lost driving the rental car around Dublin, trying to get to the General Post Office before getting out of the city. We were lucky enough, though, to spot the tall monument to Michael Collins, sometimes called the father of modern guerrilla warfare, who led the Irish rebels in the War of Independence that followed the Easter Rising and lasted until the British put forth a treaty that divided the Irish. Collins was ambushed and killed in the ensuing civil war. Another sad story. "Yeah, but he brought the English to their knees, didn't he?" Ma said. She always thought putting up a good fight was more important than a tragic death.

We didn't stop for Collins's grave, though. We were too distracted by an Ireland we'd never seen before, the Ireland whose booming economy was being called the Celtic Tiger. "The shopping bags on them!" Each time we passed someone with a bag, Ma had to comment on it. "Look, there's another one!" "Christ, is that one there?" "Look at this one; well, by Jesus, she'll have forearms like Popeye with all the bags." It got ridiculous, as Ma pointed at people coming out of corner stores with bags that probably held nothing more extravagant than milk or eggs. Sick of counting shopping bags, I was more excited about the road ahead of us, south and then westward. So we skipped the General Post Office, though I'd always wanted to see the bullet holes in the columns.

South of Dublin the country got greener within minutes. In no time we were driving through smaller and smaller towns with twisting roads, hedges, and no sidewalks. I mentioned to Ma that we were leaving the "Pale," the name given to Dublin and its environs, which had the most English during colonization. "'Beyond the Pale' meant barbaric Ireland," I said. "That's where we're going."

Ma laughed. "In all my life I never heard of that. Keep quiet now so I can listen to my news," she said, blaring the car radio. She always called the news hers, just the way Grandpa did. But even now that he was gone you could never tell Ma she was exactly like Grandpa. All the talk on the news was about the Good Friday Accords being negotiated by Ireland, England, and all parties of the North after years of Irish rebellion and English vengeance, followed by greater rebellion. Good Friday, when the Accords were to be signed, was only a couple of days away, and the commentators were talking about a time when there'd be as many happy-go-lucky shoppers in troubled Belfast as there were in booming Dublin. Along with all the optimism, though, there were reports about the South's soaring suicide rates and racist attacks on the country's first wave of immigrants, drawn to the Celtic Tiger's jobs.

"Well, my God, isn't this a historic time to be coming to Ireland?" Ma said about the Accords. She asked me to pull over so we could talk to some people about it in the local pub. But we had lots more traveling to do. And I knew the best parts — farther from the Pale — were yet to come.

We had no plans, no obligations other than to stop in at the Riordans' and to visit Danny's grave. Ma was even more determined to do that than I was. "Did you see the way Buddy's face lit up when I promised I'd play the accordion at Danny's grave?" she asked.

I thought we'd first go to Kilkenny, but we took the wrong road and ended up in Tullow. I remembered that Father John Murphy, the leader of the peasant revolts of 1798 in Wexford, had been captured and martyred in Tullow. I knew the story well because Grandpa always liked to sing "Boulavogue" whenever it was his turn, especially since the rebel martyr shared his name. " 'Arm! Arm!' he cried, 'for I've come to lead you, / For Ireland's freedom we'll fight or die.' " As a child in Nana and Grandpa's kitchen — before I started to hate all things Irish — I was excited to hear Grandpa's voice rise in rebellion against King George. "Look out for hirelings, King George of England / Search every kingdom where breathes a slave / For Father Murphy of the county Wexford / Sweeps o'er the land like a mighty wave." But, as in most of the Irish songs I grew up with, the hero we all rooted for had to die in the most bloody way, and Father Murphy was no exception. "And the yeos at Tullow took Father Murphy / And burned his body upon the rack." And here we were in Tullow, where the plaques gave even more horrific details. Father Murphy was shot, hanged, beheaded, and then burned. The English compared him to Genghis Khan because he'd led formidable troops of peasants armed with pikes and pitchforks. Ma compared him to Christ, with a death even worse than crucifixion.

We drove next into Wexford, where the United Irishmen put up one of the most promising fights against English tyranny and where the Crown's yeomen retaliated against the failed uprisings with torture like "pitchcapping" — pouring hot pitch into a cone-shaped paper "cap," which was forced onto a bound suspect's head, allowed to cool, and then torn off, taking the scalp with it. As always in Ireland, the scenery in Wexford let you think you were in a place so peaceful that blood could not possibly have been spilled there. But I knew this land ran deep with it and that we were surrounded by mass graves.

Ma liked the bits of history about putting up a good fight. But anything that had to do with English atrocities or the Irish being considered an inferior race made her change the subject. In Kilkenny I tried to tell her about the Kilkenny Statutes. I wasn't trying to show off my recent years of obsession with Irish history, I was just excited to see it all come to life. Ma said she knew all about it. "The Irish fought, they died, and by God, they'll keep fighting. What more is there to know about it?" "Yeah, but this is where it all began, in a way," I said. I explained that as far back as the fourteenth century, the Kilkenny Statutes proclaimed the Irish as an inferior race. Afraid that the Norman gentry were becoming too Irish, the Crown forbade them to speak Gaelic, to dress like the Irish, to play Irish games like hurling, or to allow Irish poets and musicians — a particularly dangerous lot — among them. It established that the Irish would be second-class citizens in their own country.

"Wasn't that a long fuckin' time ago?" Ma barked, fiddling with the car radio to try to turn up news of the Good Friday Accords in Belfast, and saying that the IRA shouldn't give up too much in the agreement. After one day of traveling with Ma, I knew it was going to be a rough week. She had to argue with anything I said sometimes. One minute she'd tell me the Irish should put it all behind them, and the next minute she'd be telling a stranger at a teahouse in Kilkenny, "Weren't those English no-good sonsabitches?" I'd noticed that most Irish I'd met were the same. Everyone knew exactly how they should feel about fighting but were confused when it came to pain.

The next day we drove into Cóbh, still called Queenstown in Grandpa's day. The coffin ships had sailed from here during the famine of the 1840s, when those who could do so left Ireland, hoping to escape the starvation and disease that were decimating the population. Most didn't survive the journey. Ireland lost a quarter of its population while England was shipping loads of food out of Ireland. Most Irish Americans I'd met had great-great-grandparents who'd come over at that time. But Cóbh was also the port Grandpa had left from when he was eighteen, after his mother died. When he told the story of his departure, he only mentioned the three days and nights of partying that preceded it and the gang of friends who rode with him on bikes all the way to the ship for his sendoff.

"That's where we moored in the middle of the night," Ma said, pointing out to the harbor as if piecing together her own connection to this port. Ma's journey to Ireland when she was seventeen had started with an eleven-day voyage from Castle Island in South Boston back to the port where her father had last seen Ireland. "When we saw the town's lights we couldn't wait to get off the ship, but we had to sit in the harbor until morning and then take a smaller boat to shore." The long journey by boat was the most fun she'd had in her life — playing her accordion, matchmaking, and instigating flirtations and fights between a Czech woman and a French man. She said she gave the French man lessons in English, pickup lines that earned him more than one belt in the mouth. Ma had bunked on the ship with an older Irish woman who drank too much and spent the hour before meeting her relatives pinching her cheeks to look healthy after all the nights of drink. I remembered having to put up with the Irish obsession with "rosy cheeks" as a kid. Nana would spit on a lint-encrusted napkin from the depths of her purse and come at me to rub my cheeks before we met up with anyone who might judge our appearance, usually friends of hers from Ireland. Ma told me that when she went to Kerry, she discovered the trick, used by men and women alike, of spitting on their red prayer books before Mass and smearing red ink on their faces for the priests, to disguise a night out on the town.

From Cóbh we headed to Bantry Bay. The farther west we went, the bumpier the roads got. And whenever I asked directions to make sure we were headed into western Cork, I got another long, snaky story. Just like in Donegal, the Irish here loved to give directions by holding up an example ("It'll be as near to you as this hand is to my face"), pointing at something in the road ("Before long it'll be as black outside as the coal sitting on that there ledge"), or stressing the might of nature ("That's a power of a storm coming!"). I could listen to the directions all day, but I got sick of Ma interrupting to talk, like it was a competition.

In Bantry I made Ma come see the shore where Wolfe Tone's heroic effort to free Ireland with help from the French fleet in 1798 was beaten back by a gale — more luck of the Irish. The French ships had to turn back, but Tone continued with his revolution until caught in Wexford and condemned to death by the Brits. Rather than give the British the pleasure of execution, though, he used a penknife to cut his own throat in his cell and suffered for a week before finally dying. We stayed in Bantry until Good Friday, then headed toward Kerry and Grandpa's town of Castleisland.

As we drove up a rocky slope into a mountainous pass I hadn't expected, the radio fluttered between English- and Gaelic-speaking stations, both talking of the peace accords being negotiated in closed meetings. The Gaelic stations played mournful uilleann pipes and laments between commentaries that neither of us could understand. Rising up out of mist and fog into clearer heights, I looked down at clouds and realized how close to the edge of a dropoff we were. The roads were twisty, and I prayed that an oncoming car wouldn't appear on one of the blind turns ahead. Mist came and went, and the weather changed from rain to sunshine in that way I'd come to love about Ireland, though not while driving above what looked like a bottomless ravine. I had no way to be sure we were on the right road into the Kingdom of Kerry. There were no signs. And at this point there was no going back. With the Gaelic radio station the only one coming through, I felt like I was in a dream. Ma was silent for once, only speaking sometimes to complain that the news was in a dead language.

After passing above the Lakes of Killarney, I knew we were

close. Ma said that her father kept coming into her head, and Davey. She told me again about Davey being sent to Castleisland to stay with Dan Murphy when he was fourteen. I knew that part of the story and knew he'd been locked up by the Royal Ulster Constabulary. But I'd never heard before that they picked him up on the streets of Belfast because they had discovered he had a false American passport. "I gave him Frankie's passport because Frankie was younger and I could get a half-price ticket for him." But Davey was six-foot-three; Ma had told him to bend his knees at the airport to be shorter. Ma said they arrested him on suspicion that he was a terrorist. I could have guessed the rest, knowing more now about the North and the fact that the RUC was a mostly Protestant police force. For years links had been made between the RUC and loyalist paramilitaries in the North, and I knew the loyalists hated Irish Americans for their allegiance to the IRA in the form of money and guns. But Ma only began to tell me that Davey was beaten by the police in the North before changing the subject to the fight she had to wage, working with politicians, to get him back home. As always when talking about Davey, Ma soon changed the subject abruptly. "When did your friend Danny Riordan die?" she asked, reminding me that he was dead.

The closer we got to Castleisland, the more I had to tell myself that I wouldn't see Danny there. These days, when I heard that someone I knew had died, it was like hearing that the person had moved far away. Like friends who had moved across the country, the dead were just beyond reach. I'd gotten good at remaining almost confused about who was dead and who lived far away. I always felt we'd cross paths again, Danny and me. And now it was sinking in that he was dead, which was hard to believe, partly because I'd only gotten the word by telephone and had not seen him in a casket.

I'd learned of Danny's death during some of Southie's darkest days. Heroin had turned the neighborhood into a ghost town, with most activities taking place indoors and too many young kids' names being added to our list for an All Souls' Day vigil. Organizing the vigil, taking the names of the dead, even those of old friends from childhood, was becoming routine to me. Hearing the details of Danny's death over the telephone right after it happened was like hearing a minor detail of his trip to Florida, where he was found dead in a swimming pool. He and his girlfriend were on vacation and staying at the home of an older lawyer she'd met when she first came to the States. Danny and his girlfriend got into an argument, and then she lay down for a nap. On waking, she found Danny floating in the pool, dead. When I got the phone call, I could have been told he was swimming in the pool, I was so numb to the news. I hung up and let it sink in for a minute or two, thinking there must be something wrong with me for not feeling what "dead" was supposed to mean.

Getting closer to Castleisland town, we passed the Torc Waterfall, which I knew of from Danny's stories. This part of Kerry was the only place I could imagine him outside of Boston, since in most of his stories this was "home."

The last time I saw Danny, I was driving to a neighborhood meeting about Southie's rampant heroin use and the almost weekly suicides and attempts. Danny tooted his horn and reached out of a van window, waving to get my attention. I hadn't seen him much in the previous year. He'd gotten in with the drug crowd in Southie and had started to avoid me. Now he was smiling and looked healthy compared to the previous times I'd seen him, when he was as skinny as a rail. We both stopped at a light, and he said he'd call me as soon as he got back from Florida. "You're looking well," he added, as Irish people often say, the way Americans say, "How are you doing?" I said thanks and changed the subject. "Ignorant fuck!" he shouted. "You're supposed to tell me I'm lookin' well too!" Danny did look great, and I decided he must have gotten clean and sober. He was beaming with pride over it, wanting me to take notice, to say something about it. I laughed and said, "Yeah, you look good!" Halfway through my words the light turned green, and off he sped, waving in a big motion out the window, all smiles and gesturing, with a closed fist to his ear, that he'd call me. I never saw him again.

For a minute after I got the call telling me he was dead, I felt the wave of numbing I was so used to. It travels from the top of your head down through your stomach and extends into your feet and hands. You feel a little dizzy from it, but it feels good the way your body just lets go of everything on its own. I had come to love the feeling. But these days the numbing wore off faster than it used to, and when it did, the guilt replaced it more immediately. The numbing and trouble-free emptiness were overcome by the thought of why Danny had avoided me so much in the year before his death. And now, as we approached his childhood home and a family that would never see him again, I was feeling the guilt again. I knew he'd stayed away because he thought I was a goody two-shoes antidrug guy, with the work I was doing in Southie.

I had my reasons for staying away from drugs, but I hated the idea that Danny might think I was judgmental about anyone else's decisions. I'd always hung out with people who were high. My community work was more out of anger at the drug trade and the dealers who got rich off people in pain. And at the Southie cops and politicians, who locked up the addicts while providing cover for the ones making all the money. And at the FBI, which, as we'd just learned from press reports, had protected our Whitey Bulger for so long.

Along with that, my work was my own alternative to the painkilling that dope gave others. I had found out that if you let yourself feel all of the pain, you can get used to it and learn to live with it. It becomes as harmless as the Christmas tree Danny brought into my house. Drugs just seemed to put all that work off for another day. Plus with all the bedlam around me in Southie then, I couldn't afford any more confusion or disorder. The suicide epidemic brought back the feelings I had after so many people were murdered in the eighties. I needed my wits about me, to be prepared for the next knock on the door telling me someone had been killed, gone off a roof, hanged himself, or overdosed. But driving closer to Castleisland, trying to justify to myself why I didn't get high, the fact of the matter remained: Danny had avoided me. I hated to think that I was perceived as "some kind of fuckin' Jehovah's Witness," that not getting high might separate me from people I wanted to be around.

A couple of kilometers outside Castleisland, we were lost at a crossroads, and we sat for a minute trying to choose the way. Ma demanded I pull over to ask directions of an older woman who was wondering who the lost Yanks were. I knew Ma only wanted to strike up a long conversation with another stranger, and I wanted to get to town before dark, so I locked the windows and tried to make like I suddenly knew where we were going. But it was too late. After cursing about the windows that didn't work, Ma opened the car door to call the woman over. I had to pull over, and I sighed, knowing we would not be back on the road for a half-hour, after Ma's interrogation to find out the woman's entire life story.

"Sure, I know them. Don't he be delivering bread to me every marnin'?" Butting in when Ma took a breath — probably to ask a personal question — the woman started straight into the directions. "When you pass me standing here, sure you'll see a great pow'r of a tree that stands in front of a house. The house has a lovely garden the length of it, so it does. This here German fella bought that house and he does have a son who's married, and the son that's married does be coming to stay in the good months with the wife and two lovely gossoons. Sure, someone — a stranger altogether — is after planting every sort of flower alongside the house, and there should be lovely roses coming up this June. Now, when you see that great big tree and the German's house with the lovely garden . . ." She paused, then said, "Ignore it altogether!" She came alive, throwing up her hand and striking the air like she wanted me to erase that house from my memory as soon as I laid eyes on it. "Keep going! Straight on!" she said, getting worked up.

"Now, a good ways down, you'll come to a house ye never seen the like of. Next to it there's a rock the breadth of the car you're sitting in right now. And when you see that house you'll say to yourself, 'Christ, what kind of a man built that there house?'"

"Was it more Germans that built that house too?" Ma asked, trying to jump in and turn it into a conversation. But the woman ignored the interruption. After once again describing the house to the last detail, she emphasized, "Ignore that house completely!" Then she assured us, cocking her head and looking yonder, "You must keep going until you pass a graveyard that's shaded by a blackthorn." She described the blackthorn — the size, the slope of the branches, the shadows it cast on which graves of old friends and neighbors — and told us to forget we'd ever laid eyes on it. "Just keep going!" she urged, "and you'll come around a slight curve. Watch that now, there do be a lot of accidents right there, with the fellas who be coming back from town with the drink in 'em." I wasn't even listening to her directions anymore. I knew I'd end up paying way too much attention to the German's house and wondering about the man who built the next house and staring too long at the blackthorn's branches to ever make it to Castleisland before dark. I just listened to the woman's downward-tumbling cadence and rolling *r*'s, reminding me how close I was to Grandpa's birthplace. We were there.

"If you come to a cross in the road, with Castleisland town below and hedges you never seen the like of on your right, then you've gone too far. You must turn around then, but don't get yerself into a ditch, for a lot of Yanks do be ending up in a ditch on account of the roads being so narrow."

"Where do you live?" Ma asked the woman, who stepped away from the car, straightened the collar of her coat, and gave a vague nod toward the glens in front of us. She backed up more with Ma's next question about her people and what their names might be. But in no time the woman turned the tables on Ma, coming back to the window and asking where we might have come from, what our relation might be to the Riordans, and how long we might be staying. Ma told the woman that her father was from the Cordal Road and asked whether she knew if his house was still there and who owned the land now. But each time Ma asked a question the woman reversed it to get information out of her. And as soon as there was a mention of land, the conversation was over and the woman didn't know much about anything at all. I said we had to be off before dark, and she gladly let us go. I drove in the general direction of Castleisland town with no idea which house had the rock, which house had the garden. I was afraid to look at anything other than the road in front of me, since I'd been told to ignore all the wondrous distractions I'd be seeing on the way. We got more lost in the labyrinth of Kerry boreens than I could have imagined. They all seemed the same after a while — narrow, bumpy roads the width of one car and surrounded by deep ditches and high hedges.

The whole rest of the way Ma complained about the woman with the elaborate directions. "That one'd do your fuckin' head in. You won't know if you're coming or going after that. And did you hear all the friggin' questions?" Ma had met her match and lost, and we knew nothing more about the woman than when we'd first laid eyes on her. Ma often said the Irish were "great talkers," like it was the highest compliment you could give someone. But her opinions about the Irish were always changing, just like Grandpa's. Now she said the one thing she couldn't stand about the Irish was how nosy they were. "Always looking for information," she said. "And then they won't tell you anything about themselves!"

After an hour lost in the maze, with Ma suspecting we'd been bamboozled by the woman, we ended up in Castleisland town before dark. Ma knew the town well and pointed to all the landmarks of her stays there. Some of the taverns where she'd played accordion were still there, like Tagney's. Ma pointed to Lyons pub, where her cousin Dan Murphy had taken her on her first night in Ireland. It was 1951, and the place had stone floors and no electricity, only candles. She said the young men were lined up on one side of the room and the women on the other side. "They were awful shy, I thought," Ma said. But in no time Ma had them dancing to her American-bred jigs and reels, and by closing time she had gained the title "the wild Yank." From the town center Ma could point in the direction of the Cordal Road, "the lonesome old place" Grandpa talked about, where she had stayed as a teenager and had the time of her life and where Davey had spent a few months right before his nervous breakdown.

We'd made arrangements in London to stay with Danny's sister Hannah and her husband, Mikey, above the town. But we knew Danny's mother and father lived in the center of Castleisland. We didn't want to get lost again, so we asked around. A scrawny kid with a dirty face said he'd take us to the Riordans', but we'd have to give him a fiver. When we got to the Riordans', as soon as they greeted us they were telling our guide to fuck off. They told us he was a no-good knacker, which I learned was just another word for tinker. They said he'd steal the eye out of your head and come back for the other one.

A large framed picture of Danny sat in the middle of the room in front of the mantel. I'd never seen Danny looking so serious. The Riordan family was gathered in the living room, crammed onto couches in front of a television set. They'd been expecting us, so everyone was there except the ones living in London. I'd never been in a roomful of Irish people so silent. Ma kept asking questions about Castleisland and which places and people were still there and mostly got yes or no answers. The TV provided an easy out from any conversation. When Ma inevitably brought the talk to Danny, Mrs. Riordan said little, then left the room and came back carrying his autopsy photos for me to see. I had to go numb to look at the bruised dead face of one of the liveliest people I'd ever known. I wondered silently why a mother would have autopsy photos. Mrs. Riordan, who told me to call her Nora, said they felt they hadn't been told the whole story around Danny's death. She said the entire right side of his body was as bruised as his face. I had to agree that I'd never heard of a drowned person looking so badly beaten.

When Danny's parents went to Florida to get the body to ship home, they felt they were given a runaround by the DA's office, which said it had lost the autopsy report. "They treated us like we were real culchie Irish who didn't know our arses from our elbows," Nora told me. Danny's father stood in a corner of the room, looking pissed off and working a toothpick with a vengeance. Catherine, the youngest, the one Danny talked about all the time, got up and stormed out of the room. There were no answers, Nora said. And they'd never heard from Danny's girlfriend again. "He hadn't a stitch of clothes on him, as naked as when he come into this world. Even all his jewelry — necklaces and rings — were gone." Nora spoke slowly and clearly, like she was talking about a battle she was still engaged in. There was no crying. It was almost as if grief were a luxury no one could have.

Hannah and Mikey showed up to take us to the grave. Hannah said she had been there earlier to tell Danny I was coming. We squeezed into the car with Catherine, who Ma had already decided was her favorite.

When we got to the grave, Catherine picked up a jug and shook it violently, splashing water all over Danny's tombstone. We were facing the stone and reading the inscription when she turned around and threw handfuls of water on us. Only when everyone blessed themselves did I realize it was holy water we'd been doused with. We stood in uncomfortable silence for a while, but I anticipated Ma breaking it soon enough.

Ma was walking around the cemetery reading the names out loud to us and mentioning that she once knew a Mary O'Brien and a Sheila O'Connor and a Margaret Murphy. Ma was astounded by the coincidences even though half the people in

Southie had those names. And when she came back to the silence at Danny's grave she carried on in a great mood about what a beautiful spot it was. Then she did what she'd told Buddy she would do, pulling the accordion onto one raised knee and breaking into "Danny Boy."

This opened every last water faucet that had been closed so tightly that evening. Hannah, Mikey, and Catherine stood frozen, staring at the gravestone with hands folded, their tears falling in steady streams. I was terrified, the way I always was when Ma opened people's faucets. I wasn't sure if Ma was being appropriate, since I didn't know Danny's family at all well. Buddy had requested the playing, but I'd figured Ma would do it when we were at the grave alone. Ma's red hair flew in all directions with the wind, exposing gray streaks at her temples, which I was seeing for the first time. She struggled to hold up the heavy accordion while standing, raising one thigh to prop it, and was soon balancing the entire spectacle on one foot. It was just past twilight, the sky was a deep dark blue, and the white stone of the religious statues shone out against the backdrop of evening. Saint Patrick leading the snakes out of Ireland, the three children of Fatima kneeling in front of a serene Mary, Jesus's crucified body floating above us, his wooden cross invisible in the night.

Ma wailed the verses and settled down to a lullaby for the last line, "I simply sleep in peace until you come to me."

We stood quietly for a few moments. I wasn't sure we'd be welcomed back at the Riordans' that night. Catherine broke the long, uncomfortable silence by soaking us all in a parting spray of holy water. Then she doused the grave. And we all went back to the cars in what seemed like a sudden descent of pitch darkness.

The next morning Ma played in the Riordans' kitchen for a few hours, and I knew we were becoming less like strangers to Mrs. Riordan. After some interrogation Ma realized that Nora's own cousin had stayed with Grandpa in Southie when

Ma was a kid. And in between songs Ma got Nora to talk more about Danny. Still she mostly focused on the details of his death and what she fervently believed had happened that day. Mr. Riordan piped in to show me pictures he took at the swimming pool in Florida, including the dumbbell weights at the side. "There's something quare about the whole thing," he said. He told me that the guy who owned the house where Danny had died was a powerful lawyer and that the story of a body found in his pool had disappeared within a day.

Mrs. Riordan looked like a fighter, and she talked about wishing she had the money to go back to Florida to find out what had happened to Danny. But her whole face changed when Ma asked her, "Was Danny everyone's favorite? I get the feeling he must have been like my Frank, the center we all gravitated to." I groaned to myself in silent frustration, wondering why Ma needed to ask a question she knew the answer to. I had already told her that he was the glue of the family. Mrs. Riordan explained with a shaky voice that he was the one everyone depended on. Catherine stormed out of the room again when voices got shaky. Then Mrs. Riordan broke down in tears as she explained to me that she had been in South Boston before Danny died. Danny had sent home newspaper clippings about the gun buybacks and other community work I was doing. When she asked him when she'd be meeting this Michael MacDonald, he said, "Oh, he wouldn't be wanting anything to do with the likes of me." She explained that Danny was convinced that I'd wanted nothing to do with him since he had gone on a binge, that I didn't associate with people like him.

The Riordans took us to Danny's grave every day during our stay in Castleisland. In the previous five years I'd probably been to my own brothers' graves once. I preferred to think they weren't there.

"See, that's where he is." Mrs. Riordan came over and stood next to me, gesturing in a straight line at the ground stretching from our feet to the stone that bore his name. Even at my own brothers' graves I had never thought about it so literally. I didn't know what to say. "You see, it's not real until you stand here in this spot and see his name there," she said. I remembered what it was like to struggle with the nonreality of it all. But by now I knew you felt that nonreality even fifteen years later, and eventually you got used to it.

"Nora, did you ever stop to think he was never your kid in the first place?" Ma asked, sitting on a gravestone nearby. "I mean, it's like they're on loan. And we just have to be thankful that we ever knew them." Nora looked at Ma and then at me with a face that seemed to say "Is this bitch for real?" But that's not what she was thinking, I realized, when I saw her look back at Ma with recognition as someone who'd been there, a few times even. Nora smiled but said she hadn't thought that way about it. Ma's voice cracked as she said that she didn't really think that way either, but she tried to, and that some days she felt like that and other days she didn't. "For a long time there were days I never thought I'd get through," she admitted.

Ma said she hadn't been to her own kids' graves in a long time, having moved to Colorado, but that at first she had to go all the time. "I'll never forget the first day it snowed after my baby Patrick died." The first thing Ma thought was that he was going to be cold in his grave. "I was going to go down with a shovel and blankets to cover the grave and keep it dry and warm." Nora looked up, nodding. "Naturally, sure, that's how a mother thinks," she said. Nora told of the first rain after Danny died, and it was the longest talk I'd heard from Nora since I'd met her. As she spoke it occurred to me that I'd never once had to think so literally about someone being in the ground, vulnerable to the elements. And that losing your child must be the worst possible thing in the world.

After the grave, Hannah took us up the Cordal Road to Grandpa's area, to visit Ma's friend the Widow Leary. We visited without warning, but Mrs. Leary knew Ma right away though she hadn't see her in years. She brought out a jug of whiskey even though it was morning, and we all had a glass. Peggy Leary said she'd never forget the first time she laid eyes on the wild Yank. She said everyone was filing out of Mass and Ma was perched on the churchyard wall wearing a leopard skirt, carrying her accordion like she was looking for a seisun. "Good thing I was getting married that week," Peggy said. Ma ended up playing at the wedding, which lasted three days and three nights. "That's how it was back then with a wedding," Ma explained. "Everyone slept all over the place on the floors, and the next morning you'd get up and start all over again."

Peggy walked us up the road for a visit with another old friend, T.J. Brennan, Grandpa's best friend from childhood. T.J. came to the gate to welcome us into his home. He was the age Grandpa would have been that year, eighty-nine, with a straight posture and the outfit of the old-timers: cap, scarf, a too-small, grimy blazer with permanent caked creases at the inner elbow, and baggy pants tucked into Wellington boots. Before Peggy Leary could even explain who we were — John Murphy's daughter and grandson — he eagerly led us into the cottage and welcomed us by taking down two bottles of whiskey. It didn't matter who we were; we were visitors all the same. And when he heard Peggy after she explained a second time, yelling "John Murphy" into his ear, he stopped his running around for cups and seats and broke into a smile of recognition at Ma, giving a quick sideways jerk of the head. He poured straight whiskey into shamrock coffee cups like the ones you see at the airport for Irish American tourists. I couldn't get over the might of his huge fists wrapped around the whiskey bottle, worker's hands like I'd never seen. His wife sat by the heat of the old-fashioned stove and smiled at us. Who we were didn't matter much to her either. Realizing T.J.'s wife couldn't hear, Ma screamed into her ear, asking if she remembered her. She just said yes to every question until Peggy nudged Ma and let her know that Mrs. Brennan had Alzheimer's. But it didn't matter. We could just as easily have been weary strangers passing, I thought, until I recognized the memories in T.J.'s eyes as he sat down to have a look at Ma. "Christ, you're very like your mother." "Did he know my mother?" Ma asked Peggy, and Peggy explained that T.J. meant Ma's grandmother, Grandpa's mother.

T.J. had grown up like a brother to Grandpa. He was one of four kids by four fathers, born to an unwed mother in turn-of-the-century rural Ireland. Grandpa's mother, Ellen Murphy — Ma's name before she started using "Helen" — took the whole family onto her land and let them build a house. "Christ, she was strong as an ox," T.J. roared with pride, like it was his own mother he was talking about. For years I'd heard the same thing from Grandpa — "Christ, she was strong as an ox!" — whenever he got close to telling the sad story of losing his mother. Ellen Murphy had the job of preparing the dead to be waked in their homes. She had a horse and trap and would pick up the body of the deceased, bring it to her home at the top of the Cordal Road, wash it and dress it up, and take it back to be laid out for the two- or three-day seisun to wake the dead. Ma said that even when she was a kid in Boston, a wake was so much fun you'd have to stop and remind yourself it was a wake, not a wedding. And in Ellen Murphy's Kerry, a time of revolution followed by bloody civil war, murders by Black and Tans, and the scourge of tuberculosis all around, the wakes, T.J. said, were just as much craic. I never heard about Grandpa's father, probably because he'd died of consumption — as they called TB — when Grandpa was still in the womb. Ellen Murphy also buried her four-year-old daughter, Nonie — a sister Grandpa never heard much about — who probably also died of TB.

"Christ, you're the spit of her!" T.J. said to Ma. "As strong as Brian Boru she was!"

Ma asked T.J. if he knew Grandpa's sister, Nonie. "The one that died," she said. But he changed the subject to talk about the Good Friday Accords that had been negotiated and how the agreement was a betrayal of every patriot that died in these hills for Ireland. Until now I'd only heard good things about the Accords. But T.J., who grew up in the years when Ireland fought to the bitter end for independence, was fuming that the Irish Republic agreed to strike its claim to the North from the constitution. Articles 2 and 3 of the Irish constitution were all that the nationalists had left to show commitment to continued struggle, after the partition of the island. Ma tried to get T.J. back to telling us about his childhood, but he didn't hear her. His huge fist pounded the table, and he said the Accords were akin to surrender.

When he finally got back to talking about Ellen Murphy, looking at Ma again like he knew her from his earliest years, he'd only repeat how strong she was, each time coming up with a new metaphor. "She was strong as ten men!" and pointing his thumb in Ma's direction like the ghost of Ellen Murphy was sitting right there next to him.

Another day in Castleisland, Ma got the idea to go look inside Dan Murphy's old house. We drove up toward Grandpa's Cordal Road, this time on our own. "There it is," Ma yelled, pointing at a house that was falling apart, with rusted tin roofs and crumbling stone walls. Getting out of the car, we both sank about six inches into the mud.

When I popped my head inside a broken side window, I saw the front door shaking and rattling with each of Ma's body slams. "What are you doing?" I shouted. By the third slam the door collapsed on the floor, with Ma on top of it. She landed on her hands and knees. "We could have just climbed in this window," I said, my head inside the empty window frame. "You're always looking for the easy way," Ma said, rising up slowly and brushing off her knees and forearms. "My God," she said, looking at the piled-up wreckage, "these are all the old lady's things," referring to Dan Murphy's mother. She lifted the biggest black iron kettle I'd ever seen and put it back where she said she remembered it hanging, above the stone fireplace that dominated the room. The pile in the middle of the floor revealed an entire life's possessions: broken crockery, a collapsed wooden chair, a black shawl, pieces of the ceiling. It looked like everything had been swept into the pile for burning. Ma shook out the shawl and put it over the back of a kitchen chair, and the chair fell over with the weight of it. She looked around and rubbed her arms slowly, like she was cold.

She told me about coming to this house for the first time when she was seventeen. "I was just off the boat, wearing a brand-new blue gingham dress and satin coat with white high heels." She laughed, remembering that when she started walking through the field in front of her cousin's house, she wasn't prepared to be "knee-deep in cow shit." She walked into the house frustrated at the state of her best outfit, threw her suitcase down, and announced she'd be staying a few weeks. "The old lady went right for the kettle and made me a cup of tea," Ma said, "and it wasn't until she'd taken my clothes to scrub clean and made me three cups of tea and loads of cake that she asked me, 'Well, now, who would you belong to?'" Ma was given a bed up in what looked like a hayloft. "But it was the most comfortable bed you ever lay in," she said. "I almost cried when I found out that the old lady was sleeping on a bunch of coats and pillows in a corner below so that I could have the good bed."

Ma reminded me that this was the house where Davey stayed years later. That's when the storytelling abruptly came to an end, and Ma decided we'd better get on the road, with the long journey ahead of us. I wanted her to tell me more about Davey's trip. But I accepted that there were some places Ma couldn't go, at least in front of her kids. Ma looked like a different person in this room. She was holding her lower back, and I noticed that she walked like she was a little sore, like an older person with arthritis. Her face had changed too, and her voice was deeper, not the high note she was always hitting for everyone else. I'd avoided looking at her while she told stories of her own past lives. Standing next to the dusty heap on the floor, I looked at the perfectly preserved picture of the Sacred Heart hanging above the fireplace, with a banner that read BLESS THIS HOME. It was the one intact thing in a house that was in ruins. I couldn't take my eyes off it.

After three days with the Riordans, it was time for us to move on, to where we didn't know. We went outside to take final pictures in the rare Irish sunshine. The Riordans lined up in front of their house, all waving, with some still red-eyed from crying. It was always difficult to tear away from anyone Irish, I'd noticed. In my own family after all the deaths, saying goodbye was hard. Whenever I visited my family in Colorado, I would cut out early and then call from the airport. But I found that all Irish from Ireland were that way, even if they hadn't gone through a lot of sudden deaths. Saying goodbye to the Riordans, though, seemed even more difficult. I knew I was the only friend of Danny's who had come to see them since he died.

But it was Ma they were mostly crying over in their farewell hugs. Hannah took me aside to tell me that having her there was like having Danny himself visit. With that we jumped into the car. Ma kept waving from the window, even though we were still only four feet from the Riordans. We drove, or wobbled, away about fifteen feet before realizing we had a flat tire. It was devastating to think we'd have to stay longer and go through the painful goodbyes again. Mr. Riordan waved us back to the curb and sent Ma and me back inside for more tea with the family, while he and his right-hand son, John, went to work with the spare. They patched the flat and held up the nail they'd plucked out of the tire. "That's a souvenir," he said. Ma thought it must be a miraculous sign, since it was Easter. But she had to explain the connection, the nailing of Christ to the cross. "And here we are with one in our tire!" Everyone looked a little puzzled but still like they wanted it to mean something, and I interrupted to say we were going to be late for Easter Mass at Grandpa's church on the Glounthane Road. This time it was a much easier getaway, but I could see in my rearview mirror that the Riordans stayed at their doorway until we turned the last corner and were out of sight.

We missed Easter Mass at Grandpa's church. But I wanted to go inside to see the room where he'd been baptized and had received his first Communion. The interior was still decorated for Easter. A purple robe was draped over the Christless cross at the altar, and long iron nails were spread out on the floor. Ma couldn't get over that we were coming across so many nails. She swiped a few and put them in her purse like they were relics of the actual crucifixion. We got into an argument over whether it was appropriate to steal rusty nails from an altar. I was tired of her insistence that everything was a sign. "It's a fuckin' nail!" I said, and my words echoed back at me in the church. I wasn't much of a churchgoer, but I still thought of the room as sacred, since it was probably the first room I'd stepped into where I could be sure Grandpa had sat with his mother, who'd always been a living presence in his stories. So the echoed curse made me cringe. After that I tried to calm down. The room probably meant even more to Ma than it did to me, so I let it all be.

When we went through the foyer to leave, we came across two Sprite bottles filled with water next to the font, so we knew they were filled with holy water. Ma said it was like they were put there for us, and for once I had to agree. We took them along to bring home.

"Hi, who are you?" Ma called over to a middle-aged woman who came out of her house across the street. The woman said her name was Wren, and she got right into the third degree with us. But Ma interrupted her. "Did you lose a Jerry Wren not too long ago? Let's see, he died last month." The woman looked like she'd seen a ghost and went running inside her house yelling, "There's a Yank out there knows Jerry!" In no time an old man, around Grandpa's age, in tweed cap and blazer, came running out. He looked much too old to be running so fast. When he got to us, he put out his hand to Ma and said nothing, still out of breath.

"Is that your son who died last month?"

"Yes!" The man's eyes welled up.

"God, and he was young," Ma said.

"Yes!" He pulled out a picture.

"Oh, what a nice face on him," Ma said, shaking her head.

"Yes!" The man was trembling now and looking to Ma like she might have a message from him, some consolation from beyond. My hair was standing on end. I didn't know how Ma could know all about this complete stranger's son. Then she explained, gripping his hand, "I saw your son's stone at the graveyard!"

"Yes! Yes!"

The old man's repeated yeses made us both think he wasn't hearing much. Ma screamed, "It's a beautiful stone!"

The man looked at Ma and started to cry. It was the first time I'd seen a man that age, one of Grandpa's peers, crying openly. I'd never seen Grandpa that way. It was almost too much to bear. I liked to think that at that late stage in life, you'd be over it all, that nothing could get to you anymore.

"The stone, it's beautiful!" Ma screamed again, thinking he didn't hear her.

"Who do you belong to?" he asked, gripping Ma's hand for dear life. She told him, at full volume, that her father was from up the Cordal Road. "John Murphy!"

"Yes! Yes!" he said, holding tighter. When he said he knew John, that's when we realized he could hear at all.

"You miss him! Your son! You miss him!" Ma yelled. Not a question but a pronouncement.

He just cranked his head to look up at Ma, his eyes filling some more. He didn't have to say yes.

"Look, he's just in another form! Do you understand?" Ma explained. I didn't know where she was going with it. The old man Wren looked down and gripped her hand, unable to say anything. Ma said, "Look! You know how you've taken many forms in this life?"

He looked up again.

"First you were a small baby. Then you were a little kid running around these glens. Then you were a young man getting married."

Mr. Wren exclaimed, "Yes!" repeatedly, getting louder with every form he'd ever taken in this world. By the excited look on him, I thought Ma was going to do him in with memories. His trembling was getting worse and he cried, but not like a child, because he was crying and smiling at the same time. "You're not the same form you were even ten years ago! It's like evolution. Throughout this life you just go from form to form! Well, it's the same when you die. Your son is just in another form! Do you hear me?"

Mr. Wren said yes about five times, gripped Ma's hand one last time, turned away, and shuffled down the path to his cottage. I couldn't tell whether he was just thrilled to meet a stranger all the way from America who acknowledged that his son had lived and died or whether Ma's words meant something to him.

Mr. Wren's gait as he walked back to his house seemed different from his panicky run when he'd first heard Ma was asking about his boy. Watching him, I still couldn't get over the fact that while I was focused on how I should and shouldn't behave at Danny's grave, Ma had been observing the details of Jerry Wren's stone. I no longer felt I'd missed out on something by not seeing the bullet-riddled columns of the General Post Office. Surrounded by these green hills, Ma made more sense to me now, and so did all the rebellion, the fights, the transformation of pain into stories that could be sung, in Ireland's history. Just moments before, getting out of the car for the church, when I saw that Ma still had her accordion slung over her shoulder, I had wanted to ask, "What the hell are you going to do with *that* on Easter Sunday?" But I no longer had to. I understood that you never know when you'll need to give whatever you've got to give.

"C'mon, Mike," Ma yelled to me as I stood, watching Mr. Wren close the door to his house. She was already in the car, the accordion held close under her arm. Looking straight ahead, Ma complained that "these goddamn boreens" of Grandpa's hills would do anyone's head in, so we'd better get on the road now in case we got lost. "Let's keep moving," she said, even though we were playing it by ear and weren't sure where we'd end up.

ACKNOWLEDGMENTS

I don't believe that "making it on your own" is possible. There is no way I could have survived as a child without welfare or the resourcefulness of my mother. (Not only was there always a full fridge, we had *two* full fridges!) But really, it is *all* welfare: all of the support we get on a daily basis from whomever we gravitate toward in our lives. A couch to sleep on, a meal, a shower, talk therapy, or a way to sneak in to see a band — these are all essentially "welfare" systems, and all kids seem incredibly capable of building them. Reme, Joe and Val, Christine Elise McCarthy (who continues to provide invaluable support and conversation), Zemlya, Ellen Deraney, Nije, Debi Winston-Buzil, Jim "Clam" Lynch, Sheena Buchholz, Madeleine and Rachel and John Steczyncki, Ziggy and Ron Hartfelder, Eileen Gallagher — these people were my extended family, and I am forever grateful to them. Many other people, whom I consider family to this day and who are not mentioned in this book, also provided crucial support in my teen years.

I am blessed by the circle of people surrounding me today, particularly during the potentially isolating process of writing a book: my editor, Deanne Urmy; Kathie and Megan Mainzer; Jade Sanchez Ventura, who was a brilliant assistant in the writing stages; Louise DeSalvo, for making that assistance happen; Peg Anderson, for her calm and steady hand; my brothers Seamus and Steven and the whole new Brooklyn family that surrounds them and therefore me (you all know who you are). Thanks to Michael Prevett at Relevant Entertainment and Ike Williams at Fish and Richardson.

I would not have been able to complete *Easter Rising* without the residencies I was granted, at the Rockefeller Foundation's Bellagio Study and Conference Center, the MacDowell Colony, the Blue Mountain Center, and the Djerassi Resident Artists' Program. I got to write some of my favorite portions of the book in some of the most beautiful places in the world, surrounded by writers, visual artists, musicians, and sculptors, all of whom contributed in one way or another to this work. We accomplish nothing alone. Some of the family I gained in these residencies are Jim and Ann McGarrell, Namita Gokhale, Jenifer Shute, Melanie Baker, Brenda Shaughnessy, Julie Gibson, and Katherine Graham.

I am grateful to my whole family: Davey, John, Mary, Frankie, Kathy, Kevin, Patrick, Seamus, Steven.

And to Ma, to the music, and to the spirit of rebellion.

PLAYLIST

CHIC, "Good Times"

EARTH, WIND, AND FIRE, "Boogie Wonderland"

SISTER SLEDGE, "We Are Family"

SEX PISTOLS, "Anarchy"

PATTI SMITH, "In Excelsis Deo"

BUZZCOCKS, "Boredom"

BLACK FLAG, "Nervous Breakdown"

RICHARD HELL AND THE VOIDOIDS, "Blank Generation"

IGGY AND THE STOOGES, "Search and Destroy"

ROCKET FROM THE TOMBS, "Sonic Reducer"

DEAD BOYS, "Sonic Reducer"

MIKEY DREAD, "Break Down de Walls"

THE CLASH, "Armagideon Time," "Police and Thieves,"
    "I'm Not Down"

WILLIE WILLIAMS, "Armagideon Time"

JUNIOR MURVIN, "Police and Thieves"

X-RAY SPEX, "Oh Bondage, Up Yours!"

MISSION OF BURMA, "That's How I Escaped My
    Certain Fate"

THE SLITS, "Heard It Through the Grapevine"

PUBLIC IMAGE LIMITED (PIL), "Death Disco"

SIOUXSIE AND THE BANSHEES, "Pull It to Bits"

GANG OF FOUR, "Not Great Men," "I Found That
    Essence Rare"

PERE UBU, "Dub Housing"

JOY DIVISION, "She's Lost Control"

BAD BRAINS, "Big Takeover"

KING TUBBY, "Dub from the Roots"

LIQUID LIQUID, "Cavern"

TRADITIONAL, "Danny Boy"

TRADITIONAL, "Black and Tan Gun"

WILLIAM B. YEATS, "Easter 1916"